ADVANCE PRAISE FOR
BOYZ 2 BUDDHAS

"David Forbes has provided a new look at an old problem: male aggression. In *Boyz 2 Buddhas*, Forbes offers a road map of how to bring to bear the wisdom of meditation and mindfulness to the turbulent lives of boys struggling to find a positive path to manhood."
    James Garbarino, E.L. Vincent Professor of Human Development, Cornell University, and Author of Lost Boys: Why Our Sons Turn Violent and How We Can Save Them

"David Forbes is one of a new wave of counselors and mental health professionals deeply concerned about the stressful lives of inner-city youth and the psychological burdens of conventional masculine attitudes. *Boyz 2 Buddhas* documents his attempt to reach urban football players through unorthodox means: teaching them meditation. And his approach works. We desperately need these innovative approaches to counseling boys who would most certainly be resistant to conventional therapeutic approaches."
    Michael Thompson, Coauthor of Raising Cain: Protecting the Emotional Life of Boys

"*Boyz 2 Buddhas* is a powerful testament to the importance of cultivating the goodness that is already inside of us in the pursuit of happiness, be it in the fields of athletic competition or the daily activities of our lives."
    George T. Mumford, Sports Psychologist and Insight Meditation Teacher

Boyz 2 Buddhas

Studies in the
Postmodern Theory of Education

Joe L. Kincheloe and Shirley R. Steinberg
General Editors

Vol. 198

PETER LANG
New York • Washington, D.C./Baltimore • Bern
Frankfurt am Main • Berlin • Brussels • Vienna • Oxford

DAVID FORBES

BOYZ 2 BUDDHAS

Counseling Urban High School
Male Athletes in the Zone

PETER LANG
New York • Washington, D.C./Baltimore • Bern
Frankfurt am Main • Berlin • Brussels • Vienna • Oxford

Library of Congress Cataloging-in-Publication Data
Forbes, David.
Boyz 2 buddhas: counseling urban high school male athletes in the zone /
David Forbes.
p. cm. — (Counterpoints; v. 198)
Includes bibliographical references and index.
1. Sports—United States—Psychological aspects. 2. High school
athletes—Counseling of—United States. 3. Masculinity—United States.
4. Violence in sports—United States. I. Title: Boys to buddhas.
II. Title. III. Counterpoints (New York, N.Y.); v. 198.
GV706.4.F67 796'.083—dc22 2003018751
ISBN 0-8204-5536-9
ISSN 1058-1634

Bibliographic information published by **Die Deutsche Bibliothek**.
Die Deutsche Bibliothek lists this publication in the "Deutsche
Nationalbibliografie"; detailed bibliographic data is available
on the Internet at http://dnb.ddb.de/.

Cover photo by Emy Öst, Brooklyn College, 2002
Cover design by Sophie Boorsch Appel

The paper in this book meets the guidelines for permanence and durability
of the Committee on Production Guidelines for Book Longevity
of the Council of Library Resources.

© 2004 David Forbes
Peter Lang Publishing, Inc., New York
275 Seventh Avenue, 28th Floor, New York, NY 10001
www.peterlangusa.com

All rights reserved.
Reprint or reproduction, even partially, in all forms such as microfilm,
xerography, microfiche, microcard, and offset strictly prohibited.

Printed in the United States of America

Table of Contents

Acknowledgments	vii
Introduction	1
I. What's Up with Boys? On the Male Question	
Chapter 1. The Boys Are Back: Mindless Masculinity	9
Chapter 2. Must Boys Always Be Boys? Mindful Masculinity	29
II. Doing Nothing for Something:	
Working with High School Male Athletes	
Chapter 3. High School Football: Life In/Out of the Zone	57
Chapter 4. Gettin' Serious	95
Chapter 5. Boyz 2 Buddhas? Findings	147
III. It Might Be Time to Move On: Integral School Counseling	
Chapter 6. Turn the Wheel: Integral School Counseling for Male Teens	167
Chapter 7. Toward Contemplative Urban Education and School Counseling	193
Bibliography	205
Index	227

Acknowledgments

I would like to thank the following people whose encouragement and support made this book possible: Carol Browner, Alberto Bursztyn, Lynn Chancer, Sherry Giles, Joe Kincheloe, George Mumford, Priya Parmar, Laura Rolle, Nancy Romer, Deborah Shanley, Shirley Steinberg, Ben Susswein, and Barbara Winslow.

I am grateful for the assistance of Alan Balkan, Mark Cinamon, Glen Hass, Dr. Howard Lucks, Rosina Montana, Dr. Henry Solomon, and Dr. Irene Strum, who enabled me to carry out the high school research project.

Thanks to the young men of this study for their cooperation, hard work, humor, and enthusiasm. I learned many things from them.

This project was made possible with the assistance of a PSC-CUNY grant. Many thanks to Sophie Appel of Peter Lang Publishing and to Elliot Lopez for production and typesetting.

Last and most important, I am grateful beyond words for the love and confidence of my wife, Iris Lopez.

Chapters 6 and 7 are an expanded and revised version of the article "Turn the Wheel: Integral School Counseling for Male Adolescents," *Journal of Counseling and Development*, Volume 81, Spring 2003, pages 142–149. ©ACA. Reprinted with permission of the American Counseling Association. No further reproduction authorized without written permission of the American Counseling Association. An earlier description of this project appears as a chapter in *Holistic Learning and Spirituality in Education* (2004, SUNY Press) edited by Jack Miller. Lines from the songs "Good Bye," "Trust," "The Conscience Rapper," and "Know Thyself" from the album *Spiral Minded* by KRS-One are reprinted with the kind permission of Kris Parker.

Please note that names of all subjects and some identifying characteristics have been changed throughout.

Introduction

Prologue: The Zone, Brooklyn, NY

At the bell, twelve beefy, boisterous high school male athletes burst into the classroom, joking, laughing, and roughhousing each other. These varsity football team members seem to be a rampant force of nature all their own. Yet, soon, each young man is seated in a circle, eyes closed, body upright yet relaxed, perfectly still. Except for a soothing voice emanating from a tape recorder and the slow, deep breathing of the students, the room is dead silent. Welcome to *the zone*.

Each week for an hour or more after school, over the course of a year, I met with these young men. Sometimes there were fewer in number, other times there were as many as nineteen. Most of them are working-class African Americans whose family backgrounds include Caribbean, Central American, African, and native-born American. There are also a number of Latinos, Arab-Americans, and Italian-Americans. They average around sixteen years of age. Many of these urban young men experience considerable stress just getting through the day. They are growing up during a time in which the meaning of masculinity is undergoing significant change. I am a white, middle-aged, male college professor and mental health professional. Together we practice meditation and also discuss topics that range from last week's football game to fathers, frustrations, and fears.

Why are they here? How is it possible to get them into a classroom on their own, let alone sit motionless and concentrate for any amount of time?

When we began, I wondered if they were there for the peanut butter and jelly sandwiches I provided as a snack. It turns out I needn't have worried. The young men had other goals in mind. They were motivated to practice meditation as a way to increase their chances of playing football in the zone. They knew that the zone is a higher state of consciousness in which the athlete is so attuned to the moment there is no thought, no effort, no self-consciousness; the mind is at one with the body and moves toward a higher goal.

More so, some also wanted to play *life* in the zone. They learned to be mindful of thoughts and feelings and experience higher states of awareness during ordinary activities. They practiced making peace with their own mind and letting go of confining concepts of masculinity and selfhood that contribute to unhappiness and ill-being. In the end, most of the young men, most of the time, attended because they were committed to doing something that could enable them to better survive and even transcend the daily exigencies of adolescent life in Brooklyn.

We didn't manage to find the zone every time. When we did, the classroom was transformed into a peaceful sanctuary, the teacher's desk into an altar, and the leftover peanut butter and jelly into offerings to our higher selves.

About This Book

In recent years my interests in the nature of masculinity, popular culture, youth counseling, meditation, and the promotion of higher human development began to converge; the result is this book. In terms of masculine gender identity development, for example, I wanted to know, how could counselors challenge and help young men overcome some of the emotional constrictions of conventional masculinity? Over the years I had worked with male adolescents in different settings and often would feel anguish myself as I came to know the harsh realities they faced as well as the narrow emotional mindset they felt necessary to adopt in order to survive them.

More recently I became heartened by our society's increasing concern over the plight of male youth that arose around the time of the Littleton, Colorado, school shooting incident. Within this responsive climate I discovered an outpouring of excellent books by authors such as James Garbarino, Daniel Kindlon and Michael Thompson, Paul Kivel, William Pollack, and Terrence Real that describe the pressures young men undergo in this culture and that offer extraordinary insights and sensitive alternatives to assisting them.

All in some way speak to many boys' and men's needs for meaning and transcendence in the face of a profound spiritual emptiness, and of the need to address boys' and men's impoverished inner life. I have found this to be a crucial but hopeful moment in our history; more than ever before, a significant number of male adolescents are receptive to exploring the realm of inner life through counseling and meditation and are open to contemplative approaches that lead to a more fulfilling way of being than that offered by conventional society.

Second, I have long been interested in popular culture, especially as a means to promote youth development and education, by working both to expose its destructive, unhealthy aspects and to tease out its transcendent possibilities. Along with many others I consider popular culture as part of the groundwork for the psychology of everyday life, certainly for youth, and am intrigued with the ways young people actively construct and negotiate meaning within it. However, of late I have become disenchanted with the postmodern turn, in particular the relativistic approach toward popular culture that abandons a quest for universals, settles for one-dimensional fragments of experience, and considers only surface analysis at the expense of depth and development.

The present study led me to look at sports as part of popular culture and their influential role in male adolescent development from a more integral perspective, and to critically sort out the parts that appeal to higher levels of awareness and deeper aspects of experience from those that exploit more sensationalist and superficial ones. Sports are a breeding ground that reproduces the troublesome consciousness of conventional masculinity among many male youth. Yet here, too, I found that there is a neglected inner dimension within sports that is accessible to youth and that can be the door that opens to a higher and more encompassing sense of self. This is the realm of the zone, and the work of writers such as Andrew Cooper and Michael Murphy, researchers like Mihaly Csikszentmihalyi, and the words of athletes no less than Michael Jordan bear witness to its presence.

Third, on a more personal level, my own evolution through a critical midlife period provided a chance for greater self-reflection. At that time I came in contact with Buddhist meditation and found it to be a viable path for self-development. Although I was always drawn to a quest for transcendental knowledge, I had felt closed off to this tradition for many years because I was unable to reconcile my valuing of critical, rational thought with what I mistakenly regarded as a prerational or irrational way of being in the world. With the aid of meditation I began to resolve some of my own issues and was able to let go of thoughts and frameworks, including ones built on notions of conventional masculinity, that were no longer working and that constricted my own awareness. I discovered that the contemplative path toward wholeness was not a regression toward some childlike state that smacked of self-centered irresponsibility, impulsive sensationalism, or glorified irrationality, but moved forward through a practice that incorporated and transcended thinking. For me, meditation led the way to greater, not less, engagement with social justice and the world as expanded parts of the self. In fact, a contemplative practice based on higher values turns out to be the most radical one I have ever undertaken. It challenges the very things on which this commodity culture depends. Robert Thurman (1994) encouraged us to contemplate patience and compassion, to develop a greater capacity for responsibility and creativity, by seeing through the greedy, socially constructed materialist culture that enmeshes us:

> Commercial interests with their advertising industry do not want people to develop contentment and less greed. Military interests in economic, political, ethnic or nationalist guises, do not want people to develop more tolerance, nonviolence, and compassion. And ruling groups in general, in whatever sort of hierarchy, do not want the ruled to become too insightful, too independent, too creative on their own, as the danger is that they will become insubordinate, rebellious, and unproductive in their allotted tasks. (p. 2)

A mindful populace detaches from clinging to temporal or nonexistent things. They realize that all living things are interconnected. Such people see that everyone's true nature is compassion and know that being fully present in this moment liberates one from the suffering of dwelling in the past or obsessing about the future.

From my own evolution I discovered the intellectual roots of the contemplative tradition. I found it to be the natural successor to critical thought and postmodern multiperspectives because it accepts their strengths and transcends their limitations. Here my personal and intellectual interests began to intersect. Through the works of David Brazier, Thich Nhat Hanh, Jon Kabat-Zinn, Anne Klein, Jack Kornfield, Stephen Levine, Robert Thurman, Chogyam Trungpa, Ken Wilber, and others, I began to see the link between approaches toward self-knowledge and human development within Western practices of counseling and psychotherapy and contemplative practices such as meditation and visualization that arise from Buddhist and other traditions. I learned how academics, counselors, developmental psychologists, and educators in North America and elsewhere had already begun to do considerable work in the area of applying holistic, transpersonal, and spiritual approaches toward higher human development. A number were grounding their work in practical research. In education I was influenced by the writing of Rachael Kessler, Jack Miller, Ron Miller, Parker Palmer, and David Purpel; in counseling and therapy by Mark Epstein, Mary Fukuyama and Todd Sevig, and John Welwood; in developmental psychology by James Garbarino, Robert Kegan, and Jane Loevinger; and in compassionate social action by Robert Aitken, Bernie Glassman, Thich Nhat Hanh, Ken Jones, Kenneth Kraft, Joanna Macy, and Pat Enkyo O'Hara.

This book describes the journey of urban male adolescents who play high school football, yet it is also an invitation to consider an integral, contemplative way of life. It is about meditation both as an educational and developmental counseling tool and as an end in itself, the mindful awareness of the present based on compassion and wisdom. With regard to male adolescent development it takes an integral perspective that includes self-awareness, social connectedness, and critical knowledge of the world. An important theme of the book is that meditation promotes spiritual well-being, which is associated with less rigid adherence to stereotypical masculinity, which is stressful. Unlike many books I have read about meditation that speak of life's problems in general terms, I have tried to provide a more detailed account of some of the specific issues that young people face. I also have tried to take a dialogical rather than a polemical approach to the theoretical positions of some academic authors with whom I at times respectfully differ, and in the spirit of mutual growth toward an integral perspective invite discussion on these issues.

I intend this book to be used in courses in school counseling, teacher education, physical education, social work, adolescent development, psychology of gender, and gender studies programs, especially ones that are open to spiritual matters. I hope, too, that it becomes a small contribution to an evolving field of contemplative studies in urban education and psychology.

In Part One, I give an overview of the problematic of masculinity and the arguments over the developmental needs of young men and how to meet them. Chapter 1 looks at some consequences of conventional masculinity and revisits the nature-nurture debate regarding the source of young males' behavior. Chapter 2 argues for an integral, developmental model as the best way to frame the issue of masculine gender identity. This leads to the quest for higher development beyond conventional masculinity, which in effect is a spiritual undertaking. In this regard, I suggest that meditation is an exceptional developmental tool that promotes the evolution of masculine gender identity for male youth.

Part Two examines my work with young men on a high school football team in Brooklyn. Chapter 3 gives a critical account of the material, social, cultural, and psychological context of football as a sport and in particular with respect to adolescent males who play it in high school. It suggests that encouraging athletes to play in the zone and be mindful of themselves provides a higher response to the limitations of young men's conventionally prescribed participation in athletics and in their everyday undertakings. In Chapter 4, I describe in detail the meditation/discussion group I led in which the young men participated and their practice of exploring the zone through mindfulness both in football and in everyday activities and relationships. Chapter 5 includes the findings and conclusions of the study.

Part Three describes a vision for future work based on the project. Chapter 6 sets forth an overarching integral model and rationale for counseling male youth in schools. Chapter 7 in brief draws the broader implications for a contemplative urban school counseling and some concluding points.

PART ONE

What's Up with Boys?
On the Male Question

Chapter One

The Boys Are Back: Mindless Masculinity

Walk with my shoes that hurt your feet
And know why I lurk the streets

—DMX (1998), "Look Through My Eyes," from *It's Dark and Hell Is Hot*

Boys are breaking news all across America. In the late 1990s, young males committed a series of violent incidents in schools that sparked a nationwide concern about the behavior and future direction of male youth that is ongoing today. During the 1997–8 school year, white male high school students murdered fellow students and teachers in Pearl, Mississippi; West Paducah, Kentucky; Jonesboro, Arkansas; and Springfield, Oregon; a year later, in April 1999, two boys killed twelve of their classmates and a teacher at Columbine High School in Littleton, Colorado, before killing themselves. In 2001, a boy killed two students in a high school near San Diego.

These events provoked an impassioned debate over what to do with troubled boys and over the very nature of masculinity. Are boys naturally aggressive and violent, and, if so, do schools need to clamp down? Or are boys themselves one more set of victims of socially tolerated norms and practices such as bullying, left to fend for themselves without adequate emotional tools and requiring more preventive and therapeutic services? The media devoted considerable coverage of the events and incited much hand-wringing and concern over these homegrown perpetrators in light of the sad and disturbing consequences. It is of course tragic itself that such events had to occur in order to alert people to the plight of many boys. For years, many poor and working-class African Americans and Latinos have faced the violence committed by some young males within their inner-city communities in fear, pain, and isolation while the rest of the country offered them little recognition, sympathy, or support. Now, many people from suburbs to small towns, along with their urban counterparts, worry about the prospect of violence at the hands of their own sons.

Yet, as Dan Kindlon and Michael Thompson (2000) pointed out, school violence per se is not the problem. School violence nationwide is down, and students are more than twice as likely to be victims of serious violent crime away from school as at school (Indicators, 2001). It is the everyday emotional violence—bullying, harsh teasing, rejection, intolerance of difference, and meanness—that has a greater negative impact on more children and that also needs to be addressed (see Mickens, 2003, April 19; Galinsky & Salmond, 2002). If any good has come of the recent cases of extreme violence, it is that they have forced many educators and parents of all stripes to stop and examine the ordinary emotional quality of the lives of boys in their own schools and backyards. A number of thoughtful mental health professionals and educators have looked beyond the media's simplistic and incorrect explanations of boys' violence, for example, that it is an inevitable outcome of male testosterone (see Garbarino, 2000; Sapolsky, 1998). These professionals have criticized the calls for tougher punishment and more prisons as being inadequate and in fact detrimental to male youth. Their point is that the well-publicized school shootings are symptoms of deeper forces that have been long festering within society that center on the questions of how and what it means to grow up to be a man in this culture. They have pleaded for more understanding of boys' experiences and for the need for genuine compassion, connectedness, and community in raising and educating boys and in preventing incidents of violence. To build on their insightful work, I believe the current crisis makes it necessary to consider an integral approach to male development, one that takes into account the larger issue of what it means to be a fully developing person. The question is how we can promote development beyond the conventional level of male gender identity in ways that are enhancing for both men and women.

The Bigger Picture:
Conventional Masculinity—Becoming Outmoded

Feminists, as well as educators, mental health professionals, and now many males themselves, are aware of some of the troublesome consequences of adhering to the norm of conventional masculinity. These include violence, sexual abuse, sexual harassment, and self-destructive activities including alcohol and drug abuse, as well as relationship inadequacies, absent fathering, and social-emotional withdrawal (Brooks & Silverstein, 1995). The more boys and men try to adhere to rigid gender stereotypes of manhood, the more stress they experience (Eisler & Skidmore, 1987). Gender role stress, the strain of keeping up with the masculine norm, in turn is related to troublesome behaviors and negative emotions such as anger and hostility and social isolation (Mahalik & Lagan, 2001).

In our society today conventional masculinity is undergoing a dynamic change. Many young males struggle with this norm that sets the standard for making it as a man. Conventional masculinity cuts both ways. Some characteristics are positive: courage, strength, heroic self-sacrifice. It provides some young males privileges; but it also hampers their development and contributes to the harm of others, males as well as females. In this respect, as Joseph Pleck (1980) argued, it is a dual system in which men not only oppress women but oppress themselves and each other. The meaning of masculinity is no longer something that can be assumed. Of course all boys grow to be men. The question today is, what kind?

Conventional masculinity goes by different names: the Boy Code (Pollack, 1998); Hegemonic Masculinity (Connell, 1995); the Culture of Cruelty (Kindlon and Thompson, 2000); Acting Like a Man (Kivel, 1999); Performance-Based Esteem (Real, 1997); the Masculine Mystique (O'Neil, 1982). Conventional masculinity pressures young males to prove their maleness, and thereby their self-worth, over and over again. Young males often feel they are never masculine enough, and so they struggle to prove their masculinity to themselves and others.

The conventional way to verify one's manhood is through thinking and acting in certain prescribed ways. One is stoical inexpressiveness: don't show vulnerability, don't show weak feelings, and don't act like a woman, because women and feminine qualities are devalued. Another is to be in control at all times, to never admit mistakes, ask for help, or show that you don't know what you're doing. A third is homophobia, the need to avoid any whiff of consciousness or behavior conventionally associated with gay men, who share with women qualities that are unacceptable to be expressed. A fourth is to act physically tough, aggressive, and intimidating toward others in order to be able to compete with other men and gain access to attractive women. The presumed reward, often at the exhausting cost of eternal emotional vigilance, is power, defined in terms of the accumulation of money, material possessions, and women, and by domination over others, namely, women and weaker males.

Men who are successful at following the norms of conventional masculinity gain dividends in terms of socially acceptable power, privilege, and material awards. Despite women's considerable efforts to gain equality, women have not achieved parity with men. Among men themselves there is a hierarchy of power and privilege in terms of class, ethnicity, and sexual orientation. However, as Connell (1996) has found, men overall continue to maintain greater advantage over women in terms of wealth and income, cultural authority, levels of education, political influence, and control of organizations. This power imbalance shows up in domestic life. Women still do most of the less valued but necessary labor in terms of housework, child-rearing, and emotional work—establishing and maintaining interpersonal relations.

Up until the September 11, 2001, attack on the World Trade Center in New York, it was clear that larger social forces were undercutting conventional masculine roles such as the strong provider and protector. Social change has made the roles less relevant as means for males to gain a sense of self. Terry Kupers's (1993) list of contributing social factors included the rise of global corporate power, the influence of the mass media, the shift from a manufacturing to a service economy, the drop in real earnings for working-class families, and fewer social support services and safety nets. As a result, some emerging forms of social relations within the workplace and the family have begun to reward behaviors other than conventional masculine means to secure power and privilege. For example, male managers and others in power learn that cooperation, nurturance, and empathy are now desirable traits. It is more acceptable for men to show caring emotions in public.

Trends in everyday life and popular culture have reflected these changes. Men such as President George W. Bush and media anchorman Dan Rather cried publicly after 9-11, a positive change in the behavior of public male figures. In movies such as *In the Bedroom* (2001, Miramax) it has become acceptable for older women to find younger, more emotionally expressive men as partners. A male actor such as Ben Stiller in *Meet the Parents* (2000, Universal) portrayed a more sensitive male in contrast to his prospective father-in-law as played by Robert De Niro. In this context, traditional masculinity takes the form of a retrograde male backlash. In a technology-oriented, service-based world, macho characters who are powerful, physical protectors such as those portrayed by Sylvester Stallone and Arnold Schwarzenegger become nostalgic embodiments of traditional, heroic roles. (It was not surprising that in 2003, Schwarzenegger was elected as a Republican for governor in California and capitalized on his movie image as the Terminator.) Terry Teachout (2002, September 15) suggested that while the popular TV series, *The Sopranos*, is a send-up of traditional morality, it manages to portray it nostalgically. Tony Soprano, the main character, lamented the loss of clear-cut conventional masculine behavior. In the first episode he asked his therapist,

> Whatever happened to Gary Cooper, the strong, silent type? That was an American. He wasn't in touch with his feelings. He just did what he had to do. See, what they didn't know is that once they got Gary Cooper in touch with his feelings, they couldn't get him to shut up. It's dysfunction this, dysfunction that. (Teachout, 2002, September 15, p.wk. 3)

The events of September 11, 2001, were a direct hit on America's sense of its own masculinity. The nation's ability to defend itself and feel secure through military and technological power suddenly was weakened and made vulnerable. Many Americans, especially political conservatives, took this opportunity to argue that masculinity needed to be rebuilt and reasserted. In the aftermath of the event media images emphasized the male gender of the firefighters, police force, and rescue squads who responded to the tragedy and glorified their physical strength and courage. As Marcus Weaver-Hightower (2002) argued, the media emphasis on dominant white masculinity also negated or minimized the presence of Others—women, people of color, and the needs of working-class public safety employees.

A male backlash to feminism and women's empowerment had already begun during the 1980s and 1900s, but conservative males used the 9-11 attack and the war against Iraq to justify machismo as a necessary political posture (see Goldstein, 2003, March 24). While figures such as President Bush and Dan Rather did feel free to cry in public, the preparation for and war with Iraq a year later negated these images. By the end of 2002, the backlash was in strong evidence. A psychologist who studies male behavior, Randolph R. Cornelius, said:

> I see it changing back. We are moving into a more of a "you've got to tough it out" phase as our culture is preparing us for war and there will be a lot of sacrifices. It's like, "We've got to get through all this, and there's no crying about it." (L. Lee, 2002, December 29, p. 2)

Those who handled George W. Bush's public image capitalized on the anxiety many males feel about the loss of masculinity in the face of women's demand for sexual equality. Richard Goldstein (2003, May 21–27) noticed how Bush is deliberately portrayed as a man struggling to carry off the feat of being macho, a process with which many threatened men identify; it further served to shore up his conservative, manly image and keep his Democratic opponents on the defensive.

For many men, September 11 may have compounded the sense of powerlessness, inadequacy, and confusion over the loss of conventional masculinity as a traditional means of defining and securing power and the privileges it provided for them. Many adult men, Susan Faludi (1999) found, already were beginning to feel disillusioned with the old formula for attaining manhood; they feel betrayed, believing that American society had broken its promise of guaranteed masculinity in return for certain behaviors. This contract was supposed to offer them manhood in exchange for hard work, masculine honor and pride in return for loyalty, and a sense of brotherhood, gained from protecting and providing for family and community. Faludi suggested that men feel let down by their fathers for their unavailability and for their inability to teach them masculine traditions, as well as by a culture that no longer honors the traditional male ways.

For many sons, as Ellen Willis (1999, December 13) argued, it may be that they are bitter because their fathers taught them the masculine norm all too well, and that what lies behind their sense of betrayal and loss is their awareness that the tradition no longer guarantees them power and privilege. Yet there is no doubt that many males do struggle with their relationships with their fathers, a poignant theme that resonates in American culture and in everyday life. Fathers are no more at fault than anyone else for trying to teach their sons means to succeed that are now outdated. They too often sacrificed themselves on the altar of conventional masculinity for the sake of their own identity. Terrence Real (1997, p. 159) has pointed out that what sons may yearn for is not their fathers' "balls"; they want their hearts; sons seek not the lost boy of their own youth as much as the one their own father discarded or was denied. It is not just about power; many men in this society feel a lost connection with their fathers and are beginning to acknowledge it to themselves and others.

Some men also will try to blame their loss of masculine privilege on mothers who feminize their sons. Here, too, the explanation, as well as the feelings of anger and disappointment, is misplaced. On the contrary, many boys may be emotionally harmed by too much early detachment from their mothers. Olga Silverstein and Beth Rashbaum (1994) explained that many of those mothers are pressured or buy into the fear that they are emasculating the males; as the mothers push their sons away the boys proceed to learn the masculine norm of cutting off their emotions and consequently suffer from the loss of a close, healthy relationship.

The larger problem is that many of the same advantages men have held by adhering to the masculine norm also prevent them from experiencing themselves as whole persons. Many men who follow conventional masculinity pay a high price. Traditional masculine roles are linked with indicators of physical illness; much of men's higher rates of disease, injury, and death are attributable to preventable behavior by men such as risk taking and lack of self-care (Courtenay, 2000). Conventional masculinity, in the words of one researcher, "is hazardous to your health" (Harrison, 1978; see also Kogan, 2000). Male adolescents' difficulties show up in problems of aggression, violence, and in self-destructive behavior such as alcohol and substance abuse. Youthful male behavior is linked with indicators of physical illness and emotional and social problems, including substance abuse and increasing body-image disturbances among male youth (Hall, 1999, August 22; McCreary, 2001; Pollack & Levant, 1995). The cost occurs both in the harm done to others and in the loss of a healthy inner life.

Violent aggression is one of the masculine qualities the U.S. government employed in the aftermath of September 11. President Bush, as Weaver-Hightower (2002) has pointed out, assumed a Wild West cowboy persona, demanded Bin Laden "dead or alive," adopted a shoot-first-negotiate-later approach, and restricted civil liberties. These tactics coming from the top leaders of society can convey the notion that this is the only way to handle conflict. The macho style of conservative politicians—toughness, strength, and order—speaks to people's current sense of anxiety and their need to feel safe and secure. Patriarchy, Richard Goldstein (2003, March 24) has argued, is now associated with survival.

Aggression, although it does not always lead to violence, is part of most men's experience of growing up in our society, what Kindlon and Thompson (2000) called the Culture of Cruelty. Many boys learn from their parents and caregivers not to cry, to be tough, to take it like a man (see Savran, 1998), and that expressing feelings is for girls. They learn that various types of intimidation and the expression of rage are socially acceptable ways to maintain power and domination over girls, gays, or weaker boys. Boys learn to compete against other boys, to intimidate them, including gays, to establish pecking orders and to victimize others through aggressive behavior—or else experience it themselves (see Kaufman, 1993; Kivel, 1999). Teasing and bullying are common behaviors among American adolescent males (Goode, 2001, April 25). Homophobia is internalized by many gay teens and contributes to self-hatred, dissociation, depression, and higher rates of suicide and high-risk behaviors. Even among many gay men, Richard Goldstein (2002, July 2) wrote, there is the emotionally harmful pressure to conform to a macho version of masculinity; it prevents gay men from expressing their full range of feelings and from being fully intimate with one another.

Even when some young men absorb the message that aggression is an admired trait in this society and can be an effective means to get what they want, they pay a price. Most are left without the emotional skills to deal with feelings other than through anger or physical acting out. Another cost is that they experience the sanction of aggression as a confusing double message. Susan Bordo (2000) noted that society and the media encourage and reward boys who display primal masculinity and aggression in sports, the military, and sexual conquests, and who learn not to take no for an answer. Yet at the same time they are told to be gentle, moral, and chivalrous with girls, and to know that no always means no. Bordo has likened this stress to the kind girls experience in hearing the double message society aims at them: you are encouraged to be successful and strong but you must at all times maintain your femininity.

Many young men undergo unresolved trauma as children that later contributes to their carrying out violent behavior as teens or adults (see Bloom, 1997). James Garbarino (2000) has reminded us that "psychological, physical, and sexual violence exists in homes and neighborhoods through the country, regardless of geography. And images of it are accessible to almost every child in America simply by turning on the television" (p. 107). Male youth who committed the spate of mass schoolyard murders were in pain that stemmed from physical or emotional abuse such as being teased or bullied. The adults around them ignored or minimized their hurt. This occurred in part because the boys were unable to communicate their feelings, as boys learn social rules that make them feel ashamed about weakness or vulnerability. The problem was compounded by their lack of connection with adults. The adults did not care enough to pay attention to what the boys were saying and doing, and did not take the lives of the young men seriously (see Smith 2001, July/August, interview with William Pollack).

Even subtle, socially acceptable forms of violence in the service of conventional masculinity can contribute to covert but damaging trauma among boys. Harsh, authoritarian parenting that does not otherwise show love and concern; relentless media and social pressure to gain peer acceptance through acquiring the most fashionable clothes or the latest media equipment; the invidious effects of poverty and lack of a vision of a viable future: these more everyday onslaughts on a child's development can damage a delicate sense of self (see Bloom, 1997). Terrence Real (1997) considered the withholding of the expression of love from a young boy until he is grown, a pattern that some fathers consider acceptable, to be a form of emotional violence that results in trauma.

Substances such as liquor, tobacco, and drugs often represent external props as means for male teens to medicate for overwhelming feelings of sorrow, anxiety, or low self-worth. Smoking among teens continues at an unacceptably high level and marijuana remains a popular drug in both suburban and inner-city neighborhoods. Binge drinking is a serious problem on a number of college campuses; heavy alcohol use among teenage boys is common. An adolescent psychologist, Dr. Alan Tepp, who works with teens in a wealthy New York suburb noted a significant increase in the amount that teens drink in the last five years (Scarsdale school, 2002, September 27). Those male teens that abuse drugs and alcohol do so in part from peer pressure to conform to a socially acceptable version of manhood, for example, holding one's liquor—although girls are now trying to keep up with the boys. In terms of prevalence, masculinity and drug and alcohol abuse seem to go hand in hand (Brooks & Silverstein, 1995). Addictions are temporary, ultimately inadequate solutions to feelings of pain or loss, lack of fulfillment, and low self-esteem and often are undeveloped means to deal with a poor sense of self and the world (see Forbes, 1994).

Addictions take other forms besides substances. Anne Wilson Schaef (1988) argued that conventional masculinity predominates a patriarchal society and is itself an addictive pattern. It keeps people out of touch with what we know and feel and is harmful to both men and women. For example, if a man tends to jump to practical, technical solutions before sitting with and experiencing the feelings associated with a personal problem, he may deny the underlying issues and become attached to quick fixes as the solution for every problem. As R. W. Connell (1996) pointed out, broader social relations are gendered and at present men overall have more power than women. The nature of state power, how production is organized, and how desire is gratified are arranged in terms of the values of conventional masculinity. For example, aggression and violence are regarded as normal, healthy, and often necessary means to solve problems before other choices are considered. Other traditionally masculine values are so common that people tend not to reflect on their pervasiveness. Competition for basic human needs; the exploitation and domination of nature; the priority given to rational, instrumental thought and the devaluation or denial of feelings, care, and nurturance; cultural forms of entertainment and advertisements that rely on violence or the exploitation of women, gays, and people of color: these reflect broader social inequities that privilege those who conform to the values and behaviors of conventional masculinity. Variants of feminism and spiritual traditions suggest other values: cooperation, the need to experience and appropriately express feelings, nurturance, and respect for nature.

An addictive pattern focuses on the attachment to an external solution to an inner need. This, too, is a quality of conventional masculinity: if I can fix every problem with an external solution, it will go away. For example, many boys experience the trauma of conditional love: they get approval only if they do what is expected of them. As a result, they experience what Terrence Real (1997) called performance-based esteem. They grow up to be men who are unable to accept themselves and who over and over again are driven to prove their intrinsic worth through external performance. This, however, is a futile means to heal the wound. Men try to defend themselves against this trauma through addiction to compulsive behaviors, some of which are socially acceptable, such as work, overachievement, spending, gambling, eating, and sexual scoring. The price for these defenses, however, can be repression, rage, loneliness, and an inability to develop intimate relationships with one's spouse and children, not to mention deep friendships with other men. In many cases, this contributes to a covert depression in which the man is sullen, withdrawn, and anguished. In all cases, male youth who must attend to external performance to validate themselves as men not only risk physical illnesses; they suffer the loss of a rich inner life.

The need for total control without outside help is another addictive pattern that many men manifest. When it comes to asking for help with regard to their own physical health, men often feel they have to do it by themselves. Many boys and men are reluctant to admit to pain or illness, and alternative, nontraditional approaches to men's health seeking are needed (Addis & Mihalik, 2003, January; Flaherty, 2000, December 12). For African American men, this tendency is compounded by distrust in medical health providers, whom many of the men feel treat them with disrespect. What is more, the masculine pressure to show strength and not reveal weakness is intensified in African American men, argued author Ellis Close:

> There is an ethic of toughness among black men, built up to protect yourself against racial slights and from the likelihood that society is going to challenge you or humiliate you in some way. This makes it very hard to admit that you are in pain or need help either physical or psychological.
> (Villarosa, 2002, September 23, p. 8)

The traditional means to attain manhood are disappearing. As Carolyn Steigmeier (2001, p. 7) pointed out, men are caught in a cultural vise between conflicting messages; one still glorifies conventional masculinity, the other promotes a more feminine consciousness associated with being a "new man."

An example of this conflict is the difficulty men have over taking paternity leave to help raise their children. Workplaces give male employees a double message. "Men are terrified to take paternity leave," according to author Suzanne Braun Levine. "While their organizations may profess to be family friendly, their bosses are giving them the message that men who take leave are not very manly, or are somehow letting down the team" (Ligos, 2000, May 31).

More men are realizing that much of conventional masculinity is outmoded and are open to consider new meanings of masculinity. As is true for men, Horne and Kiselica (1999) noted, the breakdown of conventional masculinity also creates pain and confusion for many male youth. William Pollack (1998) found that a growing number of boys want to opt out of the Boy Code. Because of the double-edged sword of conventional masculinity, men are realizing that the power and privilege they gain are not worth the cost of sacrificing their whole selves. Yet many do not know how to do this without sacrificing their sense of masculinity.

Men find it difficult to tackle this loss of conventional masculinity in conventional masculine terms. For men, the conventional way to address a problem is to confront it as something or someone outside themselves, oppose it, and vanquish it (see Faludi, 1999). Men, however, no longer can define themselves in opposition to an external enemy or Other that in this case is causing them pain. Whom to condemn and fight? Mothers? Fathers? Women? Bosses? Terrorists?

With no one to blame, men must face themselves. But many do not know how to do so. They lack the skills to talk about the downside of maintaining conventional masculinity and the uncertainties of evolving a new form of being a man. Even if they did, many do not feel they have permission to do so:

> Once socialized to be the "strong silent type" and "suck it up," men do not tend to seek help as this complex burden of expectation increases. To express confusion or raise concerns would seem to be complaining, being a baby, or worse, a sissy. Men "soldier on alone," keeping it in and keeping it all together, as best, and as long, as they can. (Steigmeier, 2001, p. 7)

The breakdown in conventional masculinity allows for the possibility of a more inclusive, egalitarian, and fulfilling vision of development. Boys and men need to adjust to the decline of patriarchal culture by developing a whole, powerful sense of themselves that no longer excludes and subordinates women. They also need to do so in a way that no longer depends on harming themselves and other men. Kupers (1993) asked, given that masculinity is all about the lines a man must not cross, what can we do to help them cross them and to prevent them from being ostracized for doing so? The more general question is how can we promote development beyond the conventional level of male gender identity in ways that empower both men and women.

Nature/Nurture Revisited

In light of the recent events of violence committed by boys, there are two camps that have come to regard the development of conventional masculinity from opposing viewpoints (Lemann, 2000, July 10). One lumps all men together and assumes that there is something essential about them—the gender role identity theory (Pleck, 1995)—they are either essentially bad or essentially good. Some claim there is something wrong with all men, that they are by nature competitive and aggressive, and that they are not inclined toward being tender, nurturing, or cooperative. This assumes that all men are biologically programmed to act this way and that all do. As Connell (1996) noted, it dismisses those men who experience pain from the conventional pressures to be stoic, competitive, and aggressive, and who want to resist those pressures and change. This antimale spin has produced its own backlash within the essentialist camp, those who argue that, yes, men are by nature competitive and aggressive, that they are all the better for it, and that we should stop repressing men's natural inclinations and cultivate these qualities in men for everyone's sake. Both positions share the assumption that all men have an essential nature.

The opposing camp, instead of assuming men have a natural, essential identity, blames society. Here also, as Brooks and Silverstein (1995) explained, there are two variants. The gender role strain paradigm shows that boys are pressured to conform to restrictive gender roles and experience the stress of trying to live up to difficult and psychologically dysfunctional gender roles. Some conclude from this that all male youth are members of a victimized group; society has damaged them by placing impossible pressures on growing up male. They regard boys as the latest injured party among many oppressed groups and believe that boys are prevented from realizing their kinder, gentler sides. This, however, ignores the fact that in conventional society boys and men tend to enjoy privileges and power over girls and women in many areas, an argument emphasized by the social constructionist hypothesis. Social constructivism places power at the cause of problematic masculine behavior; men have developed a sense of entitlement and a tendency to oppress women because they have had the power to do so. Let us examine the basic assumptions of each camp.

Nature Camp: The (Un)essential Man

Are boys inherently bad? Although Carol Gilligan (1982) does not believe this, she suggested there are essential, inherent differences between boys and girls and argued that boys and girls tend to regard moral choices "in a different voice." Boys tend to base moral principles on abstract ideas of justice, girls on interactive relations and care. She has become the heroine of the "difference" feminists who consider negative traits such as competitiveness as inherently masculine and who invidiously compare them to what they believe to be inherently feminine ones, nurturance and emotional expressiveness (Lemann, 2000, July 10). Although Gilligan's insights reflect general cultural variations in style and thinking between boys and girls, the evidence belies any universal, biologically determined difference: both boys and girls are capable of both kinds of moral reasoning. What is more, there is no clear evidence that girls and women are intrinsically more gentle or peaceful than boys and men. The feminist writer Phyllis Chesler (2002) argued that a number of women mistakenly believe in the myth of moral superiority of women even though many, including feminists, continue to employ cruel, vicious, aggressive, and competitive tactics against other women. With respect to assuming that men are naturally violent and love guns while women are peaceful and love children, Katha Pollitt (2003, March 24) pointed out: "Increasingly, the sexes don't fit the old binary oppositions: 15 percent of the military is female; many women have no kids and don't want any; many fathers are as deeply invested in hands-on parenting as mothers. Violence is no longer the sacred preserve of men: The NRA does everything short of painting guns pink to sell them to women" (p. 9).

The flip side of seeing men as inherently inadequate is to defend an essentialist, preconventional form of masculinity as good. Some proponents of the male essence camp glorify preconventional masculinity altogether. A conservative trend of the men's movement, which includes the Million Man March and the Promise Keepers, seeks a return to narrow, patriarchal traditions of masculinity. These groups idealize and uphold earlier, traditional roles of men as natural providers and protectors of the family and of women. At best, such organizations acknowledge the need for men to become self-conscious of the problematic aspects of male roles today, to take on more responsibilities such as child-rearing, and to hold themselves more accountable for some of their own behavior. However, they do so in the name of essential masculinity.

Robert Bly (1990) and his mythopoetic men's movement worried that men were going soft. He appealed to what he considered to be deep masculine qualities such as toughness as the universal, essential nature of all men. Bly's notion of soft conflates negative attributes such as passivity, weakness, reactivity, and failure to stand up for one's principles with positive attributes of tenderness, nurturance, and empathy. His movement tends to focus on personal, therapeutic, and spiritual elements. It draws some men who are in emotional pain who just want to feel better without changing sexist and political relations (Kupers, 1993; Savran, 1998). Such men's groups interpret spiritual yearning to mean a turning inward at the expense of ignoring social injustices and global inequities. They attempt to self-nurture and exonerate themselves as white men who experience themselves as victims of a changing world and who seek a purely personal retreat into the self (Savran, 1998; Kimmel & Kaufman, 1994). Such conservative factions appeal to what they think are men's natural needs and inclinations. Although these groups have formed in response to some men's legitimate emotional pain, they do not promote a progressive vision of gender equality between women and men and tend to ignore the reality of sexism and unequal power differences between men and women.

Other essentialist proponents suggest a patriarchal return to embracing ancient mythological archetypes such as the warrior through which it is presumed that by nature men are destined to wage war for the good of civilization (Moore & Gillette, 1990). This regressive approach, Kupers (1993) rightly argued, endorses an earlier form of social development that glorifies patriarchal masculinity and tries to rationalize it with an appeal to biological determinism.

One educator, Waller Newell (2000), lamented the culture's repression of what he called boys' natural inclination to manliness and sought to return boys back to what he considered to be traditional virtues of manly character. Newell appreciated men's traditional positive qualities but failed to sort them out from problematic traits that accompany patriarchal power relations. What is more, why should virtues such as honor, pride, and the legitimate expression of anger against injustice be identified as only for men?

Another nature proponent, Christine Hoff Sommers (2000), declared strong masculinity to be boys' essential nature. She defended essential masculinity against attacks by difference feminists who blame maleness for aggression and against those in the society camp who want to cultivate boys' sensitive side. She claimed that boys by nature are active, aggressive, and outgoing, while girls are inclined to be quiet, nurturing, and restrained. These led her, Edmundson (2000, October 9) argued, without any evidence to proclaim invariable, timeless truths, for example, that there always will be more women than men who prefer to stay home with children. Sommers thought that boys need to be in competitive, all-male classes and should receive character education that promotes traditional masculinity. Her arguments are ideological and no more verifiable than those strict proponents of nurture against whom she railed (see Edmundson, 2000, October 9).

As Connell (1995) pointed out, the weakness in the essentialist approach is that the choice of the essence is quite arbitrary, and a claim about a universal basis of masculinity for all males says more about the ethos of the claimant than anything else. In practical terms, the therapist Terrence Real (2002) disputed the patriarchal myth that only a man can teach a man to be a man; women therapists are just as effective in helping males. What is damaging about some arbitrary essentialist claims is that they are content to reproduce endless polarized dichotomies. While some glorify women's natural superiority over males, others reflect a hostile backlash toward women and women's efforts toward gender, as Faludi (1991) showed in her critique of Bly. Arguments that say we must return to some natural, preconventional, essential feminine or masculine identity unspoiled by society fail to meet our present needs for more evolved gender identities.

Culture Camp: Rebuilt Men

Men are socialized to believe that their masculinity is something they have to prove. There is strong evidence that men experience considerable stress in trying to live up to the norm of masculinity and that society has installed powerful social and psychological sanctions for those men who violate the male norm (Brooks & Silverstein, 1995; Pleck, 1995). The conventional norm of masculinity itself is problematic. What is hopeful about this, as Kupers (1993) pointed out, is that if gender is socially constructed, there is the possibility of change: men and women can socially construct a healthier gender role. Some men's movement associations are progressive and emphasize this cultural and social perspective. The pro-feminist men's movement includes the National Organization of Men Against Sexism (NOMAS), whose politicized men push for pro-feminist, antisexist change.

However, a number of these groups tend to ignore the legitimate personal needs of nonpolitical men who are drawn to groups such as the mythopoetic movement that do address personal issues. As a consequence, the political men's movement alienates many men who are emotionally and personally struggling with conventional masculinity. Kupers (1993) was critical of a political approach that ignores personal issues:

> [I]nstead of telling men they must give away their power, we might turn our attention to helping men cross the lines that constrict their possibilities and redefine power in a way that makes it possible for men to feel powerful and yet not be sexist or homophobic. (p. 154)

If gender is socially constructed through power relations, as social constructionists argue, then men should deconstruct their old notions of masculinity and reconstruct a new one based on gentleness and nurturance. Yet men cannot just change their thinking or behavior any time or in any way they (or women) like. Not all boys or men simply can or should, in Stoltenberg's (1990) terms, "refuse to be a man," that is, just choose to turn from conventional forms of masculinity, give up their power and self-interest, and become more expressive, gentle men. Being confronted with immediate demands to deny, repress, or change behavior and consciousness often only serves to stiffen resistance and to further entrench male power, for fear of losing one's sense of identity. If the conventional meaning of being a man lies in having power, aggressively competing with other men, and maintaining an armor of stoicism and self-control, then to be told to change one's masculine gender identity is tantamount to being asked to die.

Social constructivists assume that power is the cause of problematic male behavior; males have developed a sense of entitlement and a tendency to oppress women because they have had the power to do so. However, this position itself is problematic. First, as Brooks and Silverstein (1995) noted, for this approach to be consistent, if power relations were reversed women in turn would become more violent and oppressive. That is, as we have seen Phyllis Chesler (2002) and Katha Pollitt (2003, March 24) argue, there is nothing inherently gentle or peaceful about women; gender is socially constructed through power relations. Second, it not only challenges those feminists who assume the gentle nature of women, it places social and conscious development at the mercy of an ever-constant power struggle: if there is no higher truth, then whoever has the most power, or whichever position is the most powerful, prevails.

Some men rightly want to give up power over others. However, power with others is a desirable trait. Willpower is essential for change, but to force change without addressing emotional attachments and meanings becomes a futile endeavor that leads to repression of inner needs or the backlash of acting out in more insidious, destructive ways. It spurs resentment among some males against women and the women's rights and feminist movements. It can induce the call for a return to nature, to an ideology of mythic manhood that must reassert itself in the face of threats to its existence.

Some parents wish to raise nonsexist boys who won't want to play with guns and who will be expressive and nurturing. They, too, assume that with proper child-rearing their sons will turn out just the way they like. To their dismay, they sometimes discover that the boy displays his own temperament or proclivities in other directions, and/or that conventional gender messages and roles of the dominant society play a significant part in the way he prefers to think and act. Some in the culture camp ignore the process of development and tend to assume that environmental influences or rational directives determine meanings, consciousness, and behavior in a linear fashion. Others expect that change among males can occur by adopting and enforcing a peaceful discourse that emphasizes consensus and cooperation. However, as the feminist

Sharon Welch (1999) warned, through this technique people just as often evade real issues of power, differences, and conflicted feelings that occur among them and that need to be acknowledged, not denied.

The most sophisticated approach is a synthesis of both variants within the culture camp: males often sacrifice themselves and undergo considerable stress (gender role strain) to maintain a socially constructed masculine identity that rewards them with power and privilege (gender as social construction). As McLean (1998, p. 71) summarized it, "Men as a group are firmly in control of the power structures that determine the shape and direction of this society, yet they generally experience themselves as powerless." Another way to realize this is that a few men enjoy power, and privileges overall, and while men in general have relatively more power, it does not mean that all do.

Socializing institutions such as schools and male youth themselves construct meanings of masculinities. Schools at different levels produce and sustain conventional masculinity. McLean (1998, p. 69) argued that schools are "overwhelmingly male institutions, from their hierarchical authority structure, competitive learning styles, and combative discipline policies." Yet Connell (1996) has reminded us that there are many masculinities and that schools are not just agents but also sites for boys themselves to construct or make masculinities. To an extent, boys actively constitute and negotiate around what it means to be masculine on an everyday basis. This does not mean, however, that boys are inclined or even simply can construct meanings of gender identity any way they like; there are biological, social, psychological, and developmental factors that come into play.

Educators who subscribe to the social determinative perspective want to counteract the harmful effects of conventional masculinity. They aim to help male youth acknowledge their feelings of stress, show them the harmful effects of their power, and argue that it is in the youths' own interest to share it with others. They also help them construct more liberating narratives of masculine identity. However, as I will argue in detail later, these approaches are necessary but not sufficient for young men to develop beyond conventional masculinity.

In the aftermath of 9-11 we face a world in which old-order ways of thinking about gender, relationships, and personal meaning are no longer adequate. The conservative wish to reassert traditional patriarchal order is a futile attempt to maintain power and identity based on the fear of loss of men's selfhood and anxiety over change. A liberal approach that claims to construct and understand social relations through language does not take into account men's unexpressed emotional and spiritual needs; the development of consciousness is not a matter of constructing new identities through language. We require deeper levels of understanding and more highly evolved, integral means to address these issues today.

Chapter Two

Must Boys Always Be Boys? Mindful Masculinity

The rise and fall of a nation, even when the buildings tumble
I still stand tall

—Common (2000), "Geto Heaven, Part 2," from *Like Water for Chocolate*

Gender Identity Development

There is nothing essentially troublesome, bad, or evil about masculinity per se. Nor is there anything essentially superior about masculinity in contrast to femininity. Masculine energy is a universal force that complements femininity. The great traditions of the world all recognize these dualities as counterbalancing each other and render each as possessed of certain qualities. For example, Hindu philosophy realizes that all gods and goddesses are expressions of one underlying cosmic reality. One image of Shiva is half man, half woman; that is, there are two distinct gender manifestations of the underlying unity (Van Hyfte & Tejirian, 2002). Masculinity is considered to be active, dynamic, courageous, analytical, and powerful. Femininity traditionally is seen as receptive, quiescent, nurturing, intuitive, and tender. To be fully human means to experience a fluid, harmonious balance of both. Do these polarities mean all boys and men must possess the masculine attributes and/or girls or women do not or cannot? Or that men are not real men if they display feminine traits, and women are not feminine if they display masculine qualities? No. World cultures display a wide variety in how these characteristics play out among men and women; there are cultures such as the Semoi of Malaysia, for example, that scorn aggression and practice nonviolence by both genders, and there are cultures in which women display more traditionally masculine qualities and men more feminine ones.

There are obvious biological differences between men and women that can affect consciousness to varying degrees. Kindlon and Thompson (2000) have reminded us that men have a penis that can become erect as if it had a mind of its own; women are able to carry and give birth to a child; these and other biological differences can and do influence consciousness and personal experience. However, there is nothing essentially masculine about the behavior and consciousness of all men: there is no one essential masculine way to be a man. This is because development, as Ken Wilber (2000) has pointed out, which necessarily includes biological factors, also depends on cultural values, social institutions, and personal intentions.

It is true, however, that today and for much of the world throughout time patriarchal versions of masculinity have characterized the conventional developmental level of many cultures. A way to think about this is to consider how certain historical and environmental factors combined with biological differences to contribute to constructing the male role. Brooks and Silverstein (1995), referring to Gilmore's (1990) work, suggested that in societies not dominated by men, such as the Semoi, natural resources are available, there are no serious hazards involved in producing necessities, and there are no invaders or warfare. Most societies, however, have had to deal with scarce resources and ever-present threats to their safety from outside groups. As a consequence, they assigned the most dangerous tasks to men, presumably because of their greater physical strength. To ensure that men conform to dangerous roles, societies then place considerable sanctions on men to deny their needs for emotional connection and expressiveness in order to perform the roles of provider and soldier. As a payoff or reward for their self-sacrifice, Brooks and Silverstein (1995) argued that men display the "dark side" of their role through privilege and power by dominating women. The moral trade-off is based on the conventional assumption that might makes right, that men's biological strength allows them to possess and control women in order to maintain their lineage of property.

Yet in a shrinking, interdependent world, people have begun to evolve to the point where equality is feasible and where differences based on threats to existence and war no longer need dictate a gender hierarchy of power or values. Technological advances and more responsive social infrastructures make it possible for men to stay home and nurture children and for women, if they choose, to actively compete in almost every world arena, even weight-lifting. Society has reached the point where social life based on levels of consciousness higher than those of might makes right and of ownership based on patriarchal lineage can and may prevail. Men and women can coexist with the conscious ability to appreciate both differentiation and interdependence, both power and tenderness.

People construct culture, but not arbitrarily. There are deeper, universal structures of development that are neither random nor relativistic. Gender identity tends to develop from its preconventional, biological roots through various culturally constructed conventions and can evolve to transconventional forms. For much of the world throughout time patriarchal versions of masculinity have characterized the conventional developmental level of many cultures. Yet more evolved individuals and cultures move toward androgyny, a balanced integration of masculine and feminine qualities, and a few even evolve toward orientations that transcend conventional notions of gender identity altogether. A developmental perspective neither assumes there are just essential, biological determinants and limitations, nor that it is all a matter of social construction or a redistribution of social power. Educators and mental health professionals who take an integral, developmental approach are interested in ways that can lead to more evolved forms of identity that consider the present developmental level of men.

An integral model considers the stages of development of each sphere of human experience. The interior, subjective realm (I), the intersubjective web of cultural meanings (We), and the body of objective, third person knowledge (It) each evolves in developmental fashion through various levels (see Wilber, 2000). Each realm, as a part of the same whole, moves from a less developed to a higher level of development. That is, there is not just change but a hierarchical evolution toward optimal universal development. This is not to say that all development occurs through all realms at once in a linear, mechanistic movement: there are different aspects of development within one person or society. These streams can manifest themselves independent of each other, at their own rate, at different levels, simultaneously (Wilber, 2000). Examples of streams are moral, interpersonal, affective, gender, ego, and cognitive development.

An integral approach is in contrast to a popular model in counseling psychology, developmental-contextualism (Vondracek & Porfeli, 2002). This model does not specify the movement of growth or change toward optimal human development, which two proponents defined in circular terms: "According to the developmental-contextual framework, optimal development is defined neither by the context nor by the individual, but as a consequence of the dynamic interaction of the person within the environment" (p. 753). Developmental-contextualism appears to be a relativistic framework that does not evaluate levels of both consciousness and social context with respect to optimal development. Their language is devoid of evaluative content: "For effective behavior to occur, the person must have a responsive environment, sufficient motivation to continue working toward a chosen goal, the necessary skills to produce the desired results, and the physical/biological capabilities to implement them" (p. 754).

An integral model of development, by contrast, evaluates various streams of both interior and exterior aspects of both the individual and society—structural and cultural contexts as well as biological and psychological realms—in terms of levels that move toward higher and more integrated aspects of human development. It respects the relative autonomy of the co-varying realms of development instead of collapsing everything into one unit of analysis such as the person-in-context.

Of course, helping male youth means taking into account both their cultural and social context and their personal level of development. Yet from an integral perspective we must guard against assuming both a relative and an absolute stance that refuses to evaluate levels of depth and instead collapses these realms onto one plane.

All individual development necessarily occurs within a specific cultural context. The assumption that a white, straight, male, middle-class, Anglo culture is the universal or neutral culture for everyone must be completely rejected. With respect to ethnic cultural differences, however, it is relativistic to assume that each culture is unique and human beings in one culture have no universal qualities that they share with other human beings who grow up in other cultures. First, cross-cultural research shows that there are developmental stages that people in all cultures experience (Wilber, 2000). Second, cultures themselves can be evaluated developmentally (see Beck & Cowan, 2002). Third, at higher developed levels of consciousness there are individuals who both incorporate and transcend cultural differences, that is, who recognize and experience universal qualities shared by all.

Global youth culture—hip-hop, music, movies, fashion, sports—is a significant part of the medium in which many youth grow up today. However, culture has its limits, and there is a need to evaluate the depth and quality of that culture itself. It is relativistic to uncritically glorify youth culture and assume that culture is everything, to stop short of evaluating how well youth construct their cultural identities and to fail to consider how those culturally based constructions themselves need to evolve. Even the current trend in postmodern analysis of popular youth culture, finding how youth attempt to resist dominant meanings and construct their own, does not have a way out of the language and consciousness of popular culture itself. It is not accidental that much of popular culture today is self-referential and contains recycled allusions to earlier cultural referents; youth complain there are no alternatives to mass media culture, as MTV and commercials appropriate resistance and alternative expressions themselves. Within this realm there is nothing to resist, as Fuchs (1996) pointed out, and no alternative ways to define one's own masculinity.

A postmodern tendency is to assume that culture trumps interior life and that there is no developmental hierarchy that considers depth of meaning. One advocate of youth culture (Dolby, 2002, p. 41) claimed that "form (dance, music, clothing, narrative) is substance." If form is substance, then everything can only arise on a flat plane that allows no evaluation leading to higher development. This outlook, for example, has given rise to the conflation of fashion, by its nature a materialist endeavor concerned with surface appearance, with yoga, a spiritual practice that deepens the inner life, through the popularity of yoga wear in the fashion world. A *New York Times* article was entitled, "Yoga wear, not yoga, becomes the mantra" (La Ferla, 2002, December 15; see Betts, 2002, December 15). The message then, is: I wear yoga clothes, therefore I am deep. This is not to dismiss fashion, which can be an enjoyable, creative, and personal expression of one's self, but to not conflate its signifier role with actual depth of consciousness. Although working with young people does require a respect for their particular cultural context and constructions, it also means inviting and challenging them to find ways to evolve to a higher, deeper, universal level within their everyday lives.

With personal development, by contrast, the danger is to try to force developmental change, to compulsively create programs that are measured by socially acceptable criteria of success in reaching some absolute end. A Buddhist monk, Ajahn Sumedho (2001, p. 124), argued, "We all tend to think we've got to be doing something; we're so conditioned to do things that even meditation becomes a compulsive activity that we're involved in. 'Develop this...develop that....[...]' You don't just come in here and sit, you come in here and *develop!*" That treats spiritual practice as another version of standardized testing, as another marker for social and cultural success to which we become attached. From this end the practice of yoga becomes conflated with fashion; yoga becomes a chic, fashionable commodity, as if depth can be commercialized and purchased like any other entity or service: I practice yoga, therefore I am fashionable and socially acceptable. In terms of masculine identity development, when male youth meditate, they become aware of whatever is going on with themselves without judging the experience. At an early level of development this often means being with feelings of anger, aggressive thoughts, and uncomfortable emotions. It does not mean forcing positive thoughts up and negative ones down in order to arrive at a socially approved identity or self-image.

The next level of development can occur through mindfulness, establishing a good relationship with our own mind and being with whatever arises. It enables us to experience greater depth and higher levels while being in the present. We begin within our everyday personal and cultural constructions of meaning, and then move beyond them.

Postconventional Development

With respect to mature masculine identity development, an integral model shows the movement from preconventional, biological levels to conventional masculinity and toward the possibility of postconventional development and even beyond. There is some confusion among some counselors and others over how mature masculine identity should develop. Some in the nature camp believe that the development of masculinity depends on returning to a preconventional level, cast in essentialist or biological terms, instead of moving through conventional levels to a genuine transconventional one.

For example, two counselors, Jolliff and Horne (1999), who theorized about how to help boys in this society become mature, claimed that boys must first experience a conformist stage in early adolescence, that is, conventional masculinity. The counselors assumed that during this stage all boys must successfully master instrumental and active tasks linked to the achievement of goals through manipulation of objects in the world. "Until a man has successfully mastered the instrumental/active dimension and made those characteristics part of his conscious personality, he will not have the security to proceed further in his masculine development" (p. 20). They then argued that deep, primitive, virile drives of males exist and at this point must be acknowledged for the sake of the man and of society. Through the process of male initiation by mature males they suggested it is the task of the culture to put a young man "in touch with his deep masculine power and teach him appropriate stewardship of that power" (p. 23). Only after fully identifying with his essential, primitive maleness, for example, aggression, risk-taking, and the stoic endurance of pain, they believe, can he move away from conventional masculinity and toward integration of feminine qualities and become more whole. The counselors at another point suggested that this initiation should prepare young men to "take their proper places and proper roles as contributing members of the community" (p. 21).

Developmental research shows that a person tends to pass through preconventional and conventional forms before he or she can consciously integrate and transcend conventional gender identities and become more whole. However, the counselors' model makes a U-turn from conventional gender identity back to a preconventional version of masculinity, based on the presumed existence of essential, deep, primitive, virile drives. In this case, a young man supposedly must go back and express these primitive virile drives through manly initiation rites sponsored by mature males if he is to progress. This mistakenly elevates preconventional notions of masculinity to a romantic, higher level. The model attempts to strengthen the very source of the problem for males, prerational, impulsive drives, instead of promoting a real way for males to integrate and transcend these egocentric and primitive forces. It begs the question of how this preconventional realm can be transcended and how male initiators themselves manage to develop beyond primitive, virile drives within an American culture that itself glorifies the stoic need to endure pain, aggression, and manipulation, that is, primitive virility, and move toward the integration of feminine qualities.

Transcendence of conventional masculinity requires strengthening of higher ego skills. Among some boys it also may require acknowledging and integrating, but not celebrating, more biologically primitive qualities, for example, feelings of dominance, anger, and aggression. Allowing for the fact that these feelings exist, identifying them and being aware of them helps male youth integrate and gain healthy control over such feelings. Furthermore, it may be necessary to repair a developmental deficit in those youth by celebrating positive strengths traditionally associated with masculinity, for example, assertiveness and mastery, which are valid for both boys and girls. These practices differ, however, from uncritically glorifying all prerational impulsive, aggressive, manipulative, and stoic qualities that are also traditionally associated with masculinity. There is no evidence that this is necessary in order to become a more integrated man. There is no reason to assume that boys will not feel like real men until they accomplish a sense of mastery through the manipulation of objects in the world, nor is there any reason to assume that only boys and not girls also have a right to feel they can effect environmental change.

Counselors need to help boys and men develop an integrative sense of power. An integrated model for authentic male development is based on neither power over others, nor powerlessness, the notion that males must give up all power, but on power with others (Kipnis, 1991). It means one can be insightful, flexible, interdependent, and hold to awareness of contrasting perspectives at a higher order of synthesis. Kupers (1993) considered integrative power, rather than power based on threats, to mean the ability to get what one wants through the expressions of love, nurturing, and other positive forms of connection with people rather than through intimidation. He saw an integrative way of being as one that addresses men's emotional pain and yearning for spiritual fulfillment and also politically works to end male privilege, homophobia, and sexist gender relations. Rowan (1997) also suggested that men be initiated into a new way of being that allows for intimacy without losing a sense of power. This allows for both a sense of power and nurturance at a higher, integrative level. Higher male, as well as female, development means relatedness, shared mutual interest, and meaningful connection to community and nature over narrow self-interest and power over others, which lead to violence, depression, and impoverished self-expression (Spielberg, 1999).

Men need to find it in their interest to shift from identifying competitiveness, aggressiveness, rationality, emotional poverty, and social isolation as masculine traits toward a more evolved definition of identity. They can realize that it may be more courageous, in the most positive sense of masculinity, to share power with others, face one's fears, admit one does not know everything, and open one's self to the new and the unknown.

Schools and Male Youth

How do schools address the issue of masculinity? The relationship between schools and boys reflects the contradictions of masculinity within society. To varying degrees and among varying subpopulations based on class and ethnicity, boys experience both privileges and restrictions.

Those who receive the bulk of teacher attention are successful boys. Although there are cultural variations, boys in general demand more attention than do girls; they receive more constructive feedback and are more likely to be rewarded for calling out answers. Boys receive higher-quality instruction such as more open-ended questions, more spontaneous interaction with teachers, more formal instruction, more problem-solving interactions, and more hints. These differences were more marked in science and mathematics classes (Bailey, 1998). As a consequence, girls may learn to be classroom pleasers who listen carefully and are model citizens; boys may learn to be active, attention seeking, quick to offer answers, and self-confident (Anselmi & Law, 1998).

By contrast, schools and many boys are notorious for not getting along. Boys in general are highly overrepresented among students referred for remediation due to being labeled as having learning disabilities, hyperactivity, oppositional behavior, and conduct disorders (Horne & Kiselica, 1999). Schools historically have been seen as feminizing institutions that are hostile to boys' energy, physicality, and self-assertion. This is especially true of working-class and African American and Latino male youth (see Ferguson, 2000). Much of the attention these boys receive is negative. When I worked with groups of black male youth in a junior high school in Brooklyn, they complained that the women teachers picked on the boys and blamed them for anything disruptive, while some of the girls' more passive-aggressive behavior went unnoticed and unpunished. According to Ann Ferguson (2000), some African American young men regard fighting as a ritual performance of masculine power. These male youth especially threaten schools. Ferguson argued:

> This manifestation of physicality is the very material presence that the school seeks to exclude: black males are already seen as embodying the violence and aggression that will drive away "desirable" families and their children. Fighting on the part of black boys is more visible as a problem, so it is viewed with extreme concern and responded to more swiftly and harshly. (p. 194)

Counseling programs for male youth range between zero tolerance on aggression and violence to uncritically accepting the conventional norm of masculinity. After the tragic shooting incidents around the country, schools snapped to attention. They instituted counseling programs for handling grief over loss from violence, for resolving conflict and reducing violence, and for screening emotional problems. Some of these measures provide useful skills and assist students. However, the emphasis on zero tolerance—treating any threatening language or gesture, even one made in jest, as a serious threat—creates its own stress on students and faculty (see Leland, 2001, April 8; Mulvey & Cauffman, 2001). A zero tolerance policy allows no room to interpret the context of tone, voice, or multiple meaning, and students may be sent for psychological evaluation for any perceived indication of violence. This approach tries to resolve or contain a problem rooted in long-standing causes through a form of external, social control. It ends up being another manifestation of the very pattern it tries to eliminate: the conventional masculine tendency to deny and repress a problem or to try to abolish the external symptom through aggressive behavior.

Some counselor educators still take a normative view of male development. For example, Keys, Bemak, and Lockhart (1998) suggested that school counselors should "be able to recognize students who are functioning outside of the range of normal development and take action to secure an appropriate level of services" (p. 386). However, this takes normal development for granted and does not distinguish between conventional masculinity, presumably a part of normal development, and a healthier level of functioning for young men.

Schools, Connell (1996) has reminded us, are both agents and sites for the making of masculinities. A school shapes gender relations through its gender regime, the totality of its institutional arrangements. These include power relations such as discipline and supervisory tasks, division of labor reflected in curriculum choices, emotional rules and roles, and the use of gender symbols. A woman who worked as a fourth grade teacher in an inner-city school with a large African American population told me that when boys wanted attention or someone to play with they acted in a violent manner; violence was a form of communication for them. She observed that the school and even parents responded to boys with more anger, threats, yelling, and harsh discipline.

Schools are also one of the major sites for students to form gender meanings. Students contest, construct, and experiment with different masculinities, including conventional masculinity. In schools, homophobia is not only detrimental to gay males but serves as a cruel and effective deterrent for straight males' ability to explore a full range of emotional and social development. However, in my work with male adolescents in junior and senior high schools, I have noticed that boys' playful dissing and teasing in the halls and in the locker room, in particular, calling each other gay, simulating sexual acts, or expressing physical affection, may also be about exploring the limits of their gender role as it is about homophobia or anxiety about their own sexuality.

School counselors need to be aware of the school's particular gender regime, as Connell (1996) has urged, and help move the system as a whole toward gender equality as well as address the emotional needs of young men. They need to think through a middle path between zero tolerance, on the one hand, and acceptance of normal development, on the other. For men today, normal development, if taken to mean conventional masculinity, is unhealthy. It often means to be alienated and shut off from one's innermost core of being by social conventions (Rowan, 1997). In this sense all boys are at risk in that they are subject to the unhealthy norm of conventional masculinity. It is not that all boys are pathologized, or to be blamed but, rather, the social norm itself that is problematic. This, however, does not mean that all young men are members of a victimized, disadvantaged group, which ignores male privilege and personal responsibility, as Connell (1996) has pointed out. Instead of seeing all boys as at-risk in the pathological sense, Capuzzi and Gross (1999) suggested that it might be useful to regard and treat them all as at-promise. By addressing gender-based value conflicts in all men, counselors can intervene in a proactive or preventive way (Brooks & Silverstein, 1995). Although counselors can still distinguish between different characteristics of young men, they can encourage all of them to take positive risks such as developing conscious intimacy and trust with others (see Busch, 2003, July/August).

Spirituality—for Lack of a Better Word: Better for Men

The concern with higher development is often regarded as an aspect of spirituality. Counselors have pointed to the spiritual dimension as the next major construct within therapy, and nine of ten respondents in a national survey of counselor educator programs rated spirituality as a significant issue in counselor education (Hodges, 2000). Counselor educators encourage counselor training programs to consider religious and spiritual issues, given that spiritual experiences and practices have an important place in the psychological reality of many people (Schulte, Skinner, & Claiborn, 2002). Others argue that a curriculum based on spiritual issues can be infused into an accredited counselor education program (Burke, Hackney, Hudson, Miranti, Watts, & Epp, 1999). Even school administrators of late have been open to consider spirituality as an essential aspect of leadership (see the *School Administrator*, 2002, September).

There is growing evidence that spiritual beliefs and activities, in particular, meditation, benefit mental and physical health (Brown & Ryan, 2003; Fukuyama & Sevig, 1999; Hall, 2003, September 14; Miller & Thoresen, 2003, January). Most important for our purposes, spiritual well-being is associated with less masculine gender role stress. Mahalik and Lagan (2001) suggested that men who are more spiritual might be less susceptible to harsh masculine socialization or better able to deal with the anxiety and stress of transgressing masculine norms. If young men can be more spiritual in the best sense, they are more likely to let go of harsh, rigid conventional masculine beliefs and roles.

For lack of a better term, *spirituality* has become popular but has a number of problematic connotations that need to be clarified. First, spirituality is distinct from organized, institutionalized religions. Almost all counselors and educators take pains to make the point that recognizing spirituality is not identical with any particular religious organization, although of course religions incorporate spiritual dimensions. With respect to school settings, a counselor must not only uphold the separation of church and state but must also avoid any sense of proselytizing or promoting a particular religion. As Nel Noddings said, "Spirituality does not require an institutional connection" (Halford, 1998, December, p. 1). However, this is not to say that educators must shun discussion of religions or, more important, the yearning for greater meaning and the kinds of deeper questions that religions have posed, as well as the need for recognizing the sacred in everyday life (see also Kessler, 2000; Weaver & Cotrell, 1992).

Some counselors feel that spirituality is a mistaken attempt to extend the counseling profession's realms of influence beyond what Weinrach (2002, p. 311) called its "basic psychological and educational domain." Weinrach argued that "the spirituality in counseling movement is yet another example of the erosion of the separation between public and private space" (ibid.). Weinrach made this unsupported assertion in the context of correctly arguing for the need for the counseling profession to regard Jews as a culturally distinct group that deserves interventions to meet their unique needs and to acknowledge the existence of anti-Semitism wherever it appears. Jews, he felt, in turn "must embrace those aspects of the multicultural counseling movement that champion unconditional inclusiveness and equity for all culturally distinct populations" (p. 312). Yet Weinrach could not envision spirituality's connection with psychological and education concerns, nor did he see spirituality as capable of being inclusive and respectful of all cultures. He rightly resisted any coerced unity that would disrespect legitimate boundaries and that would impose a false unity or deny genuine differences in the name of spirituality. Yet he forfeited the chance to present a spiritual vision that embraces both cultural distinction and universality and that grasps the interrelationship between personal and public matters. These are aspects of a humanistic tradition that can be found in Jewish culture itself. Instead, he limited his awareness, and his outlook, by assuming that distinctions between cultures, as well as the separation between public and private matters, are inevitable, invariable truths.

Second, in this sense, spirituality is the higher awareness of the whole, interconnected nature of all beings and things, past, present, and future, which is itself without form. Spirituality also can be seen in part as "the animating force in life…an innate capacity and tendency to move towards knowledge, love, meaning, hope, transcendence, connectedness, and compassion" (Summit results, 1995, December). It is both a contemplative and engaged, sometimes political, activity, with the intention to end suffering in the world for everyone.

Spirituality arises within the context of everyday life. It does not refer to a separate realm apart from the material world, as in matter versus spirit. This is a dualistic notion. Educators who are proponents of materialism assume that everyday life can only be reduced to and described in positivist, observable, and empirical terms. They tend to dismiss people's most significant inner experiences that speak to issues of ultimate concern, wholeness, meaning, and universal connectedness. The holistic educator Ron Miller (1997) pointed out that

> the more children's lives are regimented, reduced, measured, and forced to conform to a meaningless routine, the more likely they will show symptoms of alienation such as "attention deficit," drug abuse, violence, and nihilistic withdrawal…[A] reductionist culture attempts to ignore these consequences ("Just say no!"), and cannot even recognize that these are *spiritual* problems. (original italics, pp. 223–224)

The flip side of this dualism shows up when some spiritual proponents dismiss the material world as meaningless or insignificant. Here it means a turning inward at the expense of ignoring the material world and social inequities. This may mean assuming an extreme, self-denying, ascetic, or unhealthy masochistic practice that sacrifices one's self to attain some vague, ethereal reward in the afterlife. Or it may be used as a means to maintain privilege and power. For example, some of the nature-based tendencies within the men's movement discussed previously consider themselves spiritual but end up trying to shore up and exonerate white males who experience themselves as victims of social forces. Although many males from different backgrounds do experience pain from social change, they mistakenly seek relief within an insular, regressive brand of spirituality (Savran, 1998; Kimmel & Kaufman, 1994). The term *spirituality*, Fukuyama and Sevig (1999) asserted, is even sometimes misused to justify harmful behavior against others such as certain cases of fundamentalism that rely on oppressive, authoritarian, self-serving, and repressive relations; these negative and unhealthy patterns can be contrasted to a transformative spirituality that leads people to confront inauthenticity and to accept themselves and all others.

Perhaps the most important distinction that needs to be made here is between prerational and transrational spirituality. The failure to distinguish these is what Wilber (2000) referred to as the pre/trans fallacy. Those who glorify a prerational or preconventional spirituality look to disregard critical thinking and other aspects of ego development in order to return to earlier, more primitive versions of spirit such as superstitions and belief in myths. Robert Bly (1990) and others who believed that males should return to a primal, mythic masculinity fall into this error. A transrational spirituality, by contrast, incorporates and transcends conventional ego development. It assumes the requirement of a healthy, self-aware ego and of higher cognitive processes such as critical thinking. Through transpersonal and mindful practices one is able to see that the ego is ultimately an empty construct and that all of reality is "inter-being" (Nhat Hanh, 1991). This is a universal truth of the highest order that requires a higher-order method to demonstrate it. It recognizes a hierarchy of consciousness development that moves from prerational to conventional to transrational awareness.

This approach per se is a challenge to postmodern relativism and to the failure of many social scientists to acknowledge a hierarchy of ultimately meaningful, universal values. For example, Gergen (2001), a proponent of postmodernism in psychology, believed that concepts of cognition and emotion are not universal but are by-products of the Western tradition. He asserted that such "universalizing tendencies approximate neocolonialism" (p. 809). He maintained that there are no universals, only cultural constructions, even in biology. Yet Gergen did believe in the need for psychological inquiry to "benefit humankind" and in enhancing cultural life by focusing on "positive possibilities" (p. 808) and hoped that colonialist universalism (a bad thing) will be replaced by a "global conversation among equals" (p. 813). That is, he holds an implicit belief in universals such as humankind, the value of benefiting it, and worldwide equality as opposed to colonialism.

Postmodernism has served to challenge false universals that were representations of limited perspectives, often of those in power, and has called for the need to consider multiple viewpoints. Yet postmodernism taken to its extreme, fearful of making objective statements that imply a hierarchy of truth, undercuts its very argument with the self-contradictory statement: there are no truths. This calls for the reply: except, apparently, yours. Because postmodernism can only fall back on infinite contexts of social construction, language, and pluralist cultural traditions, it must remain phobic of any realization of hierarchical truths, that is, some things, ideas, or actions are better or deeper or more true than others, a truth in and of itself. In this case even the fact that all humans think and feel to varying degrees and that cognition and emotion are universal categories that are amenable to cross-cultural investigation and validation must remain beyond the pale of postmodern beliefs and inquiry.

A growing number of educators and counselors do recognize the significance of spirituality. However, many do not distinguish between pre- and transrational spirituality and, as a consequence, risk squandering some of their credibility among their peers in education and the social sciences. An educator such as Philip Wexler (2000), to his credit, recognized the importance of spirituality but appears not to grasp the pre/trans fallacy and conflates the two; this undermines his important call for the creation of what he terms an emerging mystical society. For example, Wexler believed that almost all social practices that seek direct experience of the transcendental are laying the groundwork for a mystical society. Yet some are without credibility or validation as transrational practices:

> Mystical models of Kundalini energy, alchemy, yoga, and shamanistic, celestial descents, and the everyday healing and social distribution of energy associated with the sacred are being pressed forward to sociological awareness by the course of everyday social life. New Age body practices, increasingly being legitimated as "complementary medicine," are folk enactments of our still sociologically inarticulated consciousness of this broader meaning of social interaction. (p. 138)

Wexler did not seem to evaluate the kinds of experiences he cited with respect to whether they are regressive, prerational practices that celebrate magic or transrational ones; as a sociologist he appeared content to lump them together as social forms that are inevitably moving us forward rather than considering the quality of these various experiences and how they may or may not contribute to higher consciousness and a more advanced society.

His thesis is that social processes are diffusing and mixing mystical practices together with the social relations of the information age and that this is sufficient to establish the groundwork for a more advanced mystical society that is the synthesis of both. This model takes place on a flat sociological plane of analysis that does not distinguish various so-called mystical experiences in terms of historical depth of development or levels and streams of consciousness. Still, although Wexler's analysis does not help one sort out a viable means to revitalize sacred practices within the context of today's rational society, his call to do so is significant. The task remains how to promote human development within the current moment of society.

It may be best to avoid the conceptual pitfalls that accompany the use of the word *spirituality*. Following Ken Wilber (2000), it is preferable to refer to an integral approach rather than just focusing on spiritual or transpersonal issues. Integral counseling, for example, integrates interior self-development with the development of both objective, scientific knowledge of the natural world and of broader cultural communities and social organizations. In this sense it promotes an expansive, palpable, and transformative experience that both connects one with and places one at the center of all beings and things. Integral awareness constitutes a different level of knowing that extends beyond empirical or interpretive subject matter. Yet it shares with the physical and social sciences principles and verifiable methods of how we come to know what is true (Wilber, 1998b). Integral counseling is committed to contributing to the growing amount of empirical research that shows the positive influence of the mind on the body through meditation and other practices (Goleman, 2003; Hall, 2003, September 14; Seeman, Duban, & Seeman, 2003, January).

An integral counseling model reflects the stages of human development and moves from an egocentric to a sociocentric to a postconventional level. With respect to gender identity development, men may evolve from biological and genetic givens through conventional norms of masculinity to androgyny, and in rare instances experience the underlying unity beyond gender itself (Wilber, 2000). The starting point is in everyday life, in this moment.

Mindfulness Meditation and Male Adolescents

A highly developed man is mindful of the present experience and of the interdependent, changing nature of the way things are. To clarify the ambiguous commitment to *keepin' it real,* a premise of hip-hop culture, a mindful person envisions reality in ways that manifest itself beyond both conventional and even socially critical constructions of appearances. The practice of meditation and everyday mindfulness can facilitate this path. As part of an integral counseling approach, meditation helps male youth develop higher, more integrative levels of awareness. It does not presume just to help them adjust to the conventional or dominant norm of masculinity. Nor is its purpose solely to aid them in negotiating the world according to their own relative, individualistic, or group cultural values. For example, with respect to African American male adolescents, a common dilemma is how to follow the parental message to succeed in school and also avoid the oftentimes emasculating and treasonous appearances of such success (see Fordham, 1996; Herbert, 2003, July 10). A higher awareness means an ability to live beyond the dilemma of conforming to oppressive and dangerous notions of white manhood or resisting it in favor of marginalized posturing, some of which is self-destructive. To develop toward one's full potential is not another set of traits that can be accumulated or attained through training or traditional counseling or educational means. Integral counseling with males involves mindfulness in terms of personal, educational, and social development.

It is clear that in order to develop an adequate ego and participate in conventional society all children require certain basic psychological and social needs, such as appropriate validation or affirmation (Riethmayer, 2001, Spring). James Garbarino (2000) found that those young men who committed violence in their schools did not have such needs met: a number of them were not loved at home, were victimized by relentless teasing and bullying, felt powerless, and were socially isolated from other students. For many male adolescents their task is to move from an egocentric, impulsive, and defensive stage to a sociocentric one that entails cooperation and empathy for others as well as for themselves.

Mindfulness practices such as meditation that are integrated into all aspects of young men's lives are means by which they may be able to repair developmental deficits and continue to grow. Adults can teach meditation to young people in schools (see Fontana & Slack, 1997; Rozman, 1994) and teens can practice it themselves (see Gordhamer, 2001; Winston, 2003). Meditation can serve as a vital adjunct to counseling, therapy, and psychological educational programs. In one study, adolescent sex offenders gained greater self-awareness and self-control through a program of meditation and yoga (Derezotes, 2000). Teens in another study had lower blood pressure from practicing meditation as well as better concentration and fewer attendance and behavior problems in school (Meditation benefits, 2003, January 21; see also Busch, 2003, July/August). As James Garbarino has pointed out, meditation provides a middle way between acting out and repressing one's feelings and can provide a spiritual grounding for interventions aimed at counteracting some effects of early trauma (Getz & Gordhamer, n.d). That is, whether or not they reach higher, postconventional levels, the young men may be helped to move from an egocentric to a sociocentric level of development through mindful practices such as meditation. Meditation promotes spiritual well-being, which includes acceptance of self and others, compassion, and social connectedness. These are antidotes to the stress and anxiety of rigid conformity to stereotypical masculinity.

Meditation is potentially helpful in moving young men toward higher levels of development from whatever point they are at. In the following discussion, I illustrate these ways with some examples from my work with high school male athletes that I describe more fully later on.

1. Mindful behavior. Meditation provides male youth an alternative to either following through on a troublesome feeling or repressing it. It creates an important reflective space for boys who tend to act out their problems. When confronted with a stressful situation, many young men will impulsively act out rather than mindfully reflect on the consequences. At other times they will repress or deny the feeling of pressure, sadness, loss, anger, humiliation, or anxiety. These can build up as emotional and physical stress or later on explode in destructive or self-destructive behavior (Garbarino, 2000). A number of the African American students acknowledged they were often in survival mode and were struggling with dealing with their anger. By noticing what comes up in one's mind, considering it as a passing thought or feeling, and allowing one's self to sit with that thought in a compassionate way, the students learned they can be freer to assess the situation, consider the consequences, and decide what to do. One student attributed his ability to stay focused to practicing meditation during the football season and wrote: "During a game a kid was talking shit and kept cheap shooting me but I stayed under control."

By noticing how thoughts come and go, an adolescent is better able to assess the value of those thoughts and see them for what they are. A male teen who practiced meditation in a treatment center said, "I can replace unwanted thoughts much more easily now. I try not to control my feelings, just feel them. Otherwise, they can get stuffed and come out some other way, as abuse" (Derezotes, 2000, p. 105). Meditation as part of counseling may be useful in treating adolescent behavior problems (Laselle & Russell, 1993). There is recent evidence that meditation helps calm the part of the brain that acts as a trigger for fear and anger (Goleman, 2003).

Insight meditation (Vipassana) also may be a valuable tool for cognitive development. It can promote the practice of meta-cognition, the ability to think about thinking and to further categorize one's thoughts from a higher perspective. The higher stages for Kegan (1994) and Loevinger and Wessler (1970) involve the ability to reflect on one's own reflective categories, to make thinking itself an object of higher-order thought. It also can help a teen gain insight into one's self, by examining thoughts and feelings and tracing them back to broader categories of thoughts that in turn can be examined and sat with. It provides a method and practice to let go of the attachment to anger and oppositional thinking that often accompanies critical consciousness. For example, some in the group discussed the feelings of pressure in their own lives and began to develop a critical analysis of their sources. Athletes know that if they do well there are potential careers and big money at stake. With African American young men, there still exists few channels others than sports to succeed in society. There is also the macho pressure to prove one's toughness to oneself and others. Beyond these insights, meditation has helped these athletes consider how they will relate to these feelings of pressure and assess what values are most important to them.

2. Emotional deadness. Meditation helps male youth become attentive to bodily sensations and emotional feelings. Part of the gender role of conventional masculinity is that men are not taught how to recognize their feelings. When boys are asked how they feel, they often do not know how to answer (Kindlon & Thompson, 2000). Ronald Levant (1995) presented data that suggested that most boys display low-level alexithymia, being emotionally shut off. Terry Kupers (1993) coined the term *pathological arrhythmicity* to describe many men's lack of responsiveness to natural cycles: "working long hours without letting up, arriving at work each day even when not feeling well, hiding our true feelings, remaining vigilant before the prospect of attack from as-yet-undisclosed enemies" (pp. 30–31). Kupers also mentioned men's inability to let emotional experiences take their course. Some women become frustrated and upset with many men who are not able to acknowledge what it is they are feeling.

Men are not taught to be aware of their feelings as young boys. Instead, they learn to keep working at a physical task or sport and block out any cues from their body such as pain, fatigue, or stress that signals the body needs adjustment. A young male athlete needs to notice the pain and its degree of severity, given that many men are not in touch with bodily feelings or try to deny them. Meditation also can help men in this regard. Pain is a signal to the body that tells you to stop. When athletes keep playing in pain, they are in danger of losing a sense of where that line is. If a player consistently ignores pain, he can further damage his body. By noticing and attending to one's body, male teens can become more aware of sensations and feelings.

In the group, we discussed how Korey Stringer, a Minnesota Vikings football player who died of dehydration during a hot preseason practice session in August 2001, might not have been mindful of what his body was telling him. In this sense he may have been like many men who learn to ignore pain and other physical indicators of stress, fatigue, and illness. This is important for men who learn through the norm of conventional masculinity to sacrifice themselves for others through toughness and the denial of illness or pain for fear of being seen as a wimp. In the aftermath of the death of Korey Stringer professional football players from both the Baltimore Ravens and the

Philadelphia Eagles refused to play a preseason game on loose, uneven cutouts of wet turf. A professional player from the Pittsburgh Steelers, Jerome Bettis, believed that Stringer's death "served as a wake-up call for guys to listen to their bodies, look for the signs and not push themselves into death" (George, 2001, August 15). In the meditation group the young men learned to question the need to sacrifice their health for the purposes of fame or money.

Meditation helps to counter many men's addictive dependency on external fixes; these are attempts to medicate for feelings of pain or discomfort. When a man is not aware of his negative feelings, he is more likely to seek an extrinsic means to ease the pain through a quick fix, whether it be drugs, work, sex, gambling, or acting out in compulsive, aggressive, or self-destructive ways. Meditation involves sitting with and experiencing one's feelings, and not running away from them. It creates the space for one to notice the changing nature of feelings, to trace their origins, and to be mindful enough so that authentic responses to what is going on become possible.

3. Less attachment to conventional masculine identity. There is considerable pressure on men to uphold the conventional male gender role. This leads to stress on male youth who feel their identity must be constantly tested as to whether it is ever masculine enough. Through meditation, men can become less attached to identifying with traits of conventional masculinity: acting tough, not expressing nurturing feelings. They practice sitting with their thoughts and feelings as they arise, noticing them without judgment, and then letting them go. This provides a way out of the dilemma of either giving up all power or clinging to pressured expectations of manhood and allows them to develop a broader definition of self. Softening the space around a self-concept also allows other aspects of oneself to be incorporated into the notion of self. For example, assuming Korey Stringer had been aware of his physical state, he might have stopped practicing by disengaging from the notion that being a quitter makes one less of a man. Stringer had been teased by teammates the day before for a media photo of him that showed how exhausted he was during practice and that he said made him feel embarrassed.

If masculinity has to do with crossing or not crossing a line (Kupers, 1993), a meditative approach can help young men determine where that line is within whatever activity that engages them. Instead of providing judgments or censorship, I have worked with the students about learning to identify when competitive, aggressive teasing of their teammates, which is a part of their subculture, crossed over from friendly to hurtful. Some have learned to say to their teammates, "That crossed the line. That hurts." This has broken the pattern of repressing feelings that later often leads to acting them out while still allowing for the young men to be playful.

Murphy and White (1995) suggested that androgyny, the balance of male and female characteristics, is enhanced when athletes are performing in the zone. Dropping defenses helps expand higher awareness of one's full capacities and expressiveness. They suggested, "Many male athletes, even in the fiercest sports, have a strikingly feminine aspect, contrary to the old macho cliché. Freed from the need to prove themselves in this regard, they can allow a wider range of feeling and perceptions" (p. 142).

4. More openess to the Other. The letting go of clinging to a narrow, rigid self-concept of conventional masculinity opens up the self to consider compassion for and even identification with others who were previously regarded as one's opposite. This includes women, gays, other ethnic groups, enemies, and all aspects of nature. Meditation allows for the profound realization that one is a part of all beings and things in the universe, past, present, and future, and that concepts, identities, and relationships are always changing. By adopting an open, present mind and noticing what is going on in the moment independent of preconceptions, the person can become available to his or her own authentic response to the Other. This nonjudgmental acceptance and openness expands the capacity for empathy and can lead to compassion and higher moral reasoning.

In one group with the male athletes we critically analyzed the attitude of some rap lyrics toward women. While some of the young men had struggled with their own attitudes toward women, they gained more understanding of and empathy for women's experiences. They were also able to listen with less defensiveness to some of the younger players express their unhappiness about how some of the older players were treating them as part of an initiation tradition.

5. Mastery beyond ego. From the players' perspective, a way to transcend some of the problems of football is to distinguish between playing for egocentric or socially approved reasons and playing for a higher purpose. For example, playing for a sense of mastery, giving oneself over to a higher purpose, is neither self-centered (egocentric) nor conformist (conventional) but is transcendent (postconventional).

A mastery orientation does not involve attachment to one's ego. Shane Murphy (1999) distinguished between an ego and a higher-order, mastery orientation to competitive sports among children. When a child is motivated by ego, he or she values winning above all else and looking good and successful to one's peers and competitors. A child motivated by mastery understands that losing can also lead to progress and growth, that the ultimate value of competition is personal development, and that happiness come from becoming good at what you love. Meditation can help young men develop more of a mastery approach not only to sports but also to other life activities, such as test taking. As a practice it enables the ego to get out of the way of the moment and perform in flow. One athlete privately admitted he was afraid of hurting an opponent by playing too aggressively, but he also did not want to hold back. He was able to meditate on and visualize a way to play with a sense of mastery that avoided both pitfalls.

When athletes perform in the zone, they won't choke, which is thinking too much about something one knows how to do. If a person feels secure and confident and is not feeling that his or her ego is on the line, s/he can be in the moment and attend to the relevant performance cues.

6. Stress reduction, better health. One of the benefits of meditation is that a person is calmer, centered, and focused. He or she is less likely to be experiencing tension because one is more aware of what is going on with one's body and can employ breathing practices when tension is noticed. Being less tense and more relaxed in turn protects the immune system (see Goleman, 2003). This can have a salutary effect on men who rigidly adhere to stereotypical masculine gender roles that induce type A behavior, compulsivity, perfectionism, workaholism, and quickness to anger. These are linked to heart-related illnesses and death. Also, when pain is present, meditation can help by breathing into the injured part of the body and attending to the more neutral sensations that comprise the experience. Instead of denying the pain, one can learn to regard the sensation as separate from a sense of self.

7. Need for sacred space. All students, young women and men, especially in urban schools, need a time and space to center themselves and feel a sense of peace. They undergo considerable stress and pressure from their families, the physical environment, and from the media, with its relentless promotion of consumer goods marketed as necessary for social and personal power. A structured, protected time for meditation and visualization provides some students with the only quiet moment of the day during which they can connect with a deeper part of themselves and the world (see Glickman, 2003; Kessler, 2000).

Male adolescents can strengthen conventional ego skills through meditation. Mindful counseling and psychological education programs are also necessary. Practicing meditation furthers a vision of postconventional masculinity that allows young men to go beyond the ego and become less attached to it. It can help expand the meaning of self toward identification with others. An aspect of spiritual well-being, meditation may increase the chances of having peak experiences and enhance the joys of everyday life beyond those offered by conventional society. It may help move people toward what Ken Jones (2003) calls a radical social culture of awakening.

PART TWO

Doing Nothing for Something: Working with High School Male Athletes

Chapter Three

High School Football: Life In/Out of the Zone

When you wake up, then you'll know, what was up
You won't live, so corrupt, only love, you'll take up
All the chasin and rushin impatience and fussin
The racin for something the hatin and frontin is makin you NOTHIN
So, die before you die so when you die you don't die
You got to die before you die so when you die you don't die

—KRS-One (2002), "Good Bye," from *Spiritual Minded*

Stress City

The exigencies of everyday life in the United States have assumed the density and gravitational weight of negative matter. Let's assume we can freeze-frame a moment in the day and slice it up. We can find from top to bottom an infinitely complex nexus of realities that were unimagined just a few years back. What appears to be a simple scenario reveals greater complexity once it is scrutinized because it is linked to contexts, and in turn broader contexts, endlessly, and because of the interrelationship between all of the parts. Every aspect of the picture is linked to other levels of reality; one thing affects another. Yet in most cases the links remain unacknowledged and unexpressed.

A handy way to make sense of this is to consider the material, cultural, and psychological levels of reality. The material level concerns the natural world. Physical and natural sciences and economics are means to determine its objective qualities. The cultural refers to the shared meanings that people create through everyday practices and traditions. Methods such as ethnography, social theory and research, and journalism help us learn and interpret the norms and the quality of intersubjective life. The psychological, the most neglected level, involves the subjective, inner life of individuals, the personal experience of meaning, beauty, and truth. To access this realm we employ self-reflective practices such as counseling, psychotherapy, journaling, art, and meditation. Each level in turn can be evaluated along a chain of evolution that moves toward increasingly differentiated, higher-ordered, and integrated wholes.

Consider the scene out of an SUV TV commercial: mom and kids with school backpacks remove groceries from the car. This is the conventional take. Everything seems as it is. A deeper look asks the following:

At the material level: How does this car improve or limit the physical safety and comfort of the family members' bodies (does it contribute to their longevity or to their mortality through obesity, lack of exercise, and the vehicle's tendency to roll over)? How is this car, especially given its low fuel economy, affecting the environment (smog, global warming, diminution of the rain forest, ice cap melting, ozone depletion)? Where is the money coming from to finance and maintain it in terms of family (consumer debt), society (increase in traffic, accidents), and global levels (petroleum as a factor in Middle East foreign policy, steel industry tariffs, billions of dollars spent on corporate advertising)? What kinds of wasteful and harmful (overly packaged, processed, refined, transfatty) or nutritious (organic fruits, vegetables, grains) foods are in those bags? *Where does owning and using an SUV stand with respect to an optimal material environment?* (See Brown, 2003, February 8.)

At the cultural level: What does the car mean to this family (luxury, comfort, safety, power, status, success) in this community (educated, exclusive, competitive, upper middle income)? Does the woman juggle all her roles (wife, mother, school parent, soccer mom, successful businessperson), or does she need help (nanny and maid from developing world countries with their own families and concerns)? What do school and those overladen backpacks signify to the children (sometimes cool, sometimes boring but got to get As), to the family (a ladder toward the kids' professional career), and the community (high taxes but worth it) where they live? How does all that homework fit in with the kids' lives (online chats and cell phone calls to friends, hours of TV viewing, CD playing and movie watching, and weekly soccer, piano, and ballet practice)? Where's Waldo (Dad) and why is he not in the picture? *Where does the culture of SUV suburban life stand with respect to an optimal way of life?*

At the psychological level: What level of moral development do these kids have with respect to materialist values? How does Mom cope with what is going on in her head: the lack of time (it never feels like enough), the need to keep up appearances (washing the SUV, kids' orthodontia, the gardener, dry cleaner, hosiery), and how to cope with the other stuff (the uncertainty of the stock market, the refilling of Zoloft prescriptions, the looming high cost of college, the pressure on the kids to achieve and keep up, refinancing the mortgage, aging parents, husband working late again, her own goals and aspirations, her sense of self-worth, her relationship to her husband, how she relates to her relationship…) *Where does the consciousness of this family stand with respect to optimal human development?*

Now imagine you come across a high school football game on a city field on a Saturday afternoon. Here again we are presented with a scene in which there is more than meets the eye. One might consider:

At the material level: What kind of field are they playing on (is that AstroTurf safe or does it promote injuries as some professional players have experienced)? How physically fit are these kids (will they suffer any long-term injuries from playing as do many professional players? Are any taking steroids for bodybuilding? Do any have any obsessive-compulsive issues around body image, weight-lifting, or eating?) How much is this school spending on sports rather than academics (too much, too little, just enough, and who decides)? Do the students block out the noise of the el[elevated train] rumbling overhead near the field? After the game can they return to a quiet neighborhood and sleep (free of the noise of ambulance sirens, car alarms, loud radios, and gunshots)? *Where are these practices with respect to an optimal level of physical and environmental health?*

At the cultural level: What does this game mean to the boys (is it fun, or also a badge of social approval, acceptance, popularity, prowess, and a chance for an athletic scholarship to college)? How about to the parents (is it pride, or also a vicarious expression of power and the promotion of one's child as a star)? What is in it for the school (a means to enhance conformist values through school spirit, just fun, or also a better chance to get corporate sponsors if the players are successful)? What does it mean to their classmates (enjoyment of a good game, school spirit and camaraderie, peer pressure, something to do, wanna-be cool by knowing a football player)? What does it say about masculinity (you need to take pain like a man, prove your toughness and aggression, show you can win in a competitive society, show you're a team player by getting along with fellow players and following the authority of the coach)? How do sports feed into cultural assumptions about African American men (sports are one of the few channels for their success, sports pressure them to make it in college and the NFL, sports showcase them as gladiators for the entertainment of the white majority, sports are an expression of black male pride)? What is all that explicit bumping and grinding of the cheerleaders about (just cute and sexy; girls are sluts and hoes; sex has lost any sense of emotional weight and meaning, it's just an activity, especially for girls)? What is the place of spectator sports as leisure activity (as an expression of aesthetic spontaneity, grace, and heightened awareness, as a community bonding experience, as a passive consumer commodity, as a vicarious form of aggression and competition)? *Where do these practices stand with respect to providing optimal cultural values of meaningful rituals and relationships and the enhancement of a caring community?*

At the psychological level: What are these young men experiencing (anger; aggression; fear of getting injured or hurting someone else; tense from too much regimentation; frustration; fear of failing, messing up, looking bad; pressure from parents, coaches, peers; a sense of mastery, exhilaration, pleasure, heightened awareness, teamwork; unity of mind and body)? Is this an intrinsically meaningful, enjoyable experience for them or do they feel compelled to prove themselves? *With respect to optimal self-awareness and consciousness, what is their relationship to their own experience?*

Let us examine a particular urban high school football team from an integral point of view, the material, cultural, social, and psychological realms and their various levels of development.

Beautiful Brooklyn

Sometimes I feel like my only friend
Is the city I live in, is beautiful Brooklyn
Long as I live here believe I'm on fire hey

—Mos Def (1999), "Brooklyn," from *Black on Both Sides*

Brooklyn (aka BK) is many worlds. To discover it, one must first get past those nostalgic stereotypes of tough but good-natured, funny-accented working-class folks (Dem Bums fans, Ralph and Alice Kramden, Vinnie Barbarino/Tony Manero) who grew up on egg creams, Nathan's hot dogs, Junior's cheesecake, doo-wop, stickball, and, of course, the Brooklyn Dodgers. Beyond these are over two million people within neighborhoods as much divided by race, class, ethnicity, and immigrant status as they are unified by Brooklyn's sense of place, both cosmic and down home. Walt Whitman's presence hovers over the red brick and brownstone rows; the Brooklyn Bridge, glorified in Hart Crane's poem and Joseph Stella's paintings, stands proud; Jackie Robinson's courage and skill are embodied on the ball fields and playgrounds; and Betty Smith's spirited Tree (*Ailanthus altissima*, tree of heaven) still grows in Brooklyn. All the while throughout the borough an influx of immigrants—Chinese, Mexicans and other Central Americans, Yemeni and Pakistani Muslims, Russian Jews, and English (Jamaican), Creole (Haitian), and Spanish- (Dominican) speaking Caribbean islanders have helped remake Brooklyn with different flavors and hues. They have added themselves to the preexisting mix of African Americans, Arabs, Jews (Orthodox, Sephardic, Hasidic, and secular), Poles, Italians, Irish, and Puerto Ricans, to name a few, many of them also recent immigrants.

The tragic incident of 9-11 increased the anxiety level of all New Yorkers. But it also may have had a somber, unifying effect on some Brooklynites, contributing to an atmosphere of greater tolerance. Even prior to the event most residents of the borough were learning to get along with each other, often out of necessity; some have even come to enjoy it. The racial tensions between Hasidic Jews and Caribbean and African Americans that scarred Crown Heights in 1991 have abated for a while now.

Still, the gap between rich and poor is considerable. Group tensions assume different forms. With students now able to attend high schools outside their neighborhood, turf battles flare up on school grounds. Neighborhoods are in tremendous flux: in parts of Williamsburg, Bushwick, Cobble Hill, and Park Slope, young professionals, artists, and gays and lesbians priced out of Manhattan have transformed hardware stores and bodegas into chic restaurants, bars, galleries, children's bookstores, and candle boutiques and have moved into converted factory lofts across the street from impoverished

Mexican immigrants. In 2001, two young boys were charged with raping a girl in the projects of Coney Island; that same week, the city, hoping to restore Coney Island to some of its earlier luster, announced the opening of a Mets' minor league baseball stadium a few blocks away. The stadium, funded and named for Keyspan, Brooklyn's gas company, has drawn fans from all neighborhoods and social strata. The Metrotech complex has helped revive downtown Brooklyn and has attracted some Manhattan companies to relocate. Gentrification and downtown development, however, have taken priority over the need to build affordable housing.

Each cultural enclave transports you to another world. To name some: Russian Brighton Beach, Haitian/Jamaican East Flatbush, Polish Greenpoint, Puerto Rican Sunset Park, Italian Bensonhurst, Arabic Atlantic Avenue, African American Bed Stuy, Yiddish Borough Park, Chinatown in Bay Ridge, hipster/artist Williamsburg. As for music, reggae, rap, salsa, merengue, jazz, Middle Eastern, techno, rancheras, bluegrass, rock, and next wave classical, among others, all have their niches within segments of the populace. If any culture cuts across the neighborhoods, it is hip-hop, which can be found flourishing among white, black, Latino, and Asian youth throughout the borough. Brooklyn citizens, like those from the Bronx, have influenced international trends in music, sports, fashion, and attitude. Brooklyn is both a nexus of discrete, local villages worlds apart from each other and a pulsating, globalized epicenter that takes in—and on—the world.

The School and Boys *Not* in the 'Hood

Borough High School (a pseudonym) typifies the evolving, fluid changes that are occurring in some ethnic Brooklyn neighborhoods. An imposing, four-story brick building that opened in 1923, the school stands in a working-class section of modest brick homes and manicured gardens that once was largely Italian and is now seeing more Chinese and Russian as well as Middle Eastern families (see Berger, 2002, September 17). Near the school the el rumbles by overhead, American flags wave from most front doors on any holiday (a custom considered less quaint by Manhattanites since 9-11), and a pizzeria, Italian bakery, and *latticini* store ("fresh muzzarell'—fuhgedaboudit") are around the corner.

Borough High, for years almost entirely white, now draws an increasing number of diverse students. The students are overwhelmingly working class. In the halls, black, Latino, white, Chinese, Indian, and students in Muslim garb mingle freely. There are over twenty-seven languages spoken (After school advancement program, 2000). Of the approximately twenty-five hundred students, a high percentage qualify for free lunch, an index of household income. About half of entering 9th and 10th graders drop out prior to graduation. Many are from outside the neighborhood, especially Latino and black students from Flatbush, Bushwick, East New York, Canarsie, and other parts of Brooklyn. Its sports medicine program attracts some of them. Some black football players told me that one of the Borough High coaches recruited them from their junior high to play football for the school, and that other students came through word of mouth. They told me that formal recruitment is not allowed in public schools (unlike Catholic and private schools, which often have the best football teams in the city).

Most of the players on the football team are black. The surprise, however, is that relatively few are African American—a number are first-generation Americans whose parents are Guyanese, Jamaican, Barbadian (and Indian), Haitian, Dominican, Puerto Rican, Panamanian, and African. Yet what is striking is the extent to which they have assimilated to an American black youth subculture: hip-hop clothing, language, music, and mannerisms. Whether they chose to or not, their self-expression in part reflects the fact that on an everyday basis in this society the identity of being black more often than not trumps whatever cultural or ethnic background they possess. There are also a number of Latino players—Puerto Rican, Guatemalan, and Dominican. Most of the black and Latino students come from the neighborhoods further away. The Italian, Irish, Chinese, and Arab-American students live closer by.

Like many schools in the city, Borough High is not well off and for a number of years suffered from a lack of up-to-date facilities for its athletics programs. It has never had a home football field–until recently. In 2002, as part of another sports project initiated and funded in part by a Keyspan CEO, a 1958 alumnus, the lot next to the school was restored into a regulation AstroTurf field (Witt, 2002, September 23). According to the head coach, the football team has no budget whatsoever from the school. Players themselves must chip in and pay an annual fee of $255, plus $100 the first year for a jersey. Through corporate fundraising by the coaches the football team also received new weight-training equipment and computers for the coaching staff. Those high schools in the city with consistently successful football teams appear to have better-established athletic programs with higher-quality facilities, equipment, and more resources. Some benefit from corporate sponsorship. According to a local report (Witt, 2002, September 23), the field has brought the already tight-knit community closer together—residents watch the cheerleaders from their windows across the street.

How much closer, however, is not certain, as most of the football players are not from the neighborhood. This may be a mixed blessing for them. In many high schools the athletic teams represent the town, community, or neighborhood, which often leads to rivalry and hostility between their area and a local counterpart (see Bissinger, 1990). At Borough High most of these students are not part of the community, which relieves them of the pressure to represent and defend it. By contrast, there is an implicit tension over who does represent the community—the established white population from the surrounding area or the new students of color. All of this is not to say that as football players the students do not undergo intense rivalries with other young men who play for the other local schools in the league; it just occurs in different forms and in different venues. The antagonism may be carried out through trash-talking e-mails on chat rooms, through encounters on the subway or in the streets, and at parties in their own or in another neighborhood.

Race is often an unacknowledged but crucial subtext of the larger picture of being a student and football player at Borough High. In the morning, many of these black students leave their more dangerous and run-down neighborhoods and ride the subway long hours to reach the school. In their own 'hoods, they need to be on the lookout for danger just walking down the streets—gangs who wear colors, drug dealers, bullies, and muggers. On the weekend they may have been at a party at which someone was shot up, a story told to me in a matter-of-fact tone by one of the athletes.

At the other end of the train ride the male students shift from one kind of vigilance to another. They maintain their wariness as they descend the stairs from the el and walk to school through a still largely white world where the looks on some of the faces tell them they don't belong. The male students frequent a corner candy store and pizzeria beneath the el stop—but always en masse—and I cannot imagine they would feel welcome in some of the Italian specialty stores I patronize, nor have I ever seen a black person in them.

Once they get to school the young men must put away their props that make them feel a bit more secure: they remove the do-rags from their heads, hitch up their pants, and stow away their cell phones and portable CD players and headsets. As a consequence of living in two worlds, many of them continue to spend the day operating at a high level of stress (see Boyd-Franklin & Franklin, 2000). This is on top of the oftentimes petty insults and humiliations compounded from a day at school—getting handed back a poor grade, being teased for some facial or body feature, losing a dollar or hat that you put down on the desk for just a moment. The good news is that Borough High School, along with its surrounding neighborhood, is relatively safe. This is one of its draws for many of those students whose own neighborhood high schools are troubled with violence.

While the school offers them something of a respite, many working-class students from inner-city neighborhoods suffer from varying degrees of post-traumatic stress that existed in their lives before the added stress brought about by the events of September 11, 2001. The schools or anyone else rarely addresses this everyday, low-grade condition. Many of these students live in areas that are often noisy, dirty, congested, and unsafe, and at all times they must watch their backs. They come from woman-headed households with a mom who has little time to give because she must work two jobs and who must cope with financial hardships, uncertainty, and instability. They experience loss and abandonment when men walk away from the family or they bear witness to domestic violence and physical punishment. They endure the pain of separation when relatives remain far away in another country or region, or when one is in jail, suffers from drug abuse or alcoholism, has died from AIDS, or was killed in a violent manner. Such families are more likely to suffer emotional stress from health problems such as asthma and obesity and from the lack of resources to deal with them. The students from these families may experience poor sleep, depression, worry, and fear. They are anxious about a future that no longer includes blue-collar jobs requiring less education and that once allowed people who were starting out to earn a living and support a family. Along with their wealthier counterparts in the suburbs, young people in the inner city today get less adult support and increasingly feel the pressure on them to succeed. Some of the sources of this pressure are the restrictive criteria of success as defined by standards-based schooling, the images of success and perfection the media presents to them, and the harsh judgments of their own peers (see Julien, 2002, December 15).

For some of these young men who are not the best students, football, despite, or even because of, its tough, demanding physical regimen, holds a promise of glory and a ticket to success and, in comparison to the rest of their lives, looks pretty good. Being a member of the football team provides a number of them a structured, regimented subculture that, with regard to their behavior and schoolwork, holds them accountable and keeps them out of trouble.

Football: More than a Game

If we consider football from a conventional standpoint, it's just a game. The goal is to win: physically move the ball into the end zone and prevent your opponent from doing the same. The rules provide for wide latitude of tough physical play in the service of the goal. At Borough High School, as in many other schools, young males want to play football; they try out, join the team, practice, and compete on Saturday afternoons in the fall. Pain, injury, aggression, self-aggrandizement, competition, self-sacrifice, conformity, and other attitudes and behaviors of conventional masculinity—these are often present, all normal, and just part of the game.

From a broader, critical perspective, however, football is more than a game. For many Americans, it is an all-consuming obsession and reflects many of the material, cultural, and psychological conflicts of American life. Miracle and Rees (1994) felt that the football season has replaced other traditions and has become a ritual that marks time with sacred meaning, as well as a way to symbolize group, high school, or community unity and solidarity. From small rust-belt towns to inner cities, working-class boys and their families see high school football as a way out of economic hardship. Talented high school athletes are no longer just kids playing a local football game. They often receive regional and national attention from the media and from college recruiters eager to uphold or improve the reputation of their school. As a result, such players experience considerable emotional pressure. Beyond the United States, through the marketing of NFL merchandise and corporate network satellite broadcasts, football has become a globalized commodity that symbolizes America's successful masculine image of power and dominance.

Today, however, the meaning of high school football in this culture is becoming more ambiguous and uncertain. In the past much of the promotion of high school sports was driven by corporate America's need to compete and win; most people believed that high school football builds the kind of moral character necessary for a loyal, obedient, hard-working labor force that specializes in one skill. Now, some educators, corporate leaders, and government officials oppose money for extracurricular activities such as athletics at the expense of tougher academic standards needed to produce a workforce capable of competing in the global economy. This economy demands more sophisticated skills useful for technology and management rather than those promoted by football. These include flexibility, collaboration, non-specialization, and decision-making. In the face of the need for higher academic standards the stereotype of the dumb football jock has become unacceptable. A former high school teacher, Etta Kralovec (2003), argued that if we want to meet tough educational standards, then schools need to spend much less time and money on sports and more on academic work.

Nevertheless, the popularity of football and other sports in schools remains strong and competes with the value of education as a means toward success in this society. On a national level, the glorification of football players in part may be because they are specialists and football's glamour and notoriety for most is gained largely through watching television. Few Americans have ever seen a professional football game in person, and relatively few even play football of any sort, including two-hand touch, yet the Super Bowl and Monday Night Football remain some of the most popular broadcasts over recent years (Barra, 2002, September 29). Marketing of NFL paraphernalia is a successful mega-dollar business.

The myth that football is a wholesome activity that builds character remains a powerful one. Millions of Americans have attended high school football games and tend to link football to a time of nostalgic, youthful innocence, even as larger social forces are also undermining it. In other words, football remains popular in part because it symbolizes a time of relative purity and fun in one's life. High schools and their sports teams are significant means by which everyone is integrated into American society.

Yet media and corporate pressures have done much to erase the line between any innocent fun of high school football and the more cynical, materialist, and pressured worlds of college and professional football (see Beale, 2001, September 16). Students have become less interested in high school football, which has come to resemble the more hyped, commercialized aspects of collegiate and professional football (Beck, 1998, November 19). It now also shares some of the same problems, for example, athlete misbehavior, such as the publicized case of the suburban Glen Ridge, New Jersey, players in 1989 who sexually abused a retarded girl (Lefkowitz, 1998). In response, the NFL and the National Football Foundation in recent years have started a program for high school football players in urban areas, "Play It Smart" (Play It Smart, n.d.), that places in selected schools an academic coach who helps them with their academic, career, and personal plans. By working at the high school level the league hopes to contribute to the growth of more responsible, self-aware young men and prevent the kind of pro player behavior that has made negative headlines.

In parts of the United States, some people are more obsessed with football than others. In Massillon, Ohio, a blue-collar, rust-belt small town, the high school team plays in a twenty-thousand-seat stadium and some parents hold their son back a year in 8th grade so they can show up in better physical condition (Beale, 2001, September 16). In such towns football provides jobs, economic growth, and a vicarious way of life that offers people the chance to feel like a winner and for players to be heroes. Many athletes and their families become part of a network that affords them better social status and career connections. When it is played well, when moral character rather than just winning is emphasized, football, like other team sports, teaches young athletes to resolve conflict, deal with success and failure, and develop collaborative skills (see Solomon & Gardner, 2000).

At its worst football also can be brutally violent, numbing, nasty, ugly, and harmful. Professional football breeds cynicism and contempt when its sleazier side is exposed—for example, the players who are more interested in self-promotion and marketing or who commit violent and criminal acts off the field and the greedy team owners who value profit over fan loyalty. Football's conformist, groupthink mentality often tolerates or even encourages a climate of sexist, homophobic, and racist behavior among players and coaches at all levels (see Meggyesy, 1970; Messner & Sabo, 1990; Messner & Sabo, 1994). Anyone perceived as weaker is fair game. During the summer of 2003 at a football camp older players from a suburban New York high school team sodomized three junior-varsity players with broomsticks, golf balls, and pine cones; afterwards, most of the players maintained a code of silence and refused to come forward as witnesses (Roberts, 2003, September 28).

With its regimented physical aggression, football has adopted the language of war, for example, long passes as aerial bombs, gaining territory on the ground, penetrating into enemy territory, blitzing (from *blitzkrieg*), and punt coverage specialists as gunners (see Anderson, 2003, March 23). A *Nation* cover (September 30, 2002) before the Iraqi war showed George W. Bush in a football helmet and jersey about to throw a bomb with the title, "Block Bush." What is of equal significance, the game itself is often just as physically dangerous as war: many retired professional football athletes suffer lifelong, debilitating, painful injuries from playing that often lead to early deaths (for a disturbing view, see Nack, 2001, May 7). Through intensive media exposure more people become aware of athletes' injuries and illnesses as they arise. Yet, as with those maimed or killed in war, the harsh, long-term effects of an athlete's condition are seldom depicted and publicized.

Football can be emotionally harmful as well. At the high school level, as H. G. Bissinger (1990) showed, there are communities and parents who live through their children, use them up, then emotionally and physically discard them when they no longer can play. For men, obsessive following of TV sports and fandom, relentlessly encouraged by the media, is a vicarious substitute for a lost sense of power. Lionel Tiger argued that such behavior "may reveal a turbulent male preoccupation with competition and physical assertiveness that is no longer available to ordinary men" (Lipsyte, 1999, May 9).

At Borough High, as at other schools, being a football player is a significant social role. The players enjoy extra privileges and notoriety. Like male jocks at most high schools, a number of them are local celebrities and are at the top of the status hierarchy. Some young women vie for their attention, flirting with and pursuing the young men in the halls. The school itself also offers them dividends. At an end-of-the-season team meeting the coach warned the seniors not to slack off in their studying and especially in their behavior. He cited examples of how the school guards and even the administration had often let them get away with some rule-breaking in the halls during the fall because they were on the football team. A couple of players admitted to me this was so; they could hang out and play around outside of class more easily than other students. This jock hero status, often sanctioned by school and society, sometimes can lead to a backlash of resentment among others. While the male high school students who created the massacre in Littleton, Colorado, were driven by their own serious problems, they targeted the school athletes as the sources of their feelings of humiliation and pain.

By contrast, with the student athletes' fame comes responsibility. Before the opening game of the 2002 season, students and teachers alike felt free to tell the team members whom they saw in the halls or in class that "they better win." In this case, there was indeed extra pressure on the players; the opening game was getting some local media hype about the school's new field, and the athletes told me they felt the stress and were nervous about it. A few of the young men privately told me they struggled with feelings of doubt and lack of self-confidence in their personal lives and on the field. Bernard Lefkowitz (1998), who wrote about the Glen Ridge athletes, suggested that the hypermasculine style imposed on some of them by the community weighed on them and that the "jock swagger" was an easy way to hide their self-doubts.

Young athletes within organized sports experience increasing pressure from many places. Publicity from a successful football team benefits the school the team represents, and one study (Spence, 2000) reported that black athletes felt pressure always to win in order to make their high school look good. The pressure to win from school administrators and the community in order to satisfy their vicarious sense of pride can come at the expense of academic priorities and ethical integrity (see Bissinger, 1990).

Of late there are increasing problems among parents of athletes, who dream of lucrative salaries for their children and who invest their own emotions into their children's lives. Recent disturbing examples of abusive sports parents who replace fun with pressure include a father who beat another parent to death at a youth hockey practice, a father who lied about the age of his son in order to make him eligible for Little League play, and an increase in the number of parents who rage at athletic officials (see the interview with Rick Wolff in Rohde, 2001, September 6). This has led to efforts to formally legislate the behavior of spectator-parents, for example, offering a Fair Play Bill in suburban Long Island, New York, that would require all players and parents to sign personal pledges before using county playgrounds and for all teams to take sportsmanship seminars. Such external regulations, however, are hard to enforce and require that the parents, athletic organizations, and ultimately broader societal institutions evolve to another level of consciousness (see Vecsey, 2002, September 27).

What is more, it is hard to regulate parents who wield increasing influence on high school athletic programs when they can remain anonymous through Internet high school team chat rooms. In one case complaints posted about a nationally successful high school football coach led to his firing. Parents, team supporters, and school officials can log on to the Web and compare their programs to those of other schools nationwide by looking at standings through polls and by reading about other high schools' celebrity athletes (Roberts, 2002, December 22).

Further pressure comes from corporations. Companies such as Nike and Adidas sponsor high school teams that win and pressure them to keep winning in order to keep the free gear coming. Corporate sponsorship, a director of the Center for Sport, Character, and Culture at the University of Notre Dame said, "is an unfortunate trend that encourages student athletes to see themselves as a commodity" (Mancuso, 2001, December 21). Players become celebrities and tend to put athletics ahead of academics. Corporate media hype through the Internet has contributed to the pressures of high school athletes by turning some into national celebrities. ESPN.com ran the recruiting diary of a star high school football quarterback who has thrown for the national record of touchdowns (Bernstein, 2002, December 31).

The trend of corporate sponsorship blurs the line between the professional, who plays for money, and the amateur, who plays for love of the sport. Corporate sponsors are seeking out athletes as young as preschool-age (see Talbot, 2003, September 21). During the 2002–3 season one prep school basketball player, LeBron James, who planned to turn pro after high school, became a media star who appeared on the cover of two mass-media magazines. He drew more national media attention in early 2003 as the focus of a high school athletic association investigation over his ownership of an SUV Hummer worth at least $50,000 equipped with three TVs. It turned out his mother bought it for him for his eighteenth birthday and that his amateur status was not compromised. Shortly after this he was banned from playing for unwittingly taking two jerseys as gifts, then later suspended and reinstated. The hypocrisy is that James's team could accept free gear from Adidas but he himself could not accept two jerseys from a friend. The larger message of the drama and hype over LeBron James is that education matters less than the chance to make a lot of money and indulge in unbridled consumption (see Longman & Fountain, 2003, February 8; Rhoden, 2003, February 3).

No longer a part-time hobby divorced from societal pressures, high school football has become a serious enterprise for those students who want to play it. Despite its short season as a spectator sport, it requires dedication and focus from athletes all year round. A number of the students at Borough High take it seriously in hopes of getting a scholarship and playing college football. During the off-season (winter and spring) the students do weight-training and meet regularly as a team with the coach after school. Summer is the start of an intensive preparation period that includes a week away at football camp. As one young man remarked, they eat, breathe, and sleep football together. During the fall between games the athletes practice every day.

One former college football player who played in the 1960s, Michael Oriard (2001, December 23), observed that football now requires longtime, full-time commitment, and there are no longer any upper level (Division I) college players like himself who can afford to be "full-time students and part-time football players." The Borough High head football coach confirmed this even for high school: football is a year-round sport. Because of the competitive, pressurized, full-time nature of this sports culture, one talented high school senior from suburban New Jersey turned down invitations from Division I schools: "It's a 365-day schedule—the players are never at school…When you play Division I football, you're meeting people from all over the country, but they're all looking to smash your face in" (St. Louis, 2002, November 10). The demands of a full-time sports culture, including the intense competitiveness, make it next to impossible for such young men to develop their other abilities.

It is even harder on many working-class African American students. Poor and ethnic minority young men are disproportionately steered into athletics, in particular the more dangerous positions (see Messner & Sabo, 1994). For these students who must attend inner-city public schools that fail to help them nurture their intellectual abilities, provide them with good academic support, and instead channel them into sports, sports becomes their life and represents their one chance for success. Two educational reformers (Noguera & Akom, 2000, June 5) argued:

> Despite the daunting odds of success in professional sports and entertainment, many young people of color believe they have a greater chance of becoming a highly paid athlete or hip-hop artist than an engineer, doctor or software programmer. And with the rollback of affirmative action at colleges and universities, there is little doubt that students who possess entertainment value to universities, who can slam-dunk or score touchdowns, will be admitted regardless of their academic performance, even as aspiring doctors and lawyers are turned away. (p. 31)

The media contributes to the racial disparity. The most televised sports are ones in which blacks are disproportionately represented (Spence, 2000); by emphasizing the material rewards garnered by these athletes they reinforce the belief among black families and children that athletics is the only route out of poverty. Black sociologist Harry Edwards (1984) lamented how the black community has unwittingly become an accessory to the exploitation of black athletes by blindly believing in sport as the primary route to economic and social salvation.

Racism exists not just in the social structure that steers young black men into sports but within the athletic infrastructure as well. It is reflected in racial tensions between players as well as in the systematic lack of black team owners, top front-office jobs, and coaching and managerial positions. On the Borough High football team racial tensions existed between some players that lingered during the season and were not fully resolved. At various times these had a negative impact on the team's performance.

One of the most significant issues is that many young black men feel that athletics is a viable way to prove their masculinity (see Edwards, 1983; Ferguson, 2000). The bind for some is that their need to play tough, to dominate and inflict injury to others, to ignore pain and injury to themselves, further reinforces the harsh stereotype of black men as brutes or animals. One black Borough High football student told me he lived for football. During the off-season he was bored and could only think of the season when he could play and make tackles. Other players told me that a former teammate who was tragically killed during their season had "lived for football, it was all he had," and they dedicated the rest of the season to his memory. After the season a number of the black players checked off on a questionnaire that they played hard because they "had something to prove."

Football is a concentrated microcosm of the larger societal problems of conventional masculinity. Many of these problems reflect a rigid conformity and attachment to a high stakes masculine sports culture: a sense of entitlement, power, and privilege, the need to prove one is tough by ignoring one's body and playing through pain, the fear of being soft, racism, homophobia, the domination and devaluation of women, and valuing monetary and material rewards above one's health and relationships. The acceptance of doing one's best at what one loves and the sense of mastery for its own sake get lost. Instead, being a jock in this society often comes to represent a narrow, at times brutal, kind of masculinity.

Recent media attention has been drawn to high school, college, and professional athletes who have engaged in criminal misconduct. Experts have suggested the problem lies with the "masculine culture of sports, which often denigrates women and preaches conformity within groups of athletes" (Wong, 2001, December 23). Researcher Tim Curry argued that athletes are over conformists and act out exaggerated forms of masculinity in order to gain approval from their peers and increase their status within the group. His report suggested that this and other factors that sustain the masculine sports culture "help explain why athletes with a lot at stake—a scholarship, an award, a shot at a lucrative professional career—might jeopardize themselves and their teams by getting into trouble" (ibid.). The sports sociologists Robert Hughes and Jay Coakley (1991) argued that athletes' misbehavior in fact is a form of positive deviance, an acceptable norm of sports. The athletes' acts, they pointed out, stem from their uncritical acceptance of what they have been told by significant people around them who transmit the goals and norms of the masculine sports culture. Drug, steroid, and alcohol abuse, promiscuity, and aggressive behavior toward women and weaker men are associated with winning in adult society and with the image of the admired athlete. Miracle and Rees (1994) noted that this is compounded for those athletes who see sports as their only chance for success.

The conditions that contribute to such patterns of misbehavior are entrenched in many athletic teams at all levels. On college campuses these include the idolization and isolation of athletes and the adjudication of misconduct by the athletic department rather than the university. Many schools and colleges tend to keep the athletes apart from other students (see Arenson, 2003, September 15). As a result, the athletes cultivate a sense of privilege and entitlement. They end up associating only with fellow athletes and do not have the chance to socialize, participate in cultural and extracurricular activities, and interact with others, including women, under more relaxed and ordinary conditions (see Jordan & Denson, 1990). Noguera and Akom (2000, June 5) pointed out that engaging in such activities not only promotes socialization skills for students but also positively influences academic achievement.

Athletic programs in a number of institutions of higher learning are at odds with core educational values, a conflict that appears to be worsening (see Freeman, 2003, July 13). Cultivating athletes and winning teams are priorities that compete with the academic integrity of the schools (Shulman & Bowen, 2001).

Many top college athletic departments regard their school as a commodity. The athletic director of the University of Maryland said that a responsible director tries to "minimize danger to the brand," the reputation of the university, while others agreed that corporate involvement and commercialism are necessary to help market the school (Lipsyte, 2002, December 15). Football in particular is the biggest budget in college athletic programs and at the Division I level can include unnecessary perks such as chartered jets and hotel room stays on home-game nights. When sports programs are no longer for regular students but only for recruited players, college sports become less about playing for fun and building character and more about raising the school's profile in the business of sports entertainment. College football programs in particular draw enormous money, drain resources from other men's and women's sports programs, and often still end up in the red (Conniff, 2003, March 24).

When sports are seen less for their intrinsic value and more as a commodity, they become susceptible to addictive behaviors that depend on external reinforcers. Inner needs and meanings are denied as one's own behavior becomes a means to an end. By treating athletics as a commodity, sports, like an addiction, come to serve as an extrinsic fix for unmet emotional needs rather than an activity worth doing for its own sake (see Forbes, 1994). In line with this way of thinking, college student athletes become at risk of other addictions like drinking and gambling. They are more likely to binge drink than nonathletes. A fall 2002 report said it is not surprising that college student sports fans are similar to athletes in their extreme drinking; this behavior was played out in the form of riots after football games at a number of college campuses (Williams, 2002, December 10). While some colleges have set up alcohol and drug abuse prevention and antiviolence and sexual assault workshops and programs, there is still a long way to go to change the conformist masculine sports culture prevalent in colleges. This culture is reinforced by the behavior of coaches, college administrators, and parents as well as supported by a link between liquor advertising and athletic events.

Some big-time colleges have suffered betting scandals that involve their players. College coaches and administrators are concerned about their athletes who are tempted to alter the outcome of a game and gamble in order to gain a share of the profits they see all around them. The National Collegiate Athletic Association (NCAA) has a multibillion dollar deal with CBS, which operates Sportsline.com, featuring spreads on college games. In one study a sample of mostly African American Division I college male athletes said they believed the NCAA did not represent their interests, and felt exploited by their school, overworked, undercompensated, and channeled into particular areas of study, all of which create conditions ripe for point-rigging and betting (Lipsyte, 2002, December 22). These feelings occur within a commercialized climate in which schools stand to earn large sums based on the success of their teams.

There is a direct link between the endemic criminal and ethical scandals of college sports and the costly endeavor of running a program like football. Michael Sokolove (2002, December 22) explained:

> Teams that do not win do not excite their boosters, fill up stadiums, appear on national TV or get into postseason play, thereby endangering the revenue stream that supports the immense infrastructure. It is the desperation for

cash, every bit as much as the pursuit of victory, that causes university athletic departments to overlook all kinds of rule-breaking until it splatters out into the open. (p. 38)

Among those Borough High football players with whom I worked some did complain to me about other players who were more interested in their own personal statistics than in helping the team. This was on ongoing theme among the players that continued to surface. Of course, this is not surprising in an individualistic culture that encourages young men to promote themselves as marketable commodities and provides them, especially black males, with relatively few viable avenues for success.

If these problems extend from high school through college, some of them do not disappear when athletes assume the mantle of the professional; professionalism does not imply maturity or increased self-awareness. On the contrary, with the availability of enormous material and monetary rewards, the athletes' unaddressed emotional problems fester, and under the relentless media glare they are more exposed to everyone. The NFL recently has been concerned with the behavior of some its players who were brought up on rape, murder, and domestic abuse charges (Dubner, 2002, August 18). It has launched an orientation program for drafted rookies that hopes to educate them on responsible behavior off the field. However, the NFL often appears willing to overlook problems of football players when they conflict with its own bottom line interests. For example, some NFL teams still pursue a talented player despite his risk for getting into trouble (see Freeman, 2001, June 3). There is a certain level of tolerance of violent, aggressive behavior off the field. During the 2002 season, some New York Jets players were involved in an assault outside a restaurant where they had been drinking; that same day they engaged in fist fights with each other during practice in front of a dozen visiting schoolchildren (Battista, 2002, December 13). The head coach appeared more amused than angered and chalked up the behavior to end-of-the-season anxiety.

Other player problems do not appear to be addressed by the NFL rookie orientation program, for example, ignoring one's body, the fear of looking soft, the valuing of success over health. The tragic death of Korey Stringer, discussed earlier, is a case in point. Stringer's desire to continue practice was in part because he wanted to show his teammates he was too tough to quit. This is often further complicated, however, by the need for the player to win or maintain a position on the team; stopping because of an injury or fatigue jeopardizes the player's chances and makes it even less likely he would leave the field (see Berkow, 2001, August 5).

None of what occurs in the NFL was lost on the high school players. They followed the ongoing events through the news and discussed them among themselves. It is not surprising, then, that the pressure to avoid appearing weak or unmanly exists at the high school level as well. In the locker room before a practice I watched one player tape up his wrist. Another player told him, "Don't be a wuss. You don't need that much tape!" The young man hesitated, then began to unwrap some of the bandage.

A medical doctor and former professional football player has argued that there often is a conflict of interest among team doctors between caring for the players' health and the needs of the team management, who wants the player back on the field (Berkow, 2001, August 5). A team doctor might feel pressured to send a player back on the field under circumstances similar to those of Korey Stringer. One of the Borough High students missed the summer football training camp because his doctor told him he found some medically ambiguous results and wanted to do further tests. However, the doctor was unable to schedule these until after camp had begun. I overheard an upset assistant coach tell the student he could have gone to a second doctor who might have overlooked or minimized the results in order for him to get to camp.

A related case where masculine sports culture conflicts with the health of the players is the overuse of painkillers in the NFL. Several pro players said that they thought players rely too often on painkilling drugs because of pressure from their teams and teammates to play at all costs. Some internalize this pressure. A player for the New England Patriots said that shots are a necessary evil: "If you don't do whatever it takes to play, you feel like you let your teammates down. They might also look at you like you're a wimp" (Freeman, 2002, January 31). A problem with some painkillers is that the player can become addicted. Green Bay Packer quarterback Bret Favre was treated for an addiction to Vicodin (ibid.). Years of playing with pain and the long-term exposure to grueling, physical contact has resulted in many former NFL players living out their shortened life span in severe pain and disabilities (Freeman & Villarosa, 2002, September 26; Nack, 2001, May 7).

The issue of where to draw the line between playing hurt and playing injured is a critical one for all athletes at all levels. It requires mindful attention to one's body. A professional football player said, "The thing that's hard as an athlete is sometimes you get so used to playing in pain and dealing with pain that sometimes you're not sure where to draw the line of where it's too serious to play" (Freeman, 2002, January 31). Athletes often also need enough presence of mind to draw the line between courage and cowardice and between self-respect and selfishness. Meditation can help athletes become mindful in these regards.

The point here is that teams are willing to sacrifice their players' health and safety as well as their emotional integrity for the sake of winning, which enhances the bottom line. Players are pressured by and even internalize this calculus; this makes it difficult for them to draw necessary distinctions for their own well-being. The conformist adherence to the norm of masculinity serves as a means to enforce this value system and keep players in check.

In some sports, such as gymnastics, weight loss is desirable, which can lead to eating disorders such as anorexia and bulimia (see Fender-Scarr, 2001). In football the value instead is on bigger, stronger, and faster players who are more willing to use their size. Among young men in general, including athletes, an increasing trend is seeking a more desirable body shape that emphasizes muscle mass and physical bulk.

The wish to be more muscular and lose fat is associated with dieting and with the use of anabolic-androgenic steroids and dietary supplements that include ephedra, a stimulant. In terms of steroid use, there is an increase among American boys worried about their body images; among high school sophomores, use more than doubled from 1992 to 2000 (Egan, 2002, November 22). As for dietary supplements, during the 2002 NFL season six players were suspended for testing positive for ephedra, a banned substance in a dietary supplement. One sportswriter argued, "Players are responsible for what they put in their bodies, but the league creates this insatiable monster of competition" (Rhoden, 2002, November 16).

Ephedra is a legal, over-the-counter stimulant that speeds up the heart and may make a person susceptible to heat stroke. It was implicated in Korey Stringer's death as well. Pro players like New York Giants cornerback Jason Sehorn see as hypocritical the policy that a player who tests positive for ephedra is given a four game suspension, while players who test positive for cocaine or marijuana instead get medical treatment in a drug program. The league sees ephedra as influencing on-the-field competition, while cocaine and marijuana are off-the-field health issues. If the league is concerned with substances, Sehorn and others feel, it should more closely monitor the anti-inflammatory and painkiller injections that many players receive to help them play (Myers, 2002, November 21). During major league baseball spring training in 2003, a twenty-three-year-old Baltimore Orioles pitcher, Steve Bechler, died of heatstroke; Bechler was desperately trying to lose weight and was taking ephedra (see Chass, 2003, February 19; Kolata & Bogdanich, 2003, February 20; Vecsey, 2003, February 19). Sehorn got it partly right: society as a whole should be concerned with the quality of all substance use, both the use of painkilling injections and the use of ephedra, for which there arose a call to restrict sales or ban it altogether after Bechler died.

With larger players come more injuries; these include noncontact knee injuries and dislocated shoulders and elbows from blocking (Nack, 2001, May 7). The players' extreme size does not bode well for their future health. One former player for the Pittsburgh Steelers, Mike Webster, not only suffered from brain damage because of years of helmet-battering but died from heart disease, from which linemen have a significantly greater chance of dying than the general population (Freeman & Villarosa, 2002, September 26). In a rare editorial on football *The New York Times* argued:

> Heavyweight collisions can increase the risk of concussions and dislocations. Carrying all those pounds around puts additional wear on joints and cartilage and makes it more likely that today's players will suffer chronic arthritis, severe back pain and other ailments that have long plagued professional football players. That dismal prospect is unlikely to deter coaches from seeking more size on their teams, or deter athletes from seeking more pounds on their frames. (Gigantosauruses, 2002, September 29)

Research on adolescent males has indicated a link between the drive for muscularity and poorer self-esteem and symptoms of depression (McCreary, 2001). On the Borough High football team there was a clear desire to bulk up, and those players who did gain muscle mass through weight-training earned praise from their coaches and respect from their teammates. The Borough

High coach encouraged weight-lifting all year round, and in his estimation one of the reasons the team lost an important game was that the winners were more physically solid. As with other behaviors, overconcern with one's body can become an addiction, an attachment to one's self-image that hampers development. The danger here is that for male adolescents, especially African Americans, muscle mass becomes a way to prove oneself as being masculine and respected in a society that glorifies physical strength at the expense of valuing higher traits of personal character and intellect.

The rules of football have always allowed for violent hits as part of the game, even when they lead to injuries (see Messner, 1994). This is one of the contradictions of the game as it is currently played. Of late, however, dangerous hits in the NFL have increased. Coaches were instructing players to lead with their heads as a way to intimidate the opposing teams' receivers. By the middle of the 2002 season two players were suspended for helmet-to-helmet collisions; from 1993 until then only one player had been suspended for that type of hit. "I think players are leading with their helmet now more than ever before. I am seeing some extremely dangerous situations," said Gene Washington, the NFL's director of football operations (Freeman, 2002, November 1). During the 2002 season a player made a hard but legal block that landed his opponent in the hospital with a serious pelvic injury. A sports columnist acknowledged the bind the league is in by trying to solve the paradox, When is violence in a violent game unnecessary? He argued that "the NFL is attempting to modify or regulate behavior that cannot be modified or regulated…The NFL sells violence; it can't dress it" (Rhoden, 2002, November 30). This paradox cannot be solved within the rules of football as presently construed. Violence in football, Messner (1994) pointed out, is a legal, sanctioned aspect of the game, encouraged by society, and it serves as a means to affirm aggressive and powerful masculine identities. A number of the Borough High football players prided themselves on their reputation for tough play.

A related problem in football is sexism. Messner (1994) regarded present-day sports as an organizing institution for the embodiment of dominant masculinity: "Sports suppress natural (sex) similarities, construct differences, and then largely through the media, weave a structure of symbol and interpretation around theses differences which naturalizes them" (p. 96). That is, sports as currently organized builds in an exaggerated gender distinction that plays on the power of males over females and presents it as innate.

Male athletes are bestowed with a sense of entitlement that allows many of them to feel they can have their way with women. On the college level many of the top football teams playing in bowl games have had to confront accusations or formal charges of criminal behavior by their players; among the most common are rape and sexual assault (Wong, 2001, December 23). When male athletes are brought up on charges it is often the women who are blamed for perpetrating an injustice on the athlete. After professional basketball player Kobe Bryant was accused of sexual assault in 2003 a lawyer for a woman who had brought rape charges against four college football players in 1999 said, "The problem in charging an athlete is that it intensifies the rage and backlash factor so much more than the normal situation. The athlete has fans. They have easy access to the media. They have a voice" (Araton, 2003, July 20, p. sp6).

The issue of athletes' troublesome attitudes and behavior toward women may begin in high school, if not earlier. In my work with football players from Borough High, on a number of occasions I heard denigrating and objectifying comments about women, an issue that we discussed in our group sessions. One player, although not representative, got into an altercation with a young woman over a rebuffed overture after school; the police were called and he was arrested. Overall in our discussions a number of the young men were struggling to square their beliefs in the equality of women with some negative generalities they assumed about girls, which they attributed to some difficult interpersonal encounters and relationships.

Homophobia is another significant aspect of the sports culture of masculinity that also functions to regulate male athletes' values and behavior. Young straight males will monitor what they say and do and avoid anything that can be construed as gay. Gay athletes in almost all cases must stay in the closet for fear of humiliation or worse. Homophobia extends from high schools teams to professionals. During the 2002 season a former NFL player, Esea Tuaolo, in a number of media interviews came out as gay. Tuaolo described his feelings of depression and suicide at having to hide who he was, by pretending to laugh along with antigay jokes in the locker room, and his shame at not having the courage to come out. The sports columnist Robert Lipsyte (2002, October 27) argued that the symbolism of Tuaolo's action is hard to ignore, given that "pro football players have been promoted as supermasculine warriors, no women or sissies allowed." David Kopay, the first pro football player to declare he was gay twenty-seven years ago, contended that the NFL has never been sensitive to the issue and had failed to criticize homophobic remarks by other professional players (ibid.). During the 2002 football season New York Giant Jeremy Shockey, in response to a talk radio announcer's question about whether he thought there were gays in the NFL, said, "I don't know. I don't like to think about that. I hope not" (Shockey on radio, 2002, September 27).

If anxiety about homosexuality still exists among professional athletes it is not surprising to find it among high school players. Sixteen Borough High football players filled out a questionnaire I gave them that asked them to rate on a scale of one to seven how stressful they consider certain situations to be. On the item "Having a man put his arm around your shoulder," most circled numbers from low to moderately stressful; six circled the highest rating, "extremely stressful." During the groups and in the halls I did hear the occasional antigay epithet hurled at teammates. Some of the players told me that the word *faggot* has become less an antigay slur and more just a generic putdown. The white rap singer Eminem said that it is an all-purpose insult used by many kids and is "not meant to be literal" (Rich, 2002, November 2). Teens in Minnesota say that the slang of choice, "That's so gay," means anything they find silly or stupid (Cummins, 2002, December 13). This common usage, however, is disturbing proof that homophobia remains acceptable and would not be so tolerated for any other group. According to a National Mental Health Association survey gay slurs are the insult of choice among school bullies and have slipped down into middle and elementary schools (ibid.).

To some extent, the young men were more accepting of gays in the group discussions than I had expected. I also once observed some playful horsing around in the locker room in which some guys grabbed a teammate and briefly simulated sex with him. The most cutting homophobic remark I heard came from an assistant coach who was reviewing a game tape with the players and who described some of them as "little fags" for not playing tougher. Dave Meggyesy (1970), a former NFL player who wrote a strong indictment of the game, described a similar statement a coach made to him:

> This sort of attack on a player's manhood is a coach's doomsday weapon. And it almost always works, for the players have wrapped up their identity in their masculinity, which is eternally precarious for it not only depends on not

exhibiting fear of any kind on the playing field, but is also something that can be given and withdrawn by a coach at his pleasure. (p. 181)

A harsh, repressive, and critical culture can wound young men and induce a backlash of violent behavior. The sodomizing of younger players by older ones at a high school football training camp, and the subsequent code of silence by the team (Roberts, 2003, September 28), occurred in a conformist, hyper-masculine sports culture that encourages aggression and domination over those regarded as weaker. Many incidents of sexual violence are about power and control, a futile attempt to compensate for an inner sense of inadequacy.

In sum, football viewed with a critical consciousness has a different, multidimensional take. From this level of understanding much of football culture reflects unhealthy, preconventional and conventional levels of development. Rather than encourage the intrinsic, joyful, and mastery qualities of play and promote self-acceptance and the acceptance of others for whom they are, it emphasizes the commodified nature of the sport as a means to material, competitive, egoistical success or conformist validation of one's manhood and sense of self. Football is freighted with problematic meanings of masculinity and moral relationships. How one construes pain, injury, and violent, aggressive play in football, how one relates to one's teammates and to one's self, all reflect troublesome, often restrictive meanings of identity, social relationships, and personal values. Instead of an intrinsic, pleasurable process, sport often becomes a performance-based attempt to gain a sense of self. In so doing it compromises the athletes' moral integrity, self-development, and overall well-being.

Football and the Quest for the Zone

After taking a critical look at football, one well may ask what if anything is redeeming about it. Andrew Cooper (1998) made this point about society's obsession with the extrinsic trappings of sports:

> The problem with our obsession is not that we care about sports too much but that we care too little. We delight in the thrills, but we don't love the craft. We draw simple moral lessons when what is being revealed is the complexity of human nature. We confuse price with value. We want technical mastery without appreciating the traditions through which such mastery is transmitted. We demand the satisfaction that winning brings

while ignoring the meaning that winning confers. We consume sports like we consume Big Macs. And in so doing, the intrinsic joys and inner life are lost. (p. 18)

Is there a third way to consider football, neither conventional nor critical, that takes its problems into account and still helps young males find a higher sense of intrinsic pleasure and meaning in this activity? In seeking the best qualities of a sport such as football, it is not a matter of attempting to return to an earlier, more pure, or idealized version of the game. Rather, it is best to consider football as a whole, as an endeavor that reflects the varying levels of consciousness of this society at this particular time, and to look into it from a higher, integral level of awareness that can help young men develop themselves. In terms of solid, conventional values, football at its best represents hard work, sacrifice, mutual cooperation, and the effort of specialists in the service of a larger goal. There is, however, a higher level.

The aim is to find a way to express the highest qualities of the game from within our own culture, a culture that tends to stifle the need and desire to speak about the intrinsic meaning of what we do. From such a standpoint one can see the problems of football, work to change them where possible, and yet still appreciate the inner meaning that it offers. Despite the self-centered, conformist, and commodified aspects of sports today, an inner jewel still shines. At its highest level of play, football, whether high school, college, or pro, provides enormously satisfying, transcendent experiences for both players and its vicarious-living fans. While sport is not a spiritual, transcendental activity per se, with more conscious awareness it may serve to express these qualities for players, fans, and society. The inner experience of playing and watching a game, the conflict, drama, intensity, energy, and strength, touch upon some of the highest human values—self-sacrifice, courage, honor, camaraderie, and heroism.

Sport, Cooper (1998) suggested, more than any other single activity in our society, provides a glimpse into the inner life in which we become so absorbed in the task that the self is forgotten. It has the potential to connect us with the source of self-knowledge: the still point, or the no-self. In Zen, the moment of enlightenment is to forget the self. Most athletes at one time or another have had a transcendent experience while playing a sport. What they call being in the zone, or what psychologists call flow, is the feeling of effortless performance, being absorbed in the moment to such an extent that one experiences a heightened level of consciousness and ability (see Csikszentmihalyi, 1990; Jackson & Csikszentmihalyi, 1999). It is the experience of being relaxed and focused at the same time. Time may slow down; an extra level of energy surges through the body; one can anticipate events and control one's movements with exceptional skill; there is an exhilarating feeling throughout the body (see Nideffer, n.d.). Murphy and White (1995) believed that the altered perception, the ecstasy, the feats of extraordinary skill and strength that characterize playing in the zone, all suggest that higher powers exist in us all and can be cultivated toward greater purposes.

Dave Meggyesy asserted that in fact "the zone is the essence of the athletic experience, and those moments of going beyond yourself are the underlying allure of sport" (in Cooper, 1998, p. 25.) Not only does research by sports psychologists (e.g., Jackson & Csikszentmihalyi, 1999) back this up, but so do athletes' own experience within different sports. Masters World Champion ski racer Debbi Waldear described the zone as "leaving the rational mind behind to totally concentrate to driving yourself to your limits...There is nothing else but you moving on your skis" (Mims, 2001, August 25).

Professional football player John Brodie wrote:

> Time seems to slow way down, in an uncanny way, as if everyone were moving in slow motion. It seems as if I had all the time in the world to watch the receivers run their patterns, and yet I know the defensive line is coming at me just as fast as ever. (Murphy & White, 1995, p. 42)

Michael Jordan gave his account of the zone:

> You just start getting on a roll. Everything that you do is working...It's like you can do anything, you can take your time, you say anything to people, you seem to be just like you're on a playground all by yourself. (Mims, 2001, August 25)

If the zone is so desirable, why doesn't everyone get there? The point is that one cannot just will oneself into the zone. Part of the experience is that one must not be self-conscious. When the self tries to ignore and overcome itself, it just produces more self. As soon as one becomes aware of being in the zone, it dissipates. The most noted example occurred during the first game of the 1992 NBA finals when Michael Jordan, after just having hit his sixth consecutive three-point basket, turned to the TV network announcers on the sideline and shrugged. It was as if he himself could not explain what was happening. The streak was over; he had become self-conscious and was out of the zone (see Cooper, 1998).

For athletes, choking is a pitfall that arises when the athlete's self gets in the way, when under stress he or she thinks too much about something that he or she already knows how to do. Choking occurs when the more one tries to think one's way out of the situation, the worse it becomes. It occurs among student test-takers and anyone who views his or her performance as crucial to one's success or self-worth (see Nideffer, 1995). Internal and external distractions that affect concentration can take the player out of his or her game and create a downward performance cycle. On an internal level, negative thoughts, self-doubt, and dwelling on a past mistake or a future outcome are distractions a player cannot afford to entertain in the midst of a performance. Thinking about the clock running out or even anticipating winning sometimes cause players to lose their focus in the present and ignore process cues. External distractions have the same effect. Ones that some Borough High football players mentioned were the crowd noise at an away game, the trash-talking of their opponents, and the bad calls against them made by the refs. When the players let these bother them, it had the tendency to take them out of their game and lead them to committing mental mistakes.

The zone is the most desirable place to be, and one way that athletes increase their chances of reaching it is through meditation. This is in part because meditation provides a method that allows the mind to transcend itself, not through willful thinking toward a goal or by repressing thoughts or feelings, but by allowing the mind to be at rest, to be in the present. By giving oneself compassion, by watching the mind leap from one thought, feeling, or image to another and giving spacious awareness to those thoughts, feelings, and images, the mind over time begins to calm down. There are no longer a slew of thoughts that have to do with the past, future, or self-judgment; there is only the present. One begins to become less attached to the thoughts and no longer identify with them; to realize that thoughts about the self are not really one's self, and that even the self is not a permanent entity but is itself a concept that keeps changing.

The zone has its own intrinsic philosophy. It is not about playing for selfish or other ego-oriented reasons such as winning at any cost, nor for conventional reasons such as gaining social status, pleasing one's coach, or gaining approval from teammates or others. Rather, it is for the pure pleasure and mastery of the activity itself; the focus is on the moment. In this sense it comes to represent the highest level of moral development. There is no longer the need to prove oneself, to hold on to one's self-image, to dominate others, or to act in self-serving or conventional ways. One is at peace with oneself and others because the ego and even the social self has been transcended. A person becomes free to act in moral ways—selflessness, collaboration, nonhurtfulness—for their own sake.

My original goal was to employ meditation as a way for young males to develop beyond the restrictions of conventional masculinity, to help them notice, reflect on, and then, with compassion, let go of the eternally vigilant, harsh set of standards in their heads by which they judge themselves with respect to their manliness. In the end, I discovered that teaching athletes meditation was not only a starting point to play sports in the zone but a means to help them begin this courageous journey toward self-realization.

The Zone: End and Beginning

I knew that many male youth often feel they never can let up the stressful need to prove their masculinity to themselves and others. I wanted to work with young men around the problematic aspects of conventional masculinity, to help them critically consider and be mindful of their own issues of stress, pain, anger, and sadness and come up with better problem-solving means than those offered by the norm. I was convinced through my own experience with meditation that it could be a powerful tool along with a supportive group discussion format to help young men evolve to higher levels of ego, moral, and gender identity development. By creating a space around a thought or self-concept, a young person can more freely sit with his or her own experience and become less attached to rigid, stereotypical notions of what one is supposed to think or whom one is supposed to be. James Garbarino (2000), who worked with troubled youth, saw how meditation put the youth in a frame of mind that allowed them to be more open to educational efforts. A therapist who does meditation and therapy with adolescent males has found that "mindfulness training offers an exceptionally rich opportunity for young men to engage the process of identifying and sorting out what is true, important, and real" (Bankart, 2002, p. 7).

From readings as well as my own experience I know that as a meditator learns to compassionately witness thoughts and feelings and let them go, he or she may evolve from assuming a self-centered or conventional viewpoint to a more interconnected and spiritual one. Over time, a person is then more open to seeing what is happening in the moment and more able to consider alternatives to do what is best. Evidence suggests that meditation is beneficial to health, reduces stress, and helps one deal with pain (Murphy, Donovan, & Taylor, 1997). I wanted to employ meditation as a developmental tool that could promote higher levels of self-awareness and identity specifically for young males. Although I was not going to be doing therapy, I still wanted a structured, safe place that could provide the cover for young men to begin to develop some tolerance for exploring their full range of feelings. Bankart (2002) said the therapist must "provide a sturdy and flexible scaffold for helping the client confront his demons without resorting to stereotypical masculine escape and avoidance strategies" (p. 6). I told the young men that sitting with and facing what you feel takes courage, a quality that they, too, valued.

At first, I wondered how I could gain access to high school male youth and find a motivating factor that would pique their interest. I had not intended to work with athletes at first. Brooklyn College had developed an after-school program at Borough High School that seemed like a promising place to start. Many stressed-out urban teens live in families that often are overburdened and overwhelmed themselves and can provide little decent time for them. For these youth the only two places they know are the dry, irrelevant world of the school classroom and the harsh, dangerous proving ground of the streets. A good after-school program can provide the middle ground between the two. The research on after-school programs suggested that good ones make a difference in kids' lives—better grades, peer relations, emotional adjustment, and conflict resolution skills (Eccles & Templeton, 2002; Noam, 2002, November/December). Good programs have a developmental, holistic approach rather than a deficit-based or risk-behavior model and provide places of learning, growth, structure, and safety (DeAngelis, 2001, March). As Larson (2000) argued, in a voluntary structured activity such as an after-school program, unlike in most classrooms or even peer activities, students are both self-motivated and challenged to concentrate. Another way to put it is that activities for youth are satisfying and pleasurable in which there is the right amount of a challenge—not too easy or tough—with respect to their skill level (see Csikszentmihalyi, 1990). If I developed a project as part of something they were motivated to work hard at, I would more likely have both their attention and their interest.

At the school I considered recruiting for an after-school discussion and support group for guys—a young men's group. I ran the idea past the school peer mediation/conflict resolution club and the faculty sponsor, but after tossing it around they said it would be a tough sell to the males in the school. During a brainstorming session a colleague hit on the idea of seeking out members of one of the school athletic teams.

A sports team seemed like a good way to go. The meditation to improve their game performance, a legitimate goal in its own right, would be the hook to get them interested in the rest of the program. As an after-school activity, participating in organized sports in some cases benefits students emotionally and physically and leads to fewer dropout rates (see Hayes, 2002, April).

However, mere participation in sports is not enough to ensure positive benefits. It depends on the quality of the program; for example, whether the coaches compromise moral character in favor of winning over everything, and the degree to which students do sports for pleasure or as a means of self-validation. Sports need to be structured in a way that enhances higher moral development and intrinsic play. This includes building in opportunities for reflection and meditation, encouraging athletes to set goals of self-mastery and personal improvement over emphasizing winning, and providing direct instruction on moral concepts (Gano-Overway, 1999, May 3).

The quality of the sports program affects the athletes' growth. Youth in a martial arts program who practiced meditation and reflected on moral values reported lower levels of anxiety and aggression and improved social skills than those who just received self-defense skills (Trulson, 1986). Adult-controlled, highly organized formal sports tend to provide fewer benefits to youth than when they participate in informal sports; when the youth are in control they can manipulate the balance between skill level and the physical degree of challenge and find the pleasurable balance point, or flow, for themselves (Miracle & Rees, 1994). Some research shows that participation in competitive sports leads to increased anxiety and more self-centered moral reasoning (see Larson, 2000). Young people develop better overall in sports programs that emphasize skill acquisition and mastery rather than winning (Gano-Overway, 1999, May 3). Too many programs treat sports as a means to an extrinsic end, namely the pressure to win, which becomes equated with social success and manhood. This tendency undercuts the myth that sports participation per se leads to positive moral development (Miracle & Rees, 1994).

Changing the structure of the sports program is important but not sufficient if the corresponding development of consciousness does not occur. Although I was not in the position to directly influence the structure of the sports program, I at least wanted to invite the students to consider the quality of conscious awareness of these issues within their own lives. In light of the media attention focused on professional sports and the interest in it among many youth, I hoped to be able to convey my concerns about the critical problems facing young athletes today as well as provide them a place for support and growth.

The counselor educator Courtland Lee argued:

> We need to be working with the young athletes to help them identify values, set goals and develop a healthy perspective about their participation in sports, as well as to think beyond their playing days. I don't think that that is happening enough, partly because counselors don't understand how important a role they can play. Especially at the secondary level, and even in middle school, counselors need to be more focused on the needs of these young athletes. So it's no wonder that some people begin to lose sight of the fact that, first and foremost, sports should be fun for kids. (Hayes, 2002, April, p. 22)

I wanted the young men to critically examine the ethos that winning is everything, the thinking that says I am not a man unless I succeed, that sports is a means to get money, cars, and fame, and other self-centered, conformist, and materialist levels of moral reasoning. Instead, I wanted to help them focus on the mastery of play. This was the sword that would cut through the pressures to win, to prove oneself, or to receive social validation at the expense of one's moral, spiritual, and physical well-being, the mentality that characterizes much of sports in today's culture. Meditation as a practice focuses on the process, what is happening now, not thinking ahead about the ends. By letting go of thinking about winning or losing, of feeling the need to prove one's toughness or avoid one's fear, a young man is free to execute the skill of play in an unfettered way. As attachments to aspects of the ego dissolve and one loses one's self-consciousness, a higher level of awareness, the zone, may appear. This awareness, if cultivated and appreciated, can open the way for greater integration of self on a universal level. A performance enhancement project with college student athletes who practiced meditation found that meditation had a positive impact on other aspects of the students' lives (D'Andrea & Arredondo, 2003, July).

I also hoped that some of the athletes in the school could learn to become leaders. Athletes have high status in schools. Perhaps Malcom Gladwell's (2000) concept of the tipping point—a small change in a system at a crucial point leads to big changes, like an epidemic—could work in this case. A few young men who become interested in mindful practices perhaps could make the difference and cause an epidemic of growth. However, I knew that even though athletes had status, by nature they did not necessarily have more leadership ability than other students. For example, although team sports presents an opportunity for young people from different backgrounds to work together and know each other better, participation in athletics does not by itself promote inter-group harmony without its conscious cultivation from mindful adults (Miracle & Rees, 1994).

It is a challenge of course to start a new program in a public school, especially a program of this kind. I approached the principal and assistant principal, who were supportive of the idea but were not happy about a draft of a recruitment flier I had submitted. Ironically, the objection seemed to be not over any reference to meditation and spiritual matters but to the invitation to speak confidentially—with the usual professional exceptions—about personal matters that might include sex and drugs. After the principal approved a revised flier, he summoned his coaches to a meeting where I explained what I wanted to do. The football coach was interested and cooperative but was properly cautious and protective of his own relationship and time with his players and at first found it difficult to secure a weekly time to free them up. A short time later we worked out an arrangement and he invited me to address his players at a meeting after school.

At the first gathering, I was apprehensive about whether there would be enough interest. It was like George Mumford had said: you have about ten seconds to get their attention (Gordhamer, 2000, fall). That previous summer I had met Mumford, an African American sports psychologist and teacher of insight meditation. He was the man coach Phil Jackson, a practicing Buddhist, had brought in to teach meditation to the champion Chicago Bulls and Los Angeles Lakers (see Butler, 2003, summer; Lee, W. P., n.d.; Peak performance, n.d.; Shugar, 2001, October 30). George was one of my main inspirations. He insisted on forging the link between being in the zone on the court or ball field and engaging in mindful behavior the rest of the time you're alive, what Buddhists call right action. I was happy that a number of the football players had already heard of the zone. They were familiar with the word and the experience. The zone, they said, when I asked for examples, is when you're totally focused; when you feel you can do anything; when you're doing everything right.

They also knew about Phil Jackson and that he had introduced meditation to Michael Jordan. I also told them about George Mumford's work. I offered the young men a similar opportunity to get to the zone. Meditation does not guarantee that you will get there, I said, but it is a form of preparation that increases your chances. A good number were willing to try.

I, too, wanted them to play football in the zone. But I had that other aim in mind as well; I also wanted them to play life in the zone, and to come to see the two as inseparable. That was the more challenging part. To my relief they also were open to coming to a group where they could talk about stress, anger, and other topics if they so chose. Some were even interested in finding a spiritual space and some peace of mind.

I told the guys that signed parent/guardian consent forms were required and that most of the first session would be filling out questionnaires. They would be paid as subjects if they stayed with the program and completed a second questionnaire later on. I also told them I would tape-record some sessions but that no one would be identified in the project. I then handed out the fliers and consent forms. Armed with a small pilot project grant, I said I would provide snacks and handouts. As an incentive I also promised I would do my best to invite a couple of New York Giants football players who I learned were interested in the meditative aspects of yoga (Williams, 2001, June 3). We were ready to begin.

Chapter Four

Gettin' Serious

And it all seems clear to you now, you can breathe
It was different
When you couldn't see the forest from the trees

—Dead Prez (1999), "Score," from *Soul in the Hole* soundtrack

The Setup

I felt fortunate to undertake this project despite working under considerable constraints. I would have liked to collaborate more closely with the coaches as part of the athletic program. Instead, I insinuated myself into their routine, some professor type convincing an initially reluctant coaching staff to let me have access to the players. (I'm no Woody Allen, I even work out a bit and did play half a season of high school football, but I could have looked like Bret Favre for all it mattered and still not be one of the guys.) Part of the limitation was that some of the staff appeared to have a different take on the values and meaning of sports and how to work with male youth, and there was no formal mechanism to discuss philosophies and approaches in order to help us get on the same page.

I wish I could have met with the students on a formal, one-on-one basis in addition to the weekly group sessions to get to know what was going on with each one of them. Time, scheduling, and other logistical conflicts precluded that. I even might have made more headway as an authorized member of the school staff—a real teacher with the power to discipline or give out grades or a regular counselor who could help them get into college. Instead, I was a just nice guy willing to listen, offering them a new way to know themselves better, and committed to meeting with them on a regular basis.

As for the locale, rather than a fluorescent classroom with graffiti-covered desks off a busy corridor that provided an endless stream of curious female students peering in, it would have helped to meet in a quiet, secluded room with cushy chairs, perhaps accessorizing with a New Age tape, incense, and candle. True, the head coach had assured me his cooperation, the principal had given me the go-ahead, and the guys had said they were down with the program. Still, I was an outsider, not affiliated with the team, not a regular authority figure in the school, who was offering a voluntary project and only a vague promise of a vague reward—getting to play in the zone. At least the peanut butter and jelly sandwiches were real.

Starting Out

The first sessions begin in the midst of the football season; to use a metaphor from another sport, I'm already behind the curve. Seventeen guys pile into the classroom and drape themselves into the desks I had arranged in a circle. The tensions of being in a formal classroom all day are let out; this isn't real school. Lots of physical horseplay, bragging about the girls they were with at the party on Saturday night, and dissing (teasing). They are telling me who they are, but more important, telling each other, reestablishing hierarchies in a different format, and feeling nervous and excited. I note this behavior and believe it will provide important material for them to think about later on as well as afford me a chance to point out what I think is going on with them. I want to address here-and-now stuff with them as much as possible, for example, what's going on right now? What do you think Anton is feeling when he acts that way? This is a challenge to me but a crucial purpose of the group. I am also apprehensive myself and wonder whether I can pull the thing off. I aim to assume a role that is neither strict disciplinarian nor unstructured encounter group facilitator and hope that we can find a way to work together. Over time, it turns out that sometimes I am too directive, sometimes too laid-back; when we're in the flow, or zone, then everything clicks.

I get their attention and ask them to settle down. When they do, I welcome them and explain the purpose of the group. We are going to talk about things that might be on their minds as a way to unload them so they can play football with better focus. And we are going to practice meditation as a way to feel what it's like to be in the zone. First, however, I ask them to complete some questionnaires. I tell them we will be doing these again a few months from now and explain to them that this is a way to see what, if anything, they learn. Most, not all, manage to sit and fill them all out but have a hard time focusing and completing the task. I encourage them along the way. They get rewarded with pizza.

The next time we meet we establish a more formal routine. I greet them with jumbo loaves of bread, jars of peanut butter and jelly, and juice. Before I can say anything, some of them commandeer six or eight slices each. They quickly assemble the material into sandwiches, gobble them down, and drink all the juice. For the future I will have to work out a different means of distribution as well as increase the amount—these guys eat like there's no tomorrow. That's not what the Buddhists mean by living in the moment.

We put the desks in a circle and settle in. I ask them briefly to describe what the zone means to them. Some say it's a feeling of being totally focused when you play, that your mind and body are together without effort. I invite them to consider using this time we're in the group as a way to practice being in the zone as well.

I introduce one of the main themes of the group, to help them deal with the stress of growing up male in today's society. We discuss the "Act Like a Man" box developed by Paul Kivel (1999). Inside the box is a list of traits boys feel pressured to display, for example, be tough, be in control, don't cry, never ask for help, show anger, take it, intimidate others. If a boy goes outside the box, he is subject to verbal abuse, like being called a wimp, nerd, or fag, or physical abuse, getting beat up, isolated, or rejected. They recognize much of it. We discuss whether this is the only way to be a man, how a man can express his feelings in a healthy way, and whether one has to give in to the pressures in the box.

From the previous week I had compiled responses to a survey asking them to check off the five most important topics they wanted to discuss. The issue of sports and athletes had the highest number checked off, followed by violence/conflict resolution/anger, and relationships/sexuality/girls. I tell them that these are serious issues for many young men, that we will be discussing these issues, and that meditation also can possibly help them in these areas.

One student asks, What is the bigger purpose of meditation? I tell him that it is to reach a deeper level of awareness and connectedness with oneself and others. That's the zone. Meditation is not just a means to get whatever you want but is part of a wise tradition that helps us realize what is really important, not just our own self-interests, not just our cultural group or team. It's a way to help us come to terms with and get past thoughts and feelings of fear, hatred, greed, and stress and find a higher way to live right now. It may help us realize we can still be men and not have to be cruel or hard on others or ourselves.

My aim of course is not to turn them into passive, introspective, softies on the field; I want to help them find a way to play well, out of their highest, most inspired selves, with appropriately fierce strength, decisiveness, energy, and toughness. The challenge is to transform these competitive, aggressive strengths and energies into higher, more positive forms of mental awareness and mastery. Even in the heat of competition, the young men need to be in tune with the changing needs of the moment, and not misapply those qualities, which then become self-defeating. Too much rage or aggression, or too much competitiveness by way of fear of losing, contributes to loss of focus and energy, making mistakes, and creating harm. One can learn to use the fire of anger to cultivate positive, spiritual energy and mastery instead of being destructive.

Perhaps more important, the young men could learn to be mindful of these qualities in other areas of their lives, to not harm each other, young women, or themselves and instead move to being more compassionate, more responsive beings. Over time the wisdom becomes practical, knowing when and how to use one's skills, when to assert one's individuality, when to yield for the sake of others. Only later, despite my own meditation practice over the last four years, did I come to realize that I was inviting them to engage in something that goes against almost everything that our culture stands for and to which they are being conditioned. I was asking them to no longer succumb to mindless distractions, unhealthy diversions, and empty calories that are relentlessly promoted as means to fill ourselves up and keep us disconnected from ourselves, from others, and from nature. Instead, I wanted them to become intentional beings, fully present with themselves, able to see passing fads and sensationalistic pleasures for what they are; in sum to see with inner vision that which is not visible to the eye.

William, a big linesman, asks me if meditation can help you lose weight. I tell him that it might, because it helps you be mindful of what you are feeling (see Kabatznick, 1998). If I am frustrated but have been conditioned to eat every time I am upset and don't realize the connection, I am going to eat as a way to make the discomfort go away. If I pay more attention to what I am feeling, I can better determine whether I am really hungry or whether I am using food to medicate myself, that is, to try to make bad feelings go away. I can find a more skillful way to get my needs met. He thinks about it.

What kind of ground rules or agreements do you think we need in order for all of us to get along here? I ask. As usual in groups, the two big ones come up: respect and confidentiality. Listen to and treat each other fairly, and what is said here stays here. I tell them the exception: when someone discloses that a person is being harmed or is going to be harmed, by either his hand or another's, I am required to speak about it with the proper authorities in order to get that person help. They nod their heads.

We break down what respect means: listen, don't interrupt, and don't say nasty things to someone, they say. I add that this means even if someone has different ideas or opinions than yours. I introduce a topic that would become an ongoing theme for a year: dissing. I knew that dissing was a large part of male subculture, and by extension Kindlon and Thompson's (2000) male Culture of Cruelty. Add being African American (playing "the dozens" and woofing, engaging in aggressive verbal play as a form of asserting one's masculinity), coming from a harsh, critical family or neighborhood background, and having competitive teammates in a competitive sport, and you get a lot of it. What I did not realize at the time was the extent to which dissing infused so much of their interaction and how much of it was reinforced by the football culture itself (trash-talking, playing through pain, acting tough for fear of being seen as too soft or weak).

I have no problem with dissing itself, I tell them; a lot of it is common and is a way you guys relate to each other. (I am trying to work within their culture of meaning here and help them realize that dissing is often even an oblique way for them to express affection that works when they are on the same wavelength. I also see some of it as a defensive, protective activity for many boys, in particular for African American male youth. Although I would like them to find a way to go beyond defensive postures, I do not want to strip them of defenses they still need now. My hope is that over time they can find a way to learn to be more themselves that is neither caving in to conventional masculinity nor stuck in a defensive, resistant, or oppositional identity.) What

I want you to consider, I say, is there's a limit, a line that exists as to how much is okay. When you cross over that line it's neither fun nor funny anymore; it's hurtful and has bad consequences for you and the other person. It can lead to negative feelings and even affect your teamwork and play. Part of your job, I say, will be to figure out where that line is and learn to respect it. Dissing is a theme to which we return a number of times.

When the guys talk out of turn we try passing, or throwing, around an empty plastic soda bottle; only the holder gets to speak. In later sessions I replace that with a small, green rubber football, the school color. When that gets left in somebody's locker downstairs we work on trying to get everybody heard without it. Sometimes laughter and yelling take over the group dynamics. I consider it an opportunity to practice patience. Part of the meditative approach is to get them to see why they get out of control at that moment, what is it that makes it hard for them to sit and listen to and respect each other. I try to create a holding environment for some of their acting out; I cut them some slack and, unless they get too out of hand, try to stay with what's happening until it passes. This also on occasion encourages some of them to take a leadership role; they invoke the ground rules and bring the rest of the group to order without my having to step in. They may do it in a harsh way: "Yo, shut up!" I thank them for wanting to bring the group back; let's find a way to do it peacefully, I say, without yelling "shut up."

At the end of the session I introduce them to meditation through a tape by Jack Kornfield (1996), a teacher of Vipassana, or insight meditation. At one point I had asked some of them to write down the most important reasons they want to meditate. I got answers like: "learn how to calm down," "release the stress and anger," and "gain concentration." These were valid reasons in themselves; I hoped to get them to consider more spiritual ones. I chose insight meditation over an approach in which one mainly focuses on one thing, for example, a mantra, or a candle flame, in order to relax, because I want them to consider meditation not just as a means of stress reduction but also as a way to be mindful of their own experience and as a way to help them evolve.

Vipassana begins with concentrating on breathing, then moves on to noticing the changing nature of sensations, emotions, and thoughts. I hope in time they will take a meditative approach to mastering an activity without needing to see it as an extension of one's competitive ego or as an expression of power over others. With meditation they are self-conscious, doing this new activity in front of their teammates. Besides the giggling and false starts, they are curious to see who else has their eyes closed. Each session I spend some time going over their meditation posture, from head to toe, reminding some not to slouch, but to be relaxed and alert at the same time. After a while they settle down and become serious. Each week takes them a little less time to get into it. When new guys come to the classroom and participate most go through the same pattern—they are the ones who are identified as "serious" by the original guys. The regulars warn me about some of the others. "He's not *serious*, Mr. Forbes." I'm patient with some of these players, allowing the process to take hold of them in some cases, while with others I myself get taken. Sooner or later, though, those who are not "serious," those who are just there for the snacks or who are otherwise not motivated, stop coming.

We use the snack time as an opportunity to practice mindful eating. This is a struggle for them and for me; the food becomes a place where their anger, frustration, and aggression get played out. Being patient, feeling deprived and unloved, greedy and competitive, wolfing down the food, not tasting it, already anticipating the next bite before you've even chewed the first one, worrying about what the other guy has; it's all there. I point these things out as they occur. After a few sessions we figure out a way to break into squads and distribute the snacks to each group. There is a bit more peace.

I met with members of the team for ten sessions during and after the fall 2001 season. I administered pre- and post-tests for that interval. In the winter some seniors left and new members joined along with some from the fall season. I gave all of them a different battery of pre-tests. I was able to meet with them for longer sessions after school one day a week almost regularly through May (sixteen sessions). That's when we had a chance to stretch out some discussions and examine things they wanted to explore at a less pressured pace. After the guys returned from football camp in the summer we regrouped and managed to meet for shorter, more focused sessions (eleven) during the fall 2002 football season, the one we were gearing up for. The second post-tests were completed after the season.

Meditation and Football

The young men wanted to be focused before, during, and after a game. I explained to them that meditation is not about concentrating on whatever it is you want in order to get it. That's a different process and is not meditation. Some of them said that's what they did, try to force their mind to think about something. Stephen said he tries to block out or push down unwanted thoughts or feelings of being hyped. I told them meditation instead is about noticing what passes through your mind without judgment, letting those things go, and bringing yourself back to the present moment. It's treating your mind with kindness, a new experience for many of them.

True, one does focus on or attend to something; in this case it was always our breathing. If, however, a thought, feeling, or sensation comes up that is a distraction from attending to the breath, don't force it down, instead notice it without judgment, name it, then gently return back to the breathing. Be gentle with your mind. The more you are able to do this, the more the thoughts diminish, the mind calms down, and you are left in the present.

I was happy to see that a year later, at the end of their second season, those athletes who had the joined the group from the beginning and showed up most often tended to pick a questionnaire definition of meditation in these terms, "noticing what passes through your mind without judgment, and being in the present moment" ($N = 15$) over "meditation is focusing, concentrating, in order to get what you want" ($N = 8$). Those who saw meditation as focusing on one's goal tended to join the group later and did not attend as regularly.

In an early session some admitted it was stressful playing before people in the stands, in particular their family or large crowds. Pat, one of the team's best all-around athletes, quickly grasped the connection between meditation and the need to ward off distractions during a game. He recalled that at an important away game there was a big crowd with media coverage and that it was essential to find a way to block it all out:

> I think meditation should just help you focus on what's on the game, not everything that's going round outside the game…but whatever's going on on the field…Not the cheerleaders, not the fans, none of that stuff, the game, the game is why you're here.

The game itself however is full of surprises and twists that players cannot always anticipate. Ted said:

> A lot of the things that we practice don't really happen, like we would practice these plays and go over the plays, I've got this person coming my way but he wasn't supposed to come my way. That takes my focus away from what I was supposed to do, you know.

We talked about how that calls for awareness of the present and an ability to read a new situation and apply what one knows at the time, rather than a rigid attachment to one thought. The distraction comes when you choke, and think, *Uh-oh, what do I do now?* instead of being in flow, letting the mind alone so that one can draw from one's repertoire of skills. We discussed another approach to performance that requires mindfulness. Mark Epstein (1999) further distinguished reacting, just acting without thinking (being mindless), from responding, which is not thinking but is based on cultivated awareness. This is a subtle distinction that needs to be experienced firsthand. Ricardo said he knows that when he thinks too much he makes a mistake, but when he sets himself and knows what he needs to do he doesn't think about it, he just does it.

At one point I showed them a model developed by Robert Nideffer (n.d.) that divides a player's field of focus along the dimensions of broad/narrow and internal/external. The ability to shift smoothly from one quadrant to the next, for example, from seeing the whole field (broad-external) to knowing what the next play is (narrow-internal) is a function of one's mental preparation and ability to let go and be in the zone. When you can shift your focus, your breathing is deep and muscles are loose. When a player chokes and falls out of it, he can take deep breaths and direct his attention to relaxing his arms, neck, shoulders and leg muscles, then return to where he needs to focus.

After a tough loss played at the other school's field the guys talked about how they lost their concentration. One admitted that he used to be "violent" on the field but this time he hesitated before tackling an opponent. He thought too much about whether to tackle high or low, and how hard. Was the meditation having an opposite effect, getting them to think too much or becoming too sensitive? This wasn't a bad thing if it stopped the player from engaging in unnecessary roughness. But if he wanted to master the art of tackling, then the solution called for less ruminating and doubt, not more. This situation came up the following spring with another player, James.

Before one session, James spoke with me privately. He told me he felt a lot of pressure to excel; he was recruited from another school to play football and felt very pressured to prove how good he was. What was worse, he was concerned about playing too tough and hurting an opposing player. So then he lay back and didn't play well enough. He also heard his mom's voice telling him not to play too hard so that he wouldn't hurt himself and others.

I told him first that he doesn't have to give in to the pressure; he knows he's good and doesn't have to prove anything to anybody. I then asked James if he could visualize or imagine a middle way to play that was based on mastery, and drew this on the board. On top he is playing too aggressive, hurting himself or others. On bottom he is playing too soft, not playing well. Is there a middle ground where he could play well, not be ineffective, yet not be hurtful? I asked him. He said yes, he could imagine it. I encouraged him to visualize the third way of playing during practice and see how that went. Eventually he was able to do so. He told me the visualization practice helped him to have a good experience during summer training. James then went on to play a solid season during the fall.

Loss was a big issue the guys needed to look at. The ability to detach oneself from the pain of losing is rare even among many adults in this competitive society that denigrates losers of any sort. That first season I worked with them, despite winning their last game, the team learned afterward they were eliminated from the playoffs. Some of them said they cried after the game. Stephen said the disappointment was so painful he wasn't sure he'd be back next year. I shared their sense of frustration and letdown with them whenever they lost and encouraged them to use it as an opportunity to go deeper in their own awareness: sit with the feelings of pain and sadness and see how they change over time. In the end Stephen's feelings did change. The following year he came back and had a stellar season.

Thinking about what may happen after the game, especially if you're afraid of losing, can be a distraction while playing, especially if one's ego is involved. Drew reminded the group:

> Let's say you lose the game, know what I mean, like certain people's problem is, they know if they lose the game they get to face embarrassment, like last year their picture was in the *Daily News* when they lost to Tech.

We discussed this and other examples of mental mistakes. I framed these as situations where you know what you have to do but don't do it because you are distracted by a thought, especially one about yourself, instead of being keyed into the present. Even thinking, "We've won this game," before the game is over is a distraction and can lead to mental lapses that can quickly turn around the game's expected outcome. Other mental distractions could be something like a past mistake, worrying that the coach will take you out, or overanticipating what you will do with the ball even before it gets to you. On the heels of that example Stephen asked a receiver why he dropped a ball thrown right at him in Saturday's game. The young man admitted he was feeling pressured and was thinking just at that moment that he better catch the ball, and so failed to do what he had been able to do all week during practice. Stephen then helped us distinguish mental from physical:

> I will also say that a lot of it is physical mistakes too, because, you know, me, I'm a say, two or three people that were injured through the whole game, and still played, know what I'm saying, but they played injured like me. And I couldn't even defend the receiver with only one hand.

Stephen was right; sometimes things just happen. As a number of students said, if you've given of yourself 100 percent and played your A game, then you can accept that kind of loss more easily than one due to mental errors. One however still needs to be mindful of what kind of mental approach one takes toward physical occurrences, for example, whether to ignore them, blame them, or see them for what they are and deal with them accordingly. That is, it depends on your mind's relationship to physical events that are beyond your control.

After a few sessions the guys preferred to turn off all the fluorescent lights when we meditated. Some said each week was a little better; they could get into it sooner. I pointed out the parallel with their behavior, how they got into it more easily and that was like calming the mind more easily as well. As Jack Kornfield (1996) says on the guided meditation tape, training your mind is like training a puppy; the puppy wanders, you don't beat the puppy, you gently bring it back to the paper: "Stay, stay." Pat liked this analogy and said it helped him stay on target.

Meditation is not being so relaxed one falls asleep, I told them, when some did. One said that it's the same when you play: you don't want to be so relaxed; you need some "stress." I suggested that you want to be alert, a kind of positive stress; of course you don't want to be so stressed, agitated, or hyped you can't notice what's going on. In either case, the idea is to notice that you are sleepy, or wired, or whatever, and realize you are getting lost in that experience, then gently bring yourself back to your breathing. Often in the beginning I saw their minds would wander and were drawn away by distractions coming from the outside, such as school bells, sirens and shouts from the street, and kids talking in the hall. I would tell them to incorporate these into the meditation: "There's a distraction. Just notice it, then bring your mind back to focusing on your breath." I told them those could be like distractions during a game, an opponent's trash talk or a loss of down on the last play. These were the sorts of things that by thinking about them too long get you out of your focus. Over time some reported they noticed the distractions but were more quickly able to bring their minds back to the breathing.

A few weeks later Ted was elated. During practice he improved his pass receiving. "Meditation worked!" he told me. "I was able to concentrate on catching the ball, and not letting my mind get ahead of myself like I used to." I told him I was happy for him. I hoped that any positive experience would encourage him to practice meditation over time and allow him to enhance his athletic performance and own development. I wondered whether any actual results would be so sudden and mechanical, and, if so, whether they would last. Meditation is not a quick fix. His use of the word *worked* provided me a chance to make another point.

What about a drug dealer? I asked them. Should a drug dealer use meditation to stay calm and focused so he can avoid the cops and be more efficient at dealing? That's not the higher purpose of meditation, I said. Is meditation good in order to hurt your opponent or to win a game at any cost? No, most said, although some were not above regarding this notion as acceptable. I invited them again to consider the holistic nature of meditation, that it's not just another quick method or technique for any goal you want to attain but has to do with well-being and mastering living right in all areas of life.

In the spring we incorporated body scanning into the meditation, paying attention to sensations of every sort. We talked about the need to be aware of what is going on with the body, as a way to deal with pain. A young male athlete needs to notice the pain and its degree of severity, given that many men are not in touch with bodily feelings or try to deny them.

We discussed how Korey Stringer may not have been mindful of what his body was telling him. In this sense, I mentioned, he may have been like many men who learn to ignore pain and other physical indicators of stress, fatigue, and illness. I wanted them to learn to question the need to sacrifice their health through toughness and the denial of illness or pain for the purposes of fame or money, or for fear of being seen as a wimp.

Toward the end of our spring sessions we introduced visualization into the meditation practice. I had them visualize a play or skill they were working on in practice that they would execute successfully. Outside the school I ran into Charles, a junior varsity player who had missed a few sessions. He said he was struggling with taking a hand-off and tucking the football under his arm; his thinking about it kept getting in the way. I encouraged him to come back to the group and said that he could also add visualizing doing it successfully, then letting the mind go. As a group a number of them said that the visualization sessions were the best ones yet and that they got "deep" into them.

Around the same time I passed out green dots, tiny, color-coded file labels, and told the players they could place them on their cleats or anywhere else. When your eyes fall on these, I suggested, whatever you are doing, it's a reminder to breathe: take at least five deep breaths, and recenter yourself. Some guys put them on their notebooks and on the inside of their lockers.

On a different weekday I was on my way back from the high school after a field site class when I found a bunch of the guys hanging out in front of the pizza parlor under the el. Pat told me that Drew almost got in trouble from a remark he had made to a girl and that he had to hold up his cell phone in front of Drew's face to try to get him to calm down. I was puzzled until he took out the phone and showed it to me: on it Pat had placed not one but two green dots.

One important area was their struggle between self-centered play and being self-sacrificing and responsible to something larger than themselves. During the first season the guys talked about when they had first met each other during summer camp. Juan said, "I used to say Pat's stuck up in the beginning of the season. But at camp I got to know each one. In the Erasmus game Pat had my butt [protected me]."

They said that while some guys still play for themselves there are more times when guys step up for the team when someone is injured; they felt more like family now. I encouraged those who were at an egocentric level of thinking to consider a more caring way to be toward others; over time, meditation helps one expand from a selfish point of view to one that takes others into account, I said; you come to realize you're interconnected and your sense of self expands.

I also suggested that there are different ways for the team to be like a family and some are healthier than others. Juan picked up on this and said he was not impressed with the idea that family blood demands loyalty; blood is just blood and it's what you can do for each other that counts. I reinforced what Juan said, that just because you are family doesn't mean you automatically sacrifice yourself for others either. I had in mind those students who were already socially aware and were evolving to a more autonomous level of thinking.

One disappointment we all experienced was that we never heard from the three New York Giants football players who practice yoga and to whom I had written requesting they visit the team. I had shown the guys an article about how these players on the Giants had introduced yoga to their teammates during summer training camp. I was hoping they might have some spiritual practice as well and be able to help my students make some connections between practice and play. I sent around another letter that many of the students signed and sent it off again. The community relations director explained that they were very busy; the players never responded.

Male Roles: Fathers and Coaches

Growing up today is stressful, all the guys agreed; it was just not something they had thought about in terms of growing up male. I had introduced this notion with Kivel's (1999) Act Like a Man box. During various sessions we discussed some of the unexpressed rules of the Male Code that no one ever makes explicit. I suggested that there are a lot of pressures on guys to always suck it up and act tough even when they didn't feel like it. By way of example one student talked about how his uncles would play fight with him as a way to toughen him up as a child but that he wasn't into it. When I asked them if there's just one way to be a man, they said no, there are different ways. They also thought that crying was okay for guys, although the example they gave, crying after a difficult loss in football, was a bit more appropriate than one which may lead to feelings of humiliation and in which their masculinity might be challenged. Some of them drew an astute distinction between themselves and some of the boys who committed murder in Littleton and other small towns: they thought that here in the city even troubled kids had more connections and community; kids would know right away who was messed up and about to cause trouble and somehow wouldn't let it happen.

The issue of male stress and problems that young men go through came up indirectly, through other discussions about their relationships with fathers, coaches, girls, and their fellow students. In each case when it seemed like a good time I would make the explicit link with issues of gender; when race and class came in to play I would mention these as well.

Randall, an African American senior, began one session on a somber note that resonated with the group. He wanted to talk about fears, what he feared the most, and asked the others to share what they feared. Randall said that he feared failing. He was afraid he wouldn't be able to succeed at making money, to provide for his family, to be a good father, and to be successful at a career. The others shared similar fears. Ricardo said he was also afraid of when things get too good; then they won't last and things will get bad again. We sat with this feeling for a while.

Later I asked them from where did they think they picked up this fear and was there anyone in their family who handled it well; were their fathers good models for dealing with tough issues like failure? This touched a nerve, as many did not have fathers available or had poor relationships with them. (On a sentence completion question, "My father and I...," six of the twelve respondents completed the sentence by writing that they had an unhappy or difficult relationship with their father.) One said the hell with his father, he was raised by his brothers, and doesn't miss a father he never really had. He told the group that he had confronted his father and told him, "You may be my biological father, but you're not a real one." Some said that their father was a negative model and that whatever their father did, they would do the opposite: for instance, be there for their kids, take them on trips.

If your fathers are not models for being men, who, if anyone, is? Kevin, an African American senior who was one of the team leaders, responded by telling us he had a good relationship with his single mom. He said he had learned a lot from her about the value of hard work and felt comfortable confiding in her about personal matters. I reinforced this point and said many guys can grow up fine with a loving mom.

"It's also about trust in your own self," Ricardo said. "We can learn from our own mistakes."

I said I liked what Ricardo said and that the more aware you are of what you do, the more you can learn. Toward the end I suggested that they sit with their feelings about their fathers. Notice what comes up: happiness, anger, sadness. They could practice having compassion for fathers and for their own thoughts and feelings about them, noticing when judgments came up, as a way to eventually make peace with fathers and with themselves. Expanding on what Ricardo said, I suggested that they even could begin to practice fathering themselves.

Randall read a spiritual passage from Martin Luther King Jr. that addressed the injustices of society. Kevin pointed out that you can be aware of all the bad in society but you don't have to get down about it, and instead can ask what you can do to help others and yourself. I agreed with Kevin and said the point is not to stay feeling down about social conditions but to be like King, a wise, courageous role model who was in the zone much of the time: be aware of injustices and help right them where possible.

In the spring some of the guys were suspended by the coaches for talking back and acting disrespectfully to them and to some teachers. We talked about what happened and what was going on with them. We also discussed coaches and what it means to have one. Some of the guys were struggling in particular with a new assistant coach whom they described as having a more confrontational style and who played a part in the suspensions. They saw him as the new kid on the block; they felt he needed to earn their respect first before throwing his weight around. I made the analogy with Franklin, how in an earlier session he had admitted to the group that as a new student a few months ago he was uptight and on guard and felt he had to prove himself to the group until he felt more secure and accepted. Even though this coach is an adult, I said, it sounds like he's also going through something like that; he's trying hard to establish himself but it may not be the best way. I thought it was helpful that they understand where the other person is coming from. The important point, however, was to learn to get along with someone whom they may not respect just yet but who has power over them and who can get them in trouble. The issue was not blaming the other person for everything that happens but looking at their own response, their own piece in the relationship. How mindful will you be of your behavior? I asked them. We discussed some imaginary scenarios involving teachers, cops, coaches, and others and tried to role-play them but did not get far with that; that day there was too much nervous energy in the room.

Some of the guys expressed frustration that the coaches made decisions with which they disagree and about which they feel they have little say. I supported them in this and encouraged them to speak respectfully with the coaches and make suggestions and ask for what they needed. The guys said they didn't feel they could get anywhere doing so and sometimes did not feel heard. Some of the hierarchical decision-making seemed to be part of the structure of playing high school football, but it also seemed that athletes could learn to participate more democratically in team decisions if they knew how to do so. Compounding their inability to do this was the head coach's assessment of the team; he told me that this team did not have any clear leaders like last year's, and he felt he had to make more decisions for them.

I raised the issue of coaching style and what kind they liked. The following week I devised the scale below based on what they said and also based loosely on Kohlberg's (1984) stages of moral reasoning and made copies of it for more discussion:

Coaching: Where Is Your Center of Gravity?

I am most motivated by:
Level 1: Authoritarian, egocentric

Stage 1: Motivated by a tough and abusive coach. He's the coach (authority) no matter how he behaves. Motivated by fear of punishment. I play so he won't kick my ass. Motivated by fear. Or, motivated by personal reward. "I play for myself." Coach: Bobby Knight. Players: those who need some abuse.

Stage 2: Likes a tough coach; he pushes and criticizes, I get something out of it. Criticism, sarcasm, and toughness don't matter if they get me going. Doesn't matter as long as I win. End is all that matters. The coach helps me get better. I'm motivated to get better in order to win. Coach: Smith. Players: some Borough High players.

Level 2: Conventional

Stage 3: Coach cares about me, he's a good guy, I want to do well and maintain a good relationship with him, and please him, not get him upset; he's like a father; he has good motives. Coach: Jones. Players: some Borough High players.

Stage 4: Coach inspires us with good, caring values. I want to do well because I like him and also for sake of social values and good social relations, being a good member of society or group, by being a moral citizen. Motivated by sportsmanship, hard work, being a team player. May be motivated by wanting to please parents, the team, the school. Coach: Evans. Players: some Borough High players.

Level 3: Postconventional

Stage 5: I am motivated by pride as an African American or minority; I represent my group and play my best to help them gain their rights. The coach is no longer motivating me. I have my own higher values. Players: Jackie Robinson, Roberto Clemente.

Stage 6: Motivated by highest universal principles: to master and excel and become at one with the universe. I don't play for a coach. I play for my highest self, which is connected to all good powers. I'm not motivated out of fear of punishment, or for rewards (just to win), or because the coach is a good guy, or for other people, or for nice, socially acceptable values. I want to excel on the highest terms possible whether or not I win. You can use a coach as a helper, or guide but no longer in terms of motivation. You aim for the zone. Players: Marshall Faulk, Michael Jordan, Muhammed Ali.

Some players said they were impressed with the college basketball coach Bobby Knight's style of coaching: tough to the point of abuse. I felt they needed to understand this distinction and told them that he was someone who crossed the line between tough caring and abuse and that that was why he was fired from Indiana a few years ago. I found that most of the players were accepting of a level 1, stage 2 coach, and levels 2, stages 3 and 4 ones. They gave me examples of these styles as embodied by certain coaches they had played under. I said that if these were the kinds of coaching they needed, that was okay for now. I wanted to link this way of thinking about what motivates them with meditation and being in the zone and to use a different angle to have them think about the idea of playing for a higher purpose (stage 6). Certain great athletes have played from a higher, inspired place, I said, beyond any conventional notion of self.

Some of the young men said, "I play for myself." This was the kind of statement that obscured levels of developmental depth. I drew the distinction between playing for your selfish self (level 1) and playing for your highest self (level 3). Pat said he could see that at various times he is motivated to play for all the reasons in all the levels.

For young men at this age coaches are a crucial part of playing because they have a significant influence on them and can provide encouragement, expertise, and support. Most of the players needed the emotional structure of a firm but caring coach who kept their selfish impulses in check but who was not harmful. Part of the problem, which I was unable to address in an effective way, was that some of their coaches held a more authoritarian approach, what Garbarino (2000) referred to as the boot camp model, one that says kids need harsh discipline, teasing to toughen them up, and unquestioned obedience.

Within the limitations of the program I was trying to help move those players who were at the egocentric level up a notch to conventional motives, to want to play for the team and maintain good social values, and those who were already at a conventional level to evolve to more autonomous realms. When one plays in the zone the coach becomes superfluous in terms of motivation; through guidance, support, and inspiration a good coach can still help the player reach higher levels of mastery. As with fathering, at the highest level, the player coaches himself. These young men, however, still needed to feel their sadness and hurt and grieve over what they have missed. They further needed cognitive and social skills to deal with their coaches and fathers in order to move beyond blaming others for everything that happens to them, and to learn to feel entitled to be treated with respect and to properly ask for what one needs.

With Young Women

Before a meeting Ricardo arrived early and spoke with me one-on-one. He told me that the previous Saturday he had had difficulty "focusing" with a girl and that it had never happened to him before. I told him it was a normal thing that happens to most guys at one time or another. It could happen when a guy is not comfortable with the girl for whatever reason and may feel pressured to perform. He might not really like the girl, or he might like her so much that it feels like he has to make a good impression. He already suspected that it's like a "signal" that he shouldn't have sex with this particular girl. We looked into why it may have happened. In this case, he realized later that it was because he is religious and saw a cross on the girl's neck. He felt that having sex wasn't the right thing to do. I congratulated him for being aware, at least afterward, of what was going on. He appeared to be moving from a more self-interested, exploitative orientation to one that saw sex as a social act that involved moral issues and empathy. I linked it with meditation in the sense that when you're attending to what is going on with yourself and you're feeling relaxed, you can be aware of what you need and what is right. If you're unaware that you're worried about the consequences of a performance or about making an impression, or ignore the feelings that tell you this isn't right for you at this moment, you're out of the zone. If you are aware and have good, honest communication with the girl about what's going on, I told him, an incident like this can even be a way to get closer and more intimate with her if that is what you want. He felt relieved.

Without mentioning Ricardo I invited the group to talk about times when they struggled in dealing with a teacher, friend, family member, or girlfriend. "Do you ever feel you can't be yourself on a date, that you're not feeling yourself, maybe because you're anxious and not in the moment?" I asked. Stephen and others picked up on this. Stephen said he meets a lot of girls and can't always read them or figure out what they are in to. He also admitted that he doesn't always know what to do:

> In the summertime, I met this girl at a party. The next Saturday she came to my crib [home], and I'm like flirtin', I was sittin' there, thinkin', I should beat [have sex]! There's nobody in my house, I was like, nah, it's a week, yo, damn son, I should beat!

It took courage for Stephen to admit in front of others that he didn't automatically follow the norm of masculinity and take advantage of a willing young woman. I said that it was okay to feel uncertain or not wanting to have sex just because the situation allowed for it. We don't have to follow a script in our head about having to be a man or fulfilling the other person's expectations, especially if we don't think it's the right thing to do. Meditation may be able to help us be more in tune with ourselves, I suggested, and mindful of what is going on in these and other kinds of situations.

In the spring we had some discussions about girls and sex. At an early session, many of the young men were aware of the double standard with respect to guys and girls: girls are "hos [whores]," boys are "players." That is, when girls have sex with more than one guy they are considered promiscuous, but when guys do this they are admired and accepted, and that in principle this isn't equal and fair. They also admitted they had a double standard when it came to oral sex. They had a disparaging name for girls who give oral sex. I asked them if they go-down on girls. They became nervous and laughed and said no, it's nasty and unclean. I asked them why it is okay for women but not guys, and informed them that girls can be clean "down there," not just virgins and monogamous married women, as they believed.

They went on to argue that they feel they have no choice but to play girls; they can't find ones who are interested in guys like them, who are sincere but poor; girls are only into guys with money, cars, and clothes, they said, so try to get what you can because they do the same to you. I raised the issue of what relationships are about. Are most manipulative, for the purpose of exchanging pleasure and obtaining material gratification, or should they be about something more meaningful and involve intimacy and mutuality? Again, they understood the distinction and agreed that they would like to have mutuality but they say they can't find decent girls. They feel pressured to play the game and be manipulative themselves.

I went back and forth on this with them, challenging their generality about all girls and their lack of responsibility for their own behavior. I was skeptical about their justification, of course, although I sensed some truth and poignancy in their predicament. To the extent that so many young people have few skills in practicing intimacy and respectful honesty and instead are besotted with materialist values from the mass media, it makes it difficult for either young men or women to have satisfying relationships. I encouraged them not to give in to cynical, manipulative, impersonal ways of conducting relationships but to put out their highest selves, which will in turn attract the only kind of partners worth waiting for, people who will appreciate and accept them for who they are. Again to some extent it came down to the courage to know, accept, and be themselves. That way they would no longer feel the need to get sucked into playing games and mistakenly regard all young women as untrustworthy or incapable of mutual honesty. At a later date I was happy to hear some of them say they do have girls as friends with whom they do not have sex and with whom they can talk about things, and I encouraged them to consider these girls as the kind of young women with whom they may be able to develop a healthier sense of intimacy.

One afternoon Drew described a serious incident that had led to him being arrested; he was just as upset by his mother being angry with him about it as anything else. The story came out piecemeal, as some of the guys were there and witnessed it, and I had to get some of the details out of him. Holding the green football to govern who could speak was barely working. Drew said he was on the street corner near the school.

"You see a female walk by and when you turn your head she flicked a cigarette at you, know what I mean, like you some bum off the street, know what I mean? She started actin' like she wanted to fight me. What would you do, Mr. Forbes? Would you swing at her?"

"No, I wouldn't," I said, "that's not who I am. But it sounds like you were interested in her and you said something to her that she felt was disrespectful."

"I was interested in her," he admitted, "I was just tryin' to see how far I could get. The reason the thing got blown out of proportion is that she started yellin' and tryin' to act big in front of her friends."

"And tryin' to embarrass you in front of your homies," Pat interjected.

"She dropped the cigarette on me," Drew said. "What was I supposed to do, say, 'Oh you made a mistake?'"

"So you slapped her first?" some of the guys asked.

"He was just tryin' to make conversation with her," Pat said.

Drew continued. "What I said was, 'I'll bust you down with something later,' and she said, 'No. Y'all niggaz need to have a little bit more respect.' That's when I interrupted her…I smacked her after she got loud and tried to fight me in front of everybody…she was swingin' at me. I didn't want her to keep comin' after me, I just wanted her to calm down."

One of the guys asked, "Did she hit you?"

"No," Drew admitted.

Pat again came to Drew's defense. "Yo, shorty [the young woman] came at him wildin', son, you can't tell my man what he would do in that situation. She bust my man. He has to calm her down, son."

To some extent Drew expressed remorse, but he still blamed the young woman and the fact that she made him look bad in front of his homies.

There were two issues that had to be addressed: first, the provocation, and second, the response to how the girl reacted.

With respect to the first, I asked, "How many of you think that what Drew said, 'I'll bust you down with something later,' could be disrespectful to many girls?" Most guys raised their hand.

"They say worse shit than that to girls," Drew argued. "You'd all say the same thing." This was Drew's line of defense, that his behavior was not disrespectful, just normal.

"No, you don't speak for me, son," Franklin said. Another guy said that maybe he would but that it depends on how it was said.

The others were not letting Drew get away thinking he had no part to play in this. I said that even if some of the guys would say the same thing, it's not the point to compare yourself to others; just because others do it doesn't make it right.

"When you guys are really in the zone are you ever going to say something disrespectful to a woman?" I asked the group.

"No," almost all said.

"I wasn't in the zone," Drew admitted.

They were getting it about the zone—mindfulness, even Drew. It was an encouraging moment.

"You gotta see it from the girl's perspective," said Calvin managing to add a crucial point. "'Cause if you were by yourself and see nine niggaz around you and like, one of them try to approach you, she gonna probably think that you tryin' to play her in front of your boys."

Before I could pick up on this theme of empathy Stephen interrupted with something he'd been thinking about that touched on the heart of the matter. "I wanna ask a serious question: How many of y'all can't control your anger?" Stephen sensed that this was the underlying issue for many of them. His question was a bold move that was almost too much for the guys. They started talking and laughing at each other all at once. After they calmed down Drew was one of many who raised their hands in response to Stephen's question. Drew was hurt and angry about many things, including women.

"Drew admits he has a problem. That's a good start," I said. "First things first. When you say something that most guys here say could be reasonably interpreted by a young woman as disrespectful, you've got to see what's going on with you. You've got to be aware of and take some responsibility for your own feelings, thoughts, and behaviors. Instead of passing it on to someone else you've got to look at what are you feeling, what are you saying, what are the possible consequences of how you behave?"

The second issue was how to respond when someone is now coming after you and wants to escalate a fight. What's more, it will embarrass you in front of your friends, all the more so because the aggressor is a woman. Drew had focused on the young woman's behavior to justify his slapping her. It was important to help him recognize he was feeling humiliated and that he was not aware of the connection between his feelings and his abusive action. The young woman did not let his comment go without a response. In this case she retaliated by humiliating him in an aggressive way. She may have thought her behavior would level the playing field, but it also escalated the incident. Drew did say that his aim was to stop her from coming after him and to calm her down. However, he was unable to stay focused on this higher-order intention and instead shifted back to blaming the other person: "She still don't have the right to come out swinging," he said. I agreed that she didn't. Pat, however, went further than that and again justified Drew's actions on that basis. He reminded them that Drew felt disrespected by her throwing the butt at him and thought that she overreacted to what Drew had said. "Besides," Pat said, "if a woman is gonna come swinging, she has to expect the same thing back."

The guys were struggling with feeling disrespected, how to save face in front of one's peers, still do the right thing, and not make things worse. Some of what Pat and Drew said was at a primary level of moral reasoning, as was the young woman's behavior. It involves retaliation and exchange of aggression: you do it to me, I do it to you. Part of this reasoning also involves deflecting the focus away from one's own behavior and attributing its cause to someone else.

Stephen came up with a suggestion that, despite its disturbingly sexist swagger, was one moral notch higher than Drew's:

"My brother told me, 'Yo, one thing with a female, if she rush you, there's two ways you gonna make her realize she makin' a mistake. Either you yoke her up or smack the shit out of her one time.' That's why I could understand Drew's first reaction is to smack her, cause you bein' ready to reach out just to make her chill."

"Is smacking her the right way?" I asked.

"No, that's not the right way," Stephen said. "I can't judge Drew, but my first reaction to her swinging at me in that situation would be just to yoke her up, just to grab her and throw her on top of the car to stop her from wildin'. But if I lost my head and I hit her..."

"The point is," I urged, "can you get to be mindful enough so you don't lose your head?"

"It's hard, but you can," Pat said.

"Sometimes I think I could be a bigger man and walk away," Charles, a junior varsity player, managed to interject.

That's the highest response, I told them, to when someone threatens us, even when we're minding our business. There's an order of responses from low to high. The highest way is what Charles said, to be able to let it go or find a way to defuse the situation and walk away. Maybe you could have said you meant no disrespect, or even apologize. That sometimes takes a lot more courage than fighting. If you have to defend yourself, you do, but you do it in order to end the fight, not for retaliation. You may have to physically restrain the other person from hurting you or try to calm him or her down, like what Stephen said; that falls somewhere in the middle. The bottom one is to start a physical fight first. Drew got in trouble because he went for that one.

"I understand what you saying, Mr. Forbes, I thought about it," Drew said. "I understand what Calvin said, that you gotta think of the female point of view. When I was locked up [for one night] I thought about that. I said, Yo, what if that was me and I was walking down the block, and shorty tried to pull me into some shit, I could think of other ways to approach it."

Drew was capable of empathy and of taking the other's point of view. He had been hurt in his own life. I told him he needed to keep facing his anger and his underlying pain, to examine where they were coming from, and then to realize how these feelings manifested themselves in self-destructive and aggressive behaviors. He also needed other skills from which to draw in such situations.

Pat agreed that "if you really want to talk to a girl, you not gonna talk to her like, 'Yo, shorty, come here, yo.'"

I tried to get in the last word. "You can't control the other person's reaction. You have to decide the best thing to do for yourself."

"We got ten minutes, Mr. Forbes, we want to meditate."

Part of my goal, similar to Garbarino's (2000) program, was to encourage a discussion about moral issues. In one follow-up session I suggested the guys think about different ways of responding to women by looking at the lyrics of a rap song, "Never Crossed My Mind," by Skee-Lo (1995). The rapper asks his groupies, "Why must you do me?" You don't know me, he tells them; there's no "us," no relationship. We could continue, he muses, but then he can't help but wonder whose daughter this is. To all the guys in his crew who don't understand why he refrains, he says, you better think again: the next groupie could be your girlfriend.

I posed questions to the group in their terms based on my analysis of the moral reasoning represented by the different characters. The groupies are thinking at a preconventional level; they want Skee-Lo because of his instrumental value to them, as a way to gain notoriety. The guys in his crew whom he addresses are also thinking at this level; they regard sex as rewarding by itself and devoid of any mutual intimacy. It's all self-centered and instrumental. Skee-Lo is at the next level, conventional morality. Being human for him means the need to have some meaningful connection and respect between people, telling the groupies, "If I were a dog, then I might want you." He is opposed to exploiting a woman because she is someone's daughter and could be someone else's girlfriend; his reasoning appeals to empathy with another and relies on reciprocity, the awareness of the moral consequences of harming others. Skee-Lo's message is not at the highest level; there is no mention of love for its own intrinsic sake, the sexual desire for union with another based on love. But he is one moral notch above the self-centered thinking represented by the groupies and the guys in his crew, a prevalent trend in popular culture and manifested in the thinking of some of the young men.

I had modest success with this lesson perhaps in part because we looked at the lyrics and did not hear the song. Also, many young people tend to just want to listen to their music and regard it as their own rather than have it analyzed like a school lesson, although I think it is often necessary for students to engage in this exercise.

The session might have had a sleeper effect on some of the group. A few weeks later some were talking about "hos," girls who give sex to anyone. I asked them to consider what these girls were feeling, what do they need, and what are they trying to get. After thinking about it for a few moments some suggested that the young women might have low self-esteem and not much self-respect, and said, "They want love."

Racial and Ethnic Prejudice and Discrimination

Racial prejudice and discrimination on occasion would become an explicit issue for the team. That first fall I gave them a reading packet with a variety of short articles and chapters about sports, athletes, African Americans, and male development and asked them to read and discuss them together. They were reluctant to do this, however, and I chose not to press it. I realized later that this was not the setting for extending a more formal educational component to the program. Reading, assignments, and more formal discussions would have to take place in a more structured forum, possibly providing course credit that would need to be arranged in advance.

Randall, a senior who continued to come to the group even after the season ended and who was going to graduate in the spring, had read one of the articles on racism and sports on his own. He attempted to introduce it to the group. When he began reading a passage aloud in a halting manner some of the guys teased him about it, to which I put a quick stop. They did manage to get into a discussion of the content matter. Another African American senior, Edward, argued that nowadays anyone can succeed; for instance, you can go to the library and learn how to set up a business on the Internet. Randall and others argued with him and took the point of the article that blacks were still being discriminated against. They said that you need to have resources like money and knowledge about how to look things up and have networks of people who can help you with money and information. They agreed with the article that blacks were being channeled into sports and entertainment for the benefit of others who made money off of them. Although there were now more black quarterbacks, they said there were fewer general managers and head coaches in football. I showed them a graphic of a pyramid with the distribution of wealth in U.S. society that we began to discuss before we ran out of time.

Toward the end of spring, race became a more personal issue that the guys were able to talk about. I had heard rumblings about a white teammate whom I hadn't met and who was not a member of the meditation group. Some of the black players at different times had told me they felt he was racist. He called them "niggers" like he meant it in a derogatory way. They had explained to me earlier that that's different than "niggaz," which is a neutral, even affectionate usage that could be okay even for others to say, depending on how it's said. They had told me I could say the word like that, too. I had thanked them, but said I didn't want to take any chances of being misunderstood, and so they wouldn't hear me utter it.

We began a discussion about race and racism when one of the few white players, Larry, said he didn't want to talk about it because he didn't feel safe. "I'm scared, Mr. Forbes." He told the group he was hurt by their calling him a "cracker" and "redneck" and started to walk out of the room. I managed to convince him to stay. I then told the group that everyone needs to feel safe and respected in here and wanted their guarantee they would treat Larry and everyone else that way. The group took the issue seriously and settled down. A number of them assured Larry that they felt he was "one of us" when he was with them by himself. But when he was with this other white teammate he changed and started teasing them about being black, and referring to them as "you black guys." They felt hurt and betrayed by his behavior, they said, and it seemed two-faced. I pointed out that this was a case of guys crossing the line, and that they needed to hear each other.

Larry was able to stay and hear them. He acknowledged the truth in what they said. I asked them to hear that he was also hurt by some of their teasing about white guys as well. "Use psychology," I told them, hoping that both Larry and the others could learn to be mindful of a pattern that they all engaged in at times. I gave them the analogy of how you are more yourself with a girl when you're alone with her but sometimes feel you have to act in obnoxious ways with the same girl when you are in front of your homies. Some admitted that was how they behaved. Larry also needed to work at being less of a follower and sorting out what is right from giving in to the allure of privilege.

Drew said, "There's some kind of prejudice in everybody."

"That's true," I said, "and you may find this hard to believe right now but when you're in the zone you can actually get beyond the racist shit."

Pat was still feeling intensely about the issue and brought us down to earth. He challenged Larry: "Would you openly bring me to your house in Bensonhurst and take me to see all your friends and introduce me to your mom and do all that? Would you feel comfortable comin' back to my 'hood doin' the same thing around my black friends?"

Yes, Larry said, he felt he could. Pat described how he and a graduating senior, another Italian American, were able to do that together. I told him that he and his teammate were fortunate and that it would be great if we could all have that kind of relationship.

I framed the group interaction and Pat's experience as one in which people are in the zone; a higher level of awareness in which one is open to the present and not drawn away by fear to a preconceived thought or an imagined scenario. I pointed out that this is the same process we practice during meditation in attending to one's own mind. The students were able to hear each other, and Pat alluded to what many of the students wanted but did not have the words for, a way of being with oneself and others that acknowledged (that is, did not deny) but transcended socially determined categories and identities. Because we were familiar with the experience of the zone through meditation and had discussed how it manifests itself in everyday life the students could envision the connection. They could experience being with a teammate in this capacity as being in the zone, beyond self and other, from a higher vantage point. For some black students this was a way of expressing one's highest self that required neither an alienated, resistant pose to maintain their black identity nor the necessity of conforming and assimilating to another, dominant culture. In developmental terms for all students it was neither egocentric nor conventional; rather, it reflected a higher level of being that respected difference from a universal basis that transcended social categories such as race. Framing this level of awareness as the zone gave it a name, and gave the internal experience of being in the zone a face as well.

The discussion then touched on different ethnic groups. One or two of the young men made some statements about Jews, that they had much more power than most groups; one even thought that George W. Bush was a Jew. I took some time to address these specific misconceptions. I then emphasized that there are different kinds of people within each group, black, Latino, Jewish, Italian; some are prejudiced, some are mensches. I defined the Yiddish word to mean a highly decent, caring person with good values who respects all people. We were nearing the end of the session.

"Let's get in the *zone* real quick," Pat said.

Dissing and the Courage of Compassion

The young men's ability to get along with each other was an ongoing issue beyond being fellow football players on the same team. Just a little over a month after the 9-11 attacks on the World Trade Center, Ted, an Arab-American, confronted his teammates. He told them he didn't feel good about their teasing him and calling him a terrorist. After the United States attacked the Taliban government in Afghanistan, he said that some of the guys told him, "We bombed your uncle." He could put up with some teasing, he felt, but they had crossed a line and he was bothered by it.

Some of the guys were uncomfortable hearing him and laughed as he spoke, and questioned him on this. They said he was being too serious and emotional. I supported Ted and challenged them about their discomfort and asked them whether they were able to hear him in a respectful way. I said that we men are often uncomfortable with sharing feelings—would girls have laughed? They admitted, probably not. One said that Ted could take the teasing in a different, less sensitive way. I said maybe that's true, but you also need to learn to hear what he is saying and be more respectful and sensitive to what he is feeling. I suggested that it was hard for them to sit with and listen to vulnerable feelings when they come up, either in your own mind or from someone else, but that it was a new kind of courage that they could practice.

We were up against Kindlon and Thompson's (2000) notion of the Culture of Cruelty, the norm that justifies masculinity as including being cruel to women and other males, straight or gay, who disclose vulnerability, which can mean almost any feeling except anger. The anxiety among these young men at hearing another guy share a feeling of hurt was palpable.

At this time we could only scratch the surface of more complex and relevant concerns about ethnic discrimination, stereotyping, and how the anxiety we all felt after the terrorist attack contributed to these behaviors. In general, I noticed a tendency for dissing to increase when they seemed more stressed and anxious. I tried to get them to think about this link and recognize when they were feeling this way both in the group and during meditation.

When it came to the Culture of Cruelty these young men had much to think about. Outside of the group sessions I learned that some of the varsity players picked on the younger, junior varsity (JV) guys. The older players administer wedgies to the JV kids in the locker room; the JV kids also get pushed around on the subway platform when they go home after practice. The JV players saw this to some extent as an inevitable ritual that started in football camp, which even the coaches tolerate up to a point, but the JV guys felt that the varsity players took it too far.

In the group I brought up this issue of the rituals of coming down hard on the JV players. A number of the older players gave the answers I expected: it's harmless, they endured it themselves when they were JV players and now felt entitled to pass it on, and it's a way to build toughness on the field. By way of further justification they also supplied colorful examples of professional football teams reputed for performing nasty rituals and pranks among their players. They described one other local high school team they knew that does even nastier stuff.

I made the case that just because others do it doesn't make this sort of behavior right; it was unnecessary, there's no scientific evidence it leads to greater toughness, and the adults should not allow it to go on. I tried not to lecture but asked them to think about whether it's cruel, whether it really does make you tougher, and the fact that it gets the younger players upset. One JV student confirmed that the behavior goes on and spoke out against it. He added that this year, in fact, some JV guys didn't go along with it and complained to their parents who spoke to a school authority. They said that the coaches did tell the players not to do it, which I was relieved to hear, although I did not know to what extent the coaches were able to address the problem. A varsity starter, Stephen, spoke up and said that he didn't like it when he was on the JV and the varsity guys did it to him; his statement carried a lot of weight. I reminded the players of how Ted had told them he felt hurt when some of the teasing about him being an Arab-American went too far and how they were uncomfortable hearing it.

Ricardo wanted to know why I was bringing all this up. I described that this is all about being in the zone, that meditating to be in the zone is not just about doing things better but wanting to have a higher consciousness and sense of purpose. I suggested that they think about creating positive team rituals that are meaningful and not harmful. Maybe they could make history themselves and establish new traditions that could get passed down to the next generation of Borough High football players. They could take a leadership role with the JV guys, and even serve as mentors. They seemed to think about this.

I also learned from the guys that the Borough High football team was known around the league for trash-talking and being aggressive. Drew said it was a mixed reputation, that some of it was admirable in that they were also tough on the field, especially the defense, but that in other ways they were disliked. I suggested they think about changing their reputation and behavior off the field while still being solid players on the field. Stephen said during every game the opposing team players dissed him and sometimes he ignored it but other times gave in and would answer back one for one. Here I was seeing a young man beginning to move out of preconventional moral reasoning—if you attack me I will retaliate and attack you—and searching for a higher purpose and means to respond. I asked the group, Could courage also mean the courage to not respond at the same level of trash talk, and then answer back by playing better?

At heart was their sense of fragility and insecurity about feeling disrespected. They needed the courage to sit with these feelings and to see the connection between what they were experiencing and their behavior. At some point they could let go of feeling threatened by another and detach from the notion that their sense of self would dissolve at the hand of someone else. For now it was a struggle.

Although some of the guys made an art of disrespecting others, underneath they often did not have a solid sense of respect for themselves. During one spring session we learned that Larry got into trouble and was suspended from the team for a few days. A younger JV player had made a challenging, disrespectful remark. Instead of letting it go or walking away, Larry pushed the kid first.

Pat was exasperated. "You can't do that, Larry!" His reasoning was pragmatic—not because it was morally wrong but that Larry's actions could have gotten the team in trouble again with the deans: two football players fighting would have led to more disciplinary actions and meetings. Larry said he did it because he felt disrespected.

"This sounds like an ego thing," Randall said. I agreed.

"I do regret it," Larry said. He also was able to admit that he did not have the courage to walk away, and I praised him for at least acknowledging that. I encouraged him to look at what he was feeling at the time and come up with a response that could preserve his dignity and self-worth and also not get him in trouble. "For example," I said, "Larry has a right to say to this kid that he doesn't like being disrespected."

"And in front of people," someone added.

"There'll always be time for these little kids to pay," Pat said. He again was offering the pragmatic reason for refraining from hitting the other student at that time, in this case falling into the payback mentality, retaliation to even the score. I argued with Pat and another student on that one and encouraged them to take a higher stance than the other person. "If someone's at a lower level than you, you don't go down to their level. With little brothers, for example, when they do something to you, you don't feel they have to pay, because they're not as mature as you."

The courage to face one's own mind, to be able to sit with feelings of fear and sadness, I told them, is even a higher kind of courage than facing an opponent on the football field. Drew said he understood this idea and was trying to help his younger brother deal with his feelings of frustration and anger by suggesting that he meditate as well. Although some meditative traditions refer to the word "warrior," I avoided it because I wanted to minimize any ambiguity of the term that would inadvertently convey unnecessary aggression or violence. Instead, I told them a story that illustrated a certain kind of mental courage. The tale (it can be found in Gordhamer, 2001) is about citizens from a village who, upon hearing that a cruel, murderous warrior was heading their way, fled to the hills. The only one who insisted on staying was an old priest who sat in the temple. When the warrior learned of him he rushed into the temple and stood over the frail old man. "Do you know who I am?" He shouted. "I could cut off your head without batting an eye!" The priest stood his ground, calmly looked up at the warrior, and said, "And do you know who I am? I could sit here and have you cut off my head without batting an eye." The priest's kind of courage and fearlessness was something the warrior had never before encountered. It stopped him in his tracks; and the story goes that the warrior put down his sword and asked the old man to become his teacher.

Throughout the groups I encouraged the players to be mindful of what they were feeling, using the breath to center themselves. I also offered them a tool that could help them identify when the dissing was too much, the permission to tell the teammate, "I didn't like that; that crossed the line." This was in part the assertive skill of the I-message, stating what one feels instead of attacking back. During the following spring there were a number of opportunities for the young men to risk their vulnerability and confront their teammates about when they felt hurt by their teasing. I also became more aware of the social constraints on this kind of positive behavior that arise from some harsh aspects of the school culture and the football subculture themselves. I realized that they needed to be mindful of how the behavior of those in authority affected them and to learn to apply skills to cope with those who wielded social power over them.

In the spring we continued to play out the young men's feelings in the here and now. In one group guys kept getting on Franklin, a newcomer to the school and team, about his dislocated middle finger. Franklin said that the teasing did not bother him. DeVon, however, came to his defense. He said that Franklin is a sensitive guy and tries to take it like a man and deny what he feels. I praised DeVon and told him and Franklin that last fall, before they joined the group, we had talked about the pressure on guys to suck it up and that men can and should be able to express their feelings in a good way.

A little more than a month later, Franklin stood up for himself and told the group he was bothered by the teasing. I walked up and stood behind him and encouraged the others to acknowledge and say what it was he was experiencing. I moved around the room and did the same for a number of them. "Is Pat (or whoever) in the zone right now?" I would ask when someone was getting worked up. No, they said. What is he feeling? "Angry, frustrated…" "What is Manuel feeling about not getting the position he wanted?" "Disappointed."

Manuel and Pat had gotten into a heated argument about competing for a position. To his credit Manuel had added that he was willing to have the best solution for the good of the team, and I spoke with him later to see how he felt. In all, they needed to keep cultivating a sense of empathy for themselves (see Garbarino, 2000, pp. 233–234).

Had I worked with these young men in a different format, I also would have arranged for them to practice empathy and compassion in a more formal way, by engaging in a service project. One afternoon after school I came across five or six of the black players on the el station stairs, draped over the banisters, making passage difficult for people to descend to the street. They told me they would say hello to some, especially young women. To those who were lighting up a cigarette they would say, "You're too pretty to smoke." I watched as Pat offered to help a woman, possibly Chinese, with her stroller down the stairs. She declined his offer. "She looked afraid of me," he said. I concurred with his impression. In the next session I told the guys that I knew they were not troublemakers but many people do not know that and unfortunately find them to look intimidating. We spoke a bit about how young black males are often unfairly seen on the street as bad dudes and how they handle that. I thought of the idea of them improving their image in the community. If they were going to hang out at the el station and tell people not to smoke, maybe they could pass out fliers, for example, about smoking or nutrition, or subway riders' rights, with their school and team name stamped on it. I showed them some pamphlets I had brought from the student consumer rights club office at Brooklyn College. They declined. Pat said, "This is not our neck of the woods." Neither did they feel like taking the project up in their own neighborhoods, and I let it go.

Over time the group developed the new norm of dropping the mask of stoic cool to risk confronting one's teammates about a hurt feeling. This change even affected Phillip, one of the more detached students. Phillip often appeared oblivious to what his teammates said about him. At times he would come up for snacks and then leave; he made dismissive remarks about the group and once called me a "geezer" (my first time—a narcissistic injury). When I would run into him he sometimes would pretend to be mad or critical of me for something and I'd respond by laughing and agreeing with him to show I knew he was play fighting. Sometimes he contributed to the session and would stay for the meditation. Despite his teammates' disregard for him as "not serious" and as someone who brushed off anything they said about him, I let him attend, as I sensed he wanted to be connected to a certain extent and that his aloofness was a form of self-protection. One afternoon in the spring when the guys were getting on him, Phillip walked out. I said that even Phillip has feelings and that he seemed bothered by their comments. They insisted that he didn't care and had only come up for the snacks in the first place. The next session he did confront them, albeit not in the best form: he put it back on them, telling them he thought they were "rude" and "immature." Phillip did come back sporadically over the following weeks and through the fall season.

During the same session that Franklin was getting teased, James was taking some hits about his glasses. He, too, would not answer them back. I asked the group if they thought he was okay with their comments—I doubt it, I said—and reminded them of our ground rule that we respect everyone. On another front, teasing between Pat and George was escalating. Despite my efforts to get them to stop, Pat got in some jokes against George's mother's name, and George became sullen. These were two guys who needed to realize the extent to which they felt competitive with each other and figure out ways to get along if they were going to remain teammates.

The next week I learned that the team was going through a critical period. The players told me that the coaches had suspended a number of them for misconduct such as talking back and being disrespectful with them and with teachers who requested them to remove their hats. They thought it was unfair and were upset about it. However, I also spoke later with the head coach, who told me he was frustrated with some of them; for instance, he asked one student to begin studying and had to ask him five times.

There seemed to be a disconnect between the students and the school and team authorities, which fueled the players' acting out. We had begun some role playing of situations such as dealing with various authority figures, teachers, coaches, cops, to try to help them avoid getting in trouble.

The reality of the suspensions and the exposed feelings of guilt and anger about what occurred contributed to a volatile session. It started out well: Pat apologized to Franklin for teasing him about his finger, and even apologized to George. Pat talked about teasing each guy about their mother's name and said it was always mutual, but I said even among friends it can get out of hand, and you had to figure out and be sensitive to it if and when it crosses the line to hurting.

Pat was on a roll. He criticized William about not doing well in school even though he gets tutoring. I pointed out that William looked uncomfortable about this and that Pat could tell him in a helpful way rather than make it worse. Pat said last year he told Calvin, a younger JV player who was enthusiastic about meditation, to remove his hat, in the manner of a big brother enforcing a rule for the younger one's own good, and that Calvin had reacted negatively. But they worked it out later, Pat said, and now they were fine. In terms of coaches, teachers, and authorities, we got into talking about not responding back at the same low level someone treats you, but to take a higher position and not lose control and get into trouble. We talked about when cops stop you and how you have to consciously take a one-down position in order to minimize any problems. Calvin and another JV player mentioned again that the seniors really did harsh things to them like tying them up, which I said sounded terrible. We talked further about being supportive of each other and of the JV team and beginning a new tradition.

Suddenly, George's pent-up anger at Pat got the best of him. He jumped up and enacted an animated caricature of Pat's mother, who is from another culture. Pat said, "That crossed the line," and he walked out at the same time as a few others who had to leave, before I could address what happened. I later went down to the locker room and spoke with Pat, who was still upset.

The next session I had George and Pat speak with each other. The group, however, was skeptical about Pat; they didn't believe that he was hurt because he dishes it out so easily himself. I showed Pat how he paints himself into a corner; the guys don't take him seriously when he says things crossed the line, but I did tell the group that this time he really was hurt and upset.

Pat and James talked about their misunderstandings and dissing. James at last spoke up for himself. He said he didn't like being teased about certain things. I told them they should feel proud of themselves and need to keep hearing each other and respect each other if they want to work together as a team. I described to the group how there are many situations in which the stronger takes it out on the weaker down the line, and that the way to stop this destructive pattern is to be mindful of what is going on. The more one is aware of this chain reaction, the freer your mind is not to respond in a way that enslaves you. Where possible, you can take action to challenge an unjust power relationship and seek greater collaboration and equality. Pat, who was worked up at first, calmed down.

The authoritarian hierarchy from the school contributed to a pattern of which no one was mindful: the teachers and coaches demand obedience and a show of respect based on arbitrary power; the students themselves feel disrespected and, not knowing what they feel or how to deal with that, talk back to the authorities, which gets them in trouble. They then take it out on each other, which gets them more upset. The group format, a new way of relating to themselves and each other, had provided a space for the young men to express themselves and to peer into some of their feelings of hurt and sadness; I was struggling to help them find a proper way to do so that would also keep them safe. We ended the group with a meditation, still trying to be good to ourselves and mindful of what occurs. After the room emptied out, I decided I could use an extra peanut butter and jelly sandwich myself.

By the end of the spring, six guys—Ted, Pat, Franklin, James, Larry, and Phillip—in one way or another had confronted the group and told them that their dissing had crossed the line. In one of our last sessions before the summer the guys showed some promise that they could work well together. About eighteen of them piled into the classroom and on their own divided the room into the offense and the defense (some played both and sat near the middle or identified themselves with one or the other). For a good hour they got into a loud, spirited sparring match, teasing and egging the other side on about who was better and who was messing up more. At first I was reluctant to let it go on, and asked them a few times if they were okay and if this was what they wanted to do. "Yeah, Mr. Forbes." I then took the hint and became like a ref in the ring, pacing in the middle of the floor, keeping them in their seats, getting them to lower their voices somewhat, trying to limit the interruptions so they could listen to each other. They were critical and competitive but playful at the same time and at no point crossed a hurtful line. They described specific plays and challenged each other. They were clearly enjoying it, giving feedback to each other, shifting between serious discussion and loud goofing around and overall were successful at staying on task and managing the flow of exchange. The space for the most part was safe and structured and I intervened in minimal ways. I learned later from the head coach that the staff had encouraged competition between the offense and defense as a way to improve their play; what I saw was an expression of this. It was a thin line, but they stayed on the better side.

For the farewell spring meeting, before the summer and in anticipation of the fall season, I felt the guys could use a counterbalance to the previous week's dis fest. We had pizza, of course. As part of the ending ritual for the group I produced certificates for each participant who had been a regular member. On the certificate were lines for their teammates to write something positive about how the member plays football. The guys were happy to pass them around and fill them in and sign them. Even the teammate with whom some did not get along came upstairs. I invited him in, where he mingled and signed everyone's certificate. Pat said he "felt a lot of love in the room."

At the end of the spring I was amused to see the way some of the group members, led by Pat, addressed someone who was becoming upset and about to take it out on a teammate. To get someone to calm down, they would get up in his face and tell him, "Breathe!" The getting up in one's face part, especially from an adult authority, as Garbarino (2000, p. 232) mentioned, is not what a boy with a traumatic psychological history needs. In this case, the young men accepted it from their teammates, as it took on a different meaning, although the point that I kept emphasizing was, be peaceful about being peaceful.

Finally, lest there be any doubt that counseling high school male football players touches on many significant emotional issues, on the last day I encountered Juan, alone in the classroom, very upset. He had just quit the team, he told me, because according to him the coaches were only going to let him play second string. He told me how his brother and father had played football and that he would rather quit than not start because he would be too ashamed. I sat with him while he dealt with his disappointment and hurt. After a while I encouraged him to consider staying on the team because he might still have a chance to play if someone no longer played well or got injured. He said he would think about it. It turned out he later did change his mind and had wanted to return to the team but had missed summer camp and was ineligible to rejoin. Juan took the initiative to find a weekend football league and managed to keep up with his playing. He regularly attended our group sessions in the fall, kept up his meditation practice, and told us he was grateful for the support we provided him

The Game Is Why You're Here: The Big Season

The pace picked up once the season neared and then stayed that way throughout the fall. Some of the ongoing themes—getting along, coaches, racism, the thrill of victory, the agony of defeat—were recapitulated during the 2002 football season, as well as unforeseen events. Throughout the season I encouraged the players to be mindful of how they played, how they related to their own feelings about winning, losing, and feelings like disappointment and frustration, how they related to each other, and how they were living on a day-to-day basis. We continued our practice of meeting the Monday after the game, talking about whatever was important in group, and meditating.

At the end of August I greeted the team bus after the team's arrival from summer camp. In the school lot some of the players privately told me different things about how everyone, especially first-timers, had to adjust to each other. There was a racial incident with a new junior varsity player and the coaches had to intervene. Some new guys were struggling with communicating with the veterans. The new coach was still bugging them by being so strict. Later I spoke by phone with the head coach about summer camp. He told me he was disappointed there were no clear leaders emerging and that guys were still carping at each other.

At the beginning of September I ran into Stephen and James on the subway train on the way to school. They confirmed what the coach had told me. They, too, said they were concerned that there was still too much dissing and lack of communication on the team. They also said that some had expressed continued frustration with some of the coaches' decisions and how they handled them and felt that these affected the players, who already have their own stress.

That same week I encountered Phillip at another subway station. After we kidded each other he said he was upset because the coaches had overridden the team's voting him as co-captain and said it was because he was not doing well enough in school. I said I was sorry and that it must be very disappointing and frustrating. Phillip told me some of the same things Stephen and James did about the state of the team and their low morale. He said that "guys play for the coach," that coaches are important and how they and players relate to each other affects how hard the team members are willing to play. I told him I would invite a discussion of these issues in the weekly sessions and welcomed his input. He said he would come to the group and he did so.

Game 1 (nonleague)

The first game was away in Bay Ridge, a relatively wealthy part of Brooklyn. It was against a well-funded private school that has excellent athletic facilities and equipment and recruits students for football nationwide. In one group session the previous year we had been talking about how better-off schools tended to provide students with better education. Ricardo said that someone once pointed out this school to him and told him, "That's where society's leaders come from." That got him mad and upset about his own education and chances for success.

The team played hard but fell behind in the second quarter and some players were clearly discouraged at the half. From the sidelines I overheard Stephen tell them the game was not over. For the second half they came out with more resolution but still lost decisively.

The Monday after the game the head coach gave me ten minutes to address the whole team down in the locker room as a way to jump-start the weekly sessions. I wanted them to reflect on the game experience and began by asking what they were proud of and what they felt was good about the game. They said they didn't give up, were determined to come back the second half, and they weren't intimidated. I praised them on these accounts. Some then began to talk about their mental mistakes. I used this as a chance to talk about what happens when you're not in the moment and are worrying about the next play or still thinking about the last one. One player then described that he was worried about whether he would catch the ball; another said he was worried about how to tackle and lost his focus; a senior who rejoined the group during the season, Vince, said he noticed how they failed to line up right. An assistant coach who showed the most interest and knowledge about the zone pointed out how he had taken Vince aside during the game after he had appeared distracted by something and refocused him. He helped my pitch for meditation by describing how professional stars like NFL quarterback Curt Warner and Michael Jordan will often say in a postgame interview they were just in a zone, doing everything right.

Pat said it was better when players made positive statements during the game the way Stephen and Ricardo did, and he was bothered by some players who said critical things. A player stood up and faced Pat and said he thought he was speaking about him and that he would never say anything to hurt the team. The assistant coach cut them off and said he wanted to keep things general and not personal here. I managed to praise both of them for being open to hearing and speaking with each other and encouraged them to continue doing that, as how they all communicate affects how well they can play together.

The same student asked me to clarify what I meant when I said that in meditation one isn't hard on one's self and instead lets thoughts go. I sensed he was upholding the idea that you *should* be hard on yourself, certainly in terms of holding yourself to tough standards; what also ran through my mind was that he got this notion from someone who was hard on him as well. I tried to explain the distinction between going easy on your mind and still upholding the commitment to mastery; if you're too hard on yourself you get the opposite effect, but if you set your goal and then let your mind alone you are more likely to attain what you want. You see a mistake, you notice it, return to your breathing, let it go, and move on to the next moment.

One afternoon during the week I managed to speak with Stephen through the fence separating the football field from the street. Stephen was struggling with the new assistant coach. He felt frustrated because he felt the coach misinterpreted any question he had as being disrespectful and insubordinate. I told him to try not to take the coach's behavior personally. I suggested that he find a way to talk with the coach and possibly the head coach if necessary and to frame his statements not as complaints but rather in terms of wanting to have better communication.

The day before the opening league game at the new home field I met with about fifteen players. I stressed the importance of communication, using I-messages, and the need to work conflicts out. I asked them what the extra stresses and distractions were going to be tomorrow and listed them on the board. Larry said the media would be there because it was the school's first home game. Some said having girls watch them was a pressure; also, the school had bought them new equipment, and that everyone expected them to win. I told them to expect that stuff will come up around these things tomorrow, notice them, then notice how your mind reacts to them, and keep breathing. We meditated and did a visualization exercise on executing a play they wanted to perform.

Game 2 (opening home game)

On a clear September day a hopeful crowd arrived to christen the new field next to the school, and the principal addressed the fans. The opponents were a local Brooklyn team that brought their own small crowd of supporters. The Borough High defense played well and held them without a score, only a safety. Vince had an interception, and Stephen threw him a perfect touchdown pass. I noticed that Ricardo got upset on the sidelines after a fumble and some of them struggled to remain patient. Nevertheless, it was a solid victory.

In the group session that week some guys expressed concern about the offensive line and said they were getting mixed messages from the staff. I said they needed to clear that up immediately. They had difficulty focusing on the next opponent, last year's league champion. I said that they had to keep supporting each other and not criticize each other after a mistake and to bring themselves back to the present. After we meditated the guys returned to the locker room and the practice field. I took Pat aside and asked him what he thought was going on. He said a lot of the players did not know how to speak with the coaches in a way that enabled them to be heard and instead they alienated them.

Game 3 (away)

The team lost to the defending champions, who outplayed them. There were numerous mental errors, including penalties, and fumbles.

On Monday the players were very low after their loss. Pat said he was "clinically depressed." I had to laugh at his use of the phrase and asked him where he had heard that one, but I took his and everyone's feelings seriously—he was being dramatic, as I suspected. Ricardo reported that he had always had a good relationship with the tough assistant coach and that he thought that lately the coach had been getting along better with Phillip and Stephen, which I was happy to hear.

DeVon said he was in the zone the whole game. I had him tell the group what he meant. He said he wasn't thinking of anything, he just played great and felt good and was able to anticipate and respond well to what happened. DeVon also said the way to help your teammates is to tell them you have faith in them. The other good news was that the offensive line played better than the previous week and there were fewer communication mix-ups with the staff. We did a deep meditation. At the end of each meditation session the guys no longer jumped up and left as they did a year ago; they moved deliberately and more carefully.

Game 4 (away)

The game was in foreign territory, Staten Island, against one of the best teams in the league. The opponents racked up thirty-four points and held the Borough High team scoreless. Racial differences came up in the context of a quarterback controversy. The coaches replaced Stephen for the entire game with the student whom some had thought was racist. I did hear later that they had become relatively more comfortable with him; they could joke around and call him a cracker, he could say "niggaz," as they felt that he, too, was just fooling around. When he was inserted as quarterback, however, some linemen were upset with the coaches' decision. One said that he was not motivated to protect the new quarterback from getting sacked like they all were with Stephen and that the quarterback and linemen were out of sync.

There were a number of issues that came together here: the anger at the coaches' decision with which the players did not agree, their frustration at not having a say about it, the difficulty in adjusting to a new offensive leader after the season had already begun, the difference in play between the two quarterbacks, and the racial tension that was already there.

It was difficult to sort out to what extent each factor contributed to the problem. The switch roiled the team at a time when they were on a losing streak. In our session, I encouraged them to see this as an opportunity to examine every single conflict and problem that came up with them as a team, to let nothing go by that could get in the way of their playing well together, and to put it all out in the open at their weekly team meeting with the coaches. I also spoke with them about the need to examine their motivation and to play at one's best for the highest reason one can find, not just because you like or dislike your teammates. During the week I followed this up with an e-mail that said the same things. Pat said he printed it up and showed it to other guys on the team.

Game 5 (home)

The team lost to another highly ranked Brooklyn school. Because of a holiday schedule we had a small group turnout on an off-day. William, a lineman, said the team didn't follow the flow of play and was too rigid. He felt they gave their all and still lost and said that it made him cry. I supported his feeling that way and said that losing is part of life; sometimes you do your best and still lose, and that you still have your integrity by having given your all. Vince said the team did speak with the coaches and that it helped; the players expressed their feelings and the coaches considered what they had to say.

Game 6 (away)

In a game I was unable to attend the team earned their second victory of the season against another Brooklyn team. Stephen returned as quarterback. What was most significant, however, occurred earlier that week. On Tuesday, one of their teammates and best players from last year, a "super senior" who still attended the school but who was ineligible to play again, was murdered. According to the *New York Post* two men on a motorcycle pulled up next to him and shot him dead on a street in the Flatbush section in the early evening. The paper said the police were looking into whether the killing was in retaliation for another slaying earlier that week, part of a larger drug turf war that sparked three other shootings since the summer. The guys did not believe their teammate, who was known as MC, had been into drug dealing.

For these young men this tragic experience was part of growing up in a big city, something that no child should have to undergo; yet many do. The entire team was devastated. They decided to dedicate the rest of the season to his spirit and taped his number on their helmets.

In the session we set the meditation aside and talked about what happened for a long while. The guys needed the space to talk. One said that he couldn't get over how he had just seen their friend the very same day, and that he was alive one minute, and gone the next. They said they kept thinking about how at the very time their football practice had ended that day MC was shot. Stephen spoke about how he couldn't sleep and felt MC somehow was there at night in his own room ever since he had MC over to his house. Stephen had to go over to his relative's house in order to fall asleep. Drew said that even though he had lost other friends he just kept thinking about it and the image of MC being shot kept appearing over and over in his mind. They and others said they couldn't be alone after school or at night. Ricardo said he felt he had to call old girlfriends whom he was no longer interested in but would stay with them and talk with them; he recognized it was not a healthy thing to do but felt he needed to right now.

I told them their feelings and reactions were normal, to feel them, to not try to shut them down. I said it sounded like many of them were traumatized. Stephen asked me to repeat the word and wrote it down when I explained it.

The guys told me that football was MC's life and that it was all he had. They said that during this last game they all had played with more focus. When they were tired they thought about him and it served to revive them.

For these young men the death of their friend and teammate transformed him into a kind of living embodiment of what the zone is, a more concrete, personal expression of it. Through his death the young man became spirit, love, and caring. The zone took on another form for them, somewhat like Jesus, the person, rather than the rare ability to see everything as Jesus' body and spirit.

A few more guys came up to the room after suiting up and we did a meditation session. I said that the young man's love of the game and their love for him was his spirit. That spirit would always be here. On the in-breath, breathe in the love. On the out-breath, breathe out the pain, sadness, and poison. In-breath, love; out-breath, pain and sadness. We continued that way. A few of them sobbed quietly to themselves.

Afterward they had to go down to the field to practice. I went down with them and spoke with the head coach and told him I thought they needed more time to grieve and process what had happened. He was sympathetic but said that there just wasn't any more time this week in which I could meet with the team.

That night I e-mailed them and said that MC's death was sad and also very wrong and unjust, and that his life and death were as important as those of any person in the country. I restated what we had talked about in the group, normalizing the trauma and the need to feel both the love and the pain and to be mindful of what was going on with themselves and of any acting out.

Game 7 (home)

The team was clicking on both offense and defense and gained a clear victory over another Brooklyn school. After a stretch of three losses in a row they now had as many league wins as losses. There were few penalties, a good sign of being mindful. They were down at the half but were unfazed and came back. I saw Pat on the sidelines stretching and told him to breathe. He later e-mailed me: "mr. forbes thanx for coming to the game when I got angry at myself and u told me to breathe it really calmed me down and let me forget about what happened and focus on the present."

In the group we spent some time on a younger player, Bret, who had begun attending in the late spring. He spoke openly, saying that he thought the coaches were hard on him and that he felt bad about it. Pat and Vince, seniors, advised him on how to play more conscientiously during practice in order to make fewer mistakes. Bret shared that he was disappointed that his mom, who lived in the South, came up on the weekend to see the game and that it was the only one of the season in which he didn't get to play. We agreed that this was disappointing. I pointed out that Bret was sensitive and tended to take things to heart more than others, a positive quality, but sometimes one that gets in our way, especially when we take things too personally, and that he needed to be aware of that. After the session I spoke with him individually and suggested he speak with the coaches and find out what he needed to do in order to get back to playing. Also, regardless of what the coaches did, he needed to stay focused on his own goals and be aware of his feelings.

Drew got into trouble with an assistant coach by challenging him, which resulted in his being suspended from the team. Again, although it sounded like the coach was playing it tough and contributed to escalating the incident, we talked about how it was up to Drew to decide how to respond in a way that didn't get him into trouble. I said I knew Drew was struggling with feelings about himself and about sadness and hoped he could keep learning to take responsibility for his part in what happened instead of just blaming others.

The meditation went well. I pointed out to the group that a new member, Luis, might find the meditation strange and look around and get distracted, which is what happened. In contrast, the more experienced guys were doing much better than last year.

I was able to speak one-on-one with Stephen and then Ricardo on the street. Both said they were doing better in dealing with MC's death. Stephen was managing to sleep better and Ricardo realized that calling old girlfriends was not helping and stopped doing it. I encouraged him to remain mindful of this and said I hoped he could find and be with a girl he really likes and respects.

Game 8 (away)

On a cold and damp day in southeast Queens the team defeated a weaker opponent by a decisive score. They now had a four and three winning record in league play. There were lots of penalties, although Pat claimed they were mostly made by guys who didn't come up to do meditation.

During the session the guys were rowdy and excited. If they won the following week, they were in the playoffs. They reported that things were going well: everyone was now getting along, communicating, not saying negative things in the huddle, getting back to focusing after a penalty or loss of yards, and playing better at fundamentals—tackling, blocking. I said it sounded great and was happy for them.

The focus again was on Bret. They confronted him on how he had bragged at the beginning of the season that he was going to play so well but then did not follow through. I told Bret the guys were saying he needed to talk less and do more, but I also said it sounded like Bret was giving his best effort and needed some support. I again suggested he be aware of how he undermines himself and to let his playing do the talking.

Game 9 (home)

The team defeated another local school with solid efforts on both offense and defense. The first half they had a slim lead, with many turnovers, and appeared anxious. The second half they were visibly more relaxed yet focused and played well. They were going to the playoffs.

On Monday the team rankings came out on the league Web site. Borough High was tenth seeded out of forty-one in the league, with the top sixteen being in the playoffs. Their three league losses were at the hands of three teams that *Newsday* rated as second, third, and fifth best in the city, which included the Catholic and private high schools. Their preseason loss was against the number-one-rated team in the city. Their first-round opponent was ranked seventh. Borough High was the underdog.

In the group we talked about playing, communicating, and breathing. The guys were relaxed and confident about the upcoming playoff game. Before the meditation I said playing in the zone is something like what happens to the main character, Neo, in the movie *The Matrix* (1999). By coming to believe he is the One, Neo learns that the power of the Matrix is illusory; the Matrix depends on people believing it has more power than it does. DeVon said, but our opponents are real; they're not illusions created by computers. Yes, I said, but their power is not necessarily real either; you don't have to give them any extra power. Once you show you're not afraid and believe that you're the One, they may dissolve. DeVon was right; although there is some truth to the analogy, I was stretching it a bit here trying to inspire them and was getting carried away by playoff fever myself.

In the locker room the head coach went over tapes of their opponent. He warned the team that their turnovers were a serious problem and they had to work on them the whole week.

In an e-mail to the guys I wrote some tips I had researched on the physical aspects of turnovers. I then emphasized the mental side, breathing, helping to remind them in the huddle to be aware of holding and other penalties. I repeated the story of the Matrix and said they could be the One, it's up to them to believe it. I reported to them what the *New York Post* had said, that their opponents were motivated by their seniors not wanting to go out in a first-round upset. They, on the other hand, had a higher motivation to win, based on the spirit of their fallen friend and/or their highest and deepest selves.

Playoff Game, First Round (away)

The game was played in the Bronx. Borough High had opening jitters. During the first few minutes the team fumbled and the opponents scored a touchdown. But the team came back. They stopped the other team's run, caused them to lose the ball, and minimized the penalties. There was tremendous concentration by pass receivers George and Vince. George dropped one pass; on the next down they ran the same pattern and he caught Stephen's pass for a touchdown. In another crucial play Vince juggled one pass, kept his focus, then waited for the ball to come down and caught it. A few weeks before on a similar play, Vince had failed to catch the ball. Pat played an excellent game on both sides of the line, running and tackling. In the stands I overheard one of the cheerleaders point to a seagull that flew overhead. "There's MC," she said, referring to the teammate who was killed.

In the closing minutes the opposing team was threatening to score. Nevertheless, Borough High held them off and won the game by two points. They looked like a team that was in the zone: they had stayed within themselves, breathed, and trusted that over time, feelings like nervousness and disappointment can and do change. They had won five straight games, outscoring the opposition 128–35.

A Hollywood movie might have ended the story line there. In order to advance to the finals, though, the team had to face last year's champions again on their home turf.

In the group the guys were unfocused and agitated. A few were getting on each other. We were all out of the zone; I kept talking about the game and did not pay enough attention to the fact that everyone was nervous and out of sorts. Our meditation began late and an assistant coach came up and got the rest of the guys. He was also nervous and upset that some of them hadn't yet suited up. I apologized to him for keeping the guys so late. In the classroom he taped up Manuel, a reliable group member who had attended the sessions from the beginning. I told Manuel, don't be nervous, that's the coach's job.

I later e-mailed them and apologized for my own lack of mindfulness. I encouraged them to keep noticing when they were tense with each other and to catch themselves.

Playoff Game, Second Round (away)

On a cold and rainy afternoon Borough High was shut out by the defending champs. They were again outplayed by a superior team. The final four teams in the playoffs included the three to whom they had lost during the league season. I e-mailed them that night, saying that although they were sad and disappointed, they had nothing to be ashamed of and should be proud of their season and their efforts.

The following Monday I came by to run the group but most of the players were not in school. Instead, I ran into a bunch of them silently standing around looking dejected in front of the pizza parlor. As usual, I hung out with them for just a few moments; it was their turf, and being seen talking to any adult for too long spoils the scene and looks uncool. I asked how they were feeling. "Bad." I nodded and told them I'd see them at their team meeting the next day.

The head coach addressed them at their meeting down in the locker room. He told them he was proud of their hard work. Although I did not get to speak to them as a group, I spoke with a few individually. I told them to feel what they feel and arranged for a final meeting so they could fill out the questionnaires. The season was officially over. Soon enough they would learn there is life after football; at that moment, however, I was not going to be the one to try to convince them of that.

Chapter Five

Boyz 2 Buddhas? Findings

...I jumped up
Feeling my highs, and my lows
In my soul, and my goals

—Talib Kweli (2002), "Get By," from *Quality*

Formal Battery, Fall 2001

In the fall of 2001 I managed to get sixteen Borough High football players to take a battery of questionnaires, then retake them after ten weekly sessions of discussion and meditation. This was a pilot project, subject to the vagaries of adolescent mood swings and attention spans. As a consequence I had a small sample—despite my urging and promise of payment to the subjects upon completion of both the pre-tests and post-tests, a number did not finish them. Not all students attended all the group sessions. There was no control group, and a number of the tests with which I was experimenting showed no clear patterns of stability or trends. I administered the tests myself, and rather than rely on a blind rater, I also scored them. Results therefore must be considered inconclusive, qualitative at best, and not capable of being generalized to broader populations. Taking these limitations into account, on two of the most reliable tests I found evidence of growth among four students out of twelve completed responses (N = 12) to a Kohlberg (1984) moral dilemma question and among the same four students and one other who finished a subset of eighteen Loevinger (1970) sentence completion tests (N = 11).

Gender role stress. I administered a modified Masculine Gender Response Stress rating scale (Eisler & Skidmore, 1987), as some of the questions were not appropriate for high school students. The scale did not yield any significant pre-post differences. The most noteworthy result was that on the post-tests most of the young men consistently scored highest on four items that measure stress over the factor of perceived Physical Inadequacy. The item "Losing in a sports competition" garnered the most number of stressful ratings within this factor, along with other high scores on "Appearing less athletic than a friend," "Feeling you're not in good physical condition," and "Having your girlfriend say she is not physically satisfied." Four items from the factor Emotional Inexpressiveness also yielded relatively high scores, with "Having a man put his arm on your shoulder" being seen as extremely stressful among six students. In line with the anxiety over competition and performance, seven students rated as extremely stressful "Being outperformed by a woman." "Not making enough money," an item measuring the factor Performance Failure, also stood out as indicative of stress for these young men. These results are not surprising, given the level of competitiveness that many of the young men displayed and their participation in a football subculture that emphasizes the values of physical fitness and competition. Although I did not administer this test again, in the spring these preliminary results confirmed what I discovered about the group members and it served to inform some of the topic discussions. It may not be surprising that the two students with very low scores, that is, those who displayed the least amount of stress about living up to a conventional masculine role, did not return to play football, as they may have felt secure and had little to prove.

Kohlberg moral reasoning. Kohlberg's question requires responses to a moral dilemma and the reasoning behind the answers. In the scenario a fourteen-year-old boy works hard to save money to go to camp, as his father promised him he could. Then his father changes his mind and wants to use his son's money to go on a fishing trip. Should the boy refuse to give his father the money and why or why not? On the Kohlberg question most students evidenced a stable mix of preconventional and conventional responses. Four of twelve students moved up from preconventional and conventional responses to conventional and even postconventional ones on a number of questions.

On the pre-test, student A refers to the need for a promise to be kept even to a stranger because "you gave someone your word." This indicates a conventional, stage 4 approach that is based on social rules and responsibility. On the same post-test question, the student affirms the need to keep a promise "because that's being truthful," an appeal to a higher order principle beyond a social norm. In response to the most important thing a son should be concerned about in his relationship with his father, the pre-test response is, "His father's well-being," because "It's important for any relationship with a family relative." On the post-test his answer is considerably more encompassing and generalizes to others beyond the family: the most important thing, this student writes, is "LOVE," because "That's the most important thing in every relationship."

Student B's first response to whether it is important to keep a promise to someone one does not know well is, "No, because you won't see him again." In contrast, regarding whether to keep a promise to a stranger, he later writes, "Yes, becaus [sic] it reflects on you as a person." He first writes that the most important thing a father should be concerned about in his relationship with his son is "That promises should be kept" because "It puts more trust between them." He later says the most important thing is "The love," "because you need love in a relation for the relationship to stay together." This student has moved from a notion of relationship based on exchange and practicality to one of mutuality and higher sentiments and motives that extend to all relationships.

A third student, C, on the pre-test wrote that Joe "should give his father the money because his father's been taking care of him since he was a baby, so that's the least he could do." His later response goes beyond an obligation to authority and indicates a more caring, emotionally responsible awareness of the temporality and fragility of relationship: "cause his father is not always going to be there forever." With regard to the importance of a promise, the student's first response refers to the fact that "Joe worked hard to get the money and had all his hope on going to camp." His later response goes beyond this appeal to concrete exchange to justify a promise and refers to a more internalized, conventional sense of morality: "cause you shouldn't break your promise."

Finally, on one item, student D moved from a preconventional notion of authority of a father over his son to a more conventional one. His first answer is "to obey and always respect him" because "He's your father and he has more authority of you." His later response refers to a more normative, responsible morality, this time from the father's point of view: "Make sure he [the son] is doing positive things and carrying out his responsibilities" because "then he will have a better adulthood."

Loevinger sentence completion. Loevinger's sentence completion test is intended to measure ego strengths and evaluates development from preconventional stages to more conventional ones and toward increasingly autonomous and integrative levels. Most students remained at stable levels, self-protective or conformist, with mixtures of both and some indicating transition to a conscientious level. Students A, B, C, and D also showed some improvement on this test, as did one other student, which made for five out of a total of eleven completed.

On several items on the post-test, Student A moved from less conformist generalizations to more conscientious responses. For example, in response to the item *Raising a family,* he went from "is very hard" to "is hard if your [sic] young. But it can be wonderful." Conscientious responses are more comparative and contingent, as is this second response. For the item *When they avoided me* this student first wrote: "I got mad." His later response, "I realized I wasn't wanted," conveys less impulsivity and more inner-directed self-awareness. On *I feel sorry* the student first wrote "when people die" and later wrote "for homeless people." This latter answer is less banal and general than the first and implies compassion for specific people of whom the student is aware within society.

On a few items on the post-test, Student B moved from less egocentric and preconventional answers to more socially responsible ones. He first completed *When they avoided me* with "I ignore them" but later responded with "I feel bad." Similarly, in terms of a less defensive and more responsible position, *What gets me into trouble* moved from "school" to "me." *Being with other people* "makes me feel safe" suggests an opportunistic, self-protective, preconventional level; *Being with other people* "is nice," albeit banal, is a more conventional and appropriate response. Likewise, on the item *A wife should* the student first wrote, "Do what her man says to do"; later he responded with, "be loving."

Two of student C's responses are notable with respect to a shift in gender differences. *A man's job* "can only be done by a man," he first wrote. This is a stereotypical response that almost echoes the thought and is characteristic of an early developmental stage. Afterward, the young man surmised that *A man's job* "is a big responsibility," which is a more conventional answer that implies accountability to others. *Women are lucky because* "they get my attention" is a self-serving, egocentric viewpoint this student provided on the pre-test. His later answer, "they are very fragile," could imply sensitivity to feelings and vulnerabilities and in any event is a shift from self-reference to an awareness of the other. This response also may align with the previous notion that it is men who must bear the brunt of responsibility and the need to be tough and cannot afford to be fragile in the world. On the item *When they avoided me*, he first says, "I make them notice me," then later qualifies this with "I try my best to make them notice me," suggesting a somewhat more humble, qualified, socially conscious awareness.

On *Being with other people*, student D went from "makes you feel good" to "is the best way to express your feelings to other people," a shift from a self-serving, hedonistic level to a more related and conscientious awareness. *Women are lucky because* "They have alot [sic] of love" replaces "that [sic] won't have to struggle like men." Here the answer is less self-referential, refers to feelings, and is not contingent on the vagaries of fate. *I feel sorry* "for the people who have to struggle," the pre-test response, while it shows concern for others, is also banal, general, and fatalistic; in contrast, *I feel sorry* "when I do something wrong to somebody or myself," the later completion, is more autonomous, self-critical, and conditional, and hence more developed.

Student E went from a self-referential level to a more conventional one. Two early egocentric responses are *Raising a family* "would be my pride and joy" and *Being with other people* "make [sic] me feel good." The word *important*, a more socially related concept, then appears in both post-test responses: *Raising a family* "is important," and *Being with other people* "make [sic] me feel important." Social meaning and value take precedence over feeling good. Completing the sentence *The thing I like about myself is* went from "the way I carry myself in a upright [spelled uprigth]" to "my attitude," a shift from a bodily state to a mental one. Finally, the pre-test response to *I feel sorry*, "For when I cry," reflects conceptual confusion [sic] and echoes the thought; the later response is "for the...bad thing I have done," a more cogent and responsible sentence completion.

Survey, Fall 2001 (N = 16)

Frequency of meditation. On the written survey, when asked if they meditate during the week on their own, twelve of fifteen said they did at least once a week. Most said they did before and during a game. One wrote, "I meditate 3 time [*sic*] a week and before my game. Anytime it feels like too much stress. I do it more now since the class."

Helpfulness of meditation. In response to the question "If so how does meditation help you?" all sixteen wrote positive answers. Most mentioned it helps them relieve stress, focus, concentrate, "calms me down," "gives me clear thoughts," "keeps my mine [*sic*] clear for all unnesary [*sic*] things that [are] around me," and "to concintrate [*sic*] on what I am doing now than worry about what [is] going to happen and controlling my thinking."

Asked if they had more awareness of their thoughts and feelings than they had before they learned meditation practices, and if so, when, thirteen said yes. Some answers were, "Half of the time when I'm getting along with others when I'm about to say things I don't want to say," "Yes[,] playing in football I am more mindful of my opponent's tendencies and weakness." "After I learned I control myself better. I think of the consequences," and " I feel that I get better at handling pressure and expressing myself."

In terms of having more control of thoughts and feelings, eleven said they did: "Yes[,] when I learned meditation I learned how to make second thoughts, and try to help myself make the right decisions without having to say to myself in the future, why did I do this or that;" "Yes[,] during a game a kid was talking shit and kept cheap shooting me but I stayed under control;" "Yes[,] I don't think of stress no more;" "Yes[,] concentrating in school," "Yes" (circled school, getting along with others, handling pressures), and "Mostly with football, I feel a lot more relaxed."

Helpfulness of discussions. In terms of which discussions were helpful, nine wrote positive statements on applying meditation to playing football, including: "The discussion of how to stay focused," "Just to be in the Zone and be aware of everything around you," and "The one we had before the [X] game." (This was a thrilling away game in which Borough High almost upset a highly ranked team.)

Regarding being mindful about teasing/dissing teammates and younger players, five indicated the discussions were helpful, including: "I've learned how to put myself in there [sic] shoes and think of there [sic] feelings."

With respect to discussing leadership, eight responded positively, including, "I'm going to be one my senior year," "If I don't set an example for the young guys who will?" and "Now that I am a senior I need to take that role on."

On treating girls with respect, eight found the discussions helpful. Some wrote, "Girls are equal," "give respect get it," and "I understand females can be equal."

Nine indicated the discussion on being aware of feelings like fear of failing was useful. Comments included, "Is something that a lot of us have in common," and "I learn mistakes are going to be made no matter what." Fewer (five) responded to the reference to having the courage to sit with feelings like stress and unhappiness. One wrote, "Let it losse [loose] by taking [talking] to someone." Fewer still (three), perhaps due to its painful content, chose to mark as helpful the discussion on dealing with fathers and trying to be a "father to yourself." One just wrote, "I do what I gotta do."

Formal Battery, Spring and Fall 2002

Despite my efforts, I again ended up with a small sample of completed standardized questionnaires (N = 12). For my own end-of-program written survey I had a higher participation (N = 23). Students took pre-tests in March of 2002 and the post-tests in December after the season. I gave them another Kohlberg question in written form, the one about the druggist with a costly drug that a husband needs to save his wife's life. The husband could not afford the drug and the druggist would not sell it cheaper or let him pay later. The desperate husband considers stealing the drug for his wife. Students again completed eighteen Loevinger sentences, and this time took the Sex Role Inventory (SRI), developed by Sandra Bem (1974), and the Personal Orientation Inventory (POI) of Shostrum (1996). For the completed POI, the sample was N = 10.

Results again must be considered inconclusive and not generalizable, due to a small sample and lack of a control group among other reasons. On the Kohlberg question most students evidenced a stable mix of preconventional and conventional responses. Two of twelve showed some positive change. The strongest growth again was in the Loevinger responses, with seven of twelve showing evidence of development moving from some impulsive and self-protective levels through conformist and conscientious levels. The SRI also showed some change toward less stereotypical masculine gender role among a number of students.

The SRI. The Sex Role Inventory asks the test taker to indicate on a scale of 1 to 7 how well each of sixty characteristics describe himself or herself, with 1 for never or / almost never true and 7 for always or almost always true. Twenty items are typically masculine and twenty are feminine traits; the others are filler items. Six of the twelve students' scores changed in the direction of less masculine sex type. That is, although these scores did not reach the range that would indicate a shift to an androgynous role, they changed in terms of less stereotypical gender identification. Of note is that for seven of twelve students there was a change in the desired direction on two particular items that reflect the aim of the program. On the post-test, seven students rated a masculine trait, "aggressive," with lower scores than they did on the pre-test. On the feminine item, "sensitive to needs of others," seven students, some overlapping with the others, increased their scores on this trait.

Kohlberg question. Two students showed some movement on this question. Student F first felt that the husband should steal the drug "to save her [the wife's] life," that is, the drug has instrumental value. His later response is based on a more altruistic motive: "For the love [of] his wife." Asked if the husband should steal the drug if he doesn't love his wife, the student first wrote, "No. He would just be messing it up for the others who have the same disease." This instrumental reasoning shifts to "Yes, because theres [sic] an innocent life at steak [sic]," an appeal to an altruistic or good motive. In response to the questions, Is it important for people to do everything they can to save another's life, Why or why not, the student first wrote, "In certain surcumstances [sic] no, if someone collaspes [sic] in front of a train while you are standing there you should try to save that person[']s life." That is, it is contingent on physical happenstance. Later, the student responds, "Yes it is because that person your

[sic] saving may just thank you in the long run," an answer that implies an element of social nicety and appreciation beyond reciprocity and exchange (e.g., they might return the favor someday).

On a few post-test responses, student H introduced an appeal to both altruism and rules that govern everyone's behavior; both reflect higher stages of reasoning than his earlier instrumental ones. He first wrote that the husband should not steal the drug for a stranger "because the person could probably have the money to pay for the drug." He later said, "Yes, because it would be kindness and probably the law would let him go for [t]his reason." Asked if it is important for people to do everything they can to save another's life, his early instrumental reply was, "Yes it is because in the end it might be worth it." In contrast he later said, "Yes it is because if you don't that would be on your conscience that another could be saved by you." He first said that the most responsible thing for the husband to do is to "get more money and buy the drug because if he doesn't it could probably cost him his freedom." The second time he gave the same answer but then said it is because "any other way would be wrong if illegal," a less instrumental reason that appeals to the more general rule of law. This student also lowered his overall score on the Bem SRI, that is, from more stereotypical masculine role to less, and improved on the Loevinger (see later).

Loevinger sentence completion. While five students remained stable, seven of twelve students showed some growth from early stages, mainly from self-protective to conformist levels. To give an idea of a student at the next level, conscientious, which few if any students exhibited, consider some of the responses of one young man who began the pre-test and unfortunately did not finish it. Although one of the youngest students in the group, he was already exhibiting characteristics of a leader and was highly motivated to get into the zone: *A man feels good when* "his self-confidence his [sic] high, and when he can supports [sic] himself and his families. The family he had when he was growing up and the family he has right now." *When I get mad* "I tend to keep it to myself (the problem), and then talk it over with someone that is close to me, and the person can keep me calm." *At times he worried about* "when it [sic] my time to go to heaven and leave all the beautiful things in the world such as, my family, friends, girls, and most importantly, my life." These responses are more complex, nuanced, contingent and less banal and have a broader temporal context than those of almost any of the other students.

Student A continued to show change from the fall. On six of the eighteen items his answers indicate a transition from conventional to more conscientious ego development. For example, *Rules are* "laws that you must obey" became "for a good cause," a more internalized reason; he went from *My father and I* "love basketball" to the less concrete, more qualitative, "have a special relationship"; on *When I get mad* "I go to my room," a behavior, to "I'm not easy to talk to," a self characteristic from the other's viewpoint; and from *At times he worried about* "his well-being" to "his family," a more interpersonal concern. This student also lowered his overall score on the Bem SRI.

Student F showed some movement on items such as *At times he worried about* "his looks and what other people thought" to "the stupidest things," a change from concern with physical appearance and need for approval to a more self-critical evaluation. *My main problem is* "talking out of place," the first response, changes to "I have little patience," one that is less concerned with staying out of trouble and more self-reflective. On the pre-test, the student completed the question *When he thought about his mother, he* "felt ashamed of the past"; on the post-test, he "gave the situation a second thought," a more reflective, comparative response. Earlier, the student wrote *I just can't stand people who* "talk it but don't live it"; later he is bothered by people who "act out of character," which suggests thinking about a more stable, more highly organized pattern of behaviors. His SRI score also changed in the direction of lower masculine sex type.

Student G moved from a self-protective to a more conventional and responsible ego level on six items. For example, *When his wife asked him to help with the housework* "he said that was her job"; on his later response, "he agreed." *My main problem is* "controlling my temper" became a more mature "taking care of responsibilities." At first, *When I am criticized* "I ignore it"; later, "I am under control." Earlier, *When he thought of his mother, he* "was happy"; he changed this to "was grateful," a shift from simple hedonism to a more interpersonal quality that takes the other into account. Finally, a radical shift in personal responsibility and locus of control occurred with *Crime and delinquency could be halted if* "people wouldn't create problems that make you commit crimes" to "you were more responsible."

Student H also showed growth toward a more responsible, socially aware ego in at least six items. For example, *When I get mad* "I play videogames" later becomes "I trie [sic] to control myself." First, *He worried about* "what's gonna happen tomorrow [sic]; later, "his girl." *My conscience bothers me if* "I do something that's unlike me," a self-referential response, becomes, "I die to someone I care about [sic]." Finally, *Crime and delinquency could be halted if* "you ocupie [sic] yourself," in the context of his other egocentric responses, moves up to the more conformist, "you follow the right crowd."

Student I changed some of his self-centered, preconventional responses from the fall and showed evidence of growth on five items, most in line with his other conventional responses. He went from *When I get mad* "I fight" to "I try to get in the zone." *A husband has a right to* "slap his wife" becomes "know were [sic] his wife is going." *When he thought of his mother, he* "slap her" changes to "had happy feeling." *The worst thing about being a man* "is responsibility" replaces the earlier "nothing." And *At times he worried about* "me" expanded to "life."

Student J evolved on a number of items, including, *When I am criticized*, shifting from "I just look and laugh" to "I think to myself if what is being said is true." *My main problem* went from an exterior concern, "I am concerned about my looks" to an interior one, "not being felt appreciated," as did *My conscience bothers me if* "someone criticizes me about my looks," which changes to "I'm not doing the right thing." *Crime and delinquency could be halted if* "people's childhoods were better" suggests seeing the self as predetermined by fate; the second response, "if there were more things for us to do," allows for more possibilities and alternatives.

Last, on several post-test responses, Student K shored up his conventional level on items such as *Rules are* "obeyed"; earlier they were "annoying." *When I get mad* "I beat people up" evolved to "I yell." Along the same lines of moral development, *When I am criticized* shifts from "I retaliate" to "I feel bad." *He felt proud that he* "has lots of money" became "tried his best." Self-satisfaction yields to feelings for another: earlier, *When he thought of his mother, he* "is happy"; later, he "loved her." This student also lowered his score on stereotypical masculinity on the SRI. One other student (L) lowered his overall SRI masculinity score.

Personal Orientation Inventory. This test aims to measure self-actualization. It is a norm-referenced test (including norms for high school students) and with established validity and reliability. It consists of 150 questions that provide two choices for each item. Most of the students found the inventory to be tedious. Many did not complete the pre-test; ten completed both the pre- and post-tests (N = 10). Four students improved their scores on a number of subcategories and one showed mixed improvement. The remaining five students, except on a few items, had lower post-test scores. Further research would require identifying the characteristics of the youth who improved and those who did worse. One study (Lepuschitz & Hartman, 1996) found limitations in conventional research methodology regarding personality variables believed to be influenced by meditation. The authors concluded that more qualitative research methods might be better used to see if meditative practices influence individuals in different ways based on their diverse backgrounds.

Survey, Fall 2002 (N = 23)

Familiarity with meditation practice. Most students indicated that they had heard of meditation before the group began (twelve of twenty-three). As I mentioned earlier, most (fifteen) showed they understood that meditation is about noticing what passes through the mind without judgment rather than focusing and concentrating in order to get what you want, an answer given mostly by those who attended fewer sessions. Most (sixteen) said they meditated on their own, usually before a game. Some (eight) also said they did so more than one time a week. Almost all (twenty) said they planned to meditate during the off-season with the most frequent response of three times a week.

Helpfulness of meditation. All (twenty-three) wrote positive responses about how meditation helps them. The highest number of responses (eight) referred to helping one concentrate and focus. Helping them with anger was the second most frquent response, followed in decreasing order by getting in the zone, helping one stay calm, and providing time to self-reflect. For example, "In school, meditation helps me to focus on a test or the teacher. With football, it makes me a more focused and stronger person"; "It help [sic] me just stay in the zone and not get mad"; "It help [sic] me hold down my tempers"; "Keeps me in the zone, out of trouble with friends, family and conflicts with strangers"; "Keep my cool in school. No fights with friends. Keep me knowing myself. Keeps me in the zone"; "It help [sic] keep my attitude and tenseness down. Also give [sic] me time to think"; "Stay open minded"; "Keep in tune with myself"; and "Gets me focused during the game and not get angry. Meditation help [sic] me get in the zone and get more focused. It help [sic] me concentrate on the things I am thinking about [and] avoiding the distractions."

Asked if they felt they had more awareness of their thoughts and feelings now than they had before they learned meditation practices, twenty-one students concurred. For example, "Yes. I feel I have more awareness during a [sic] everyday situation, fighting, football, etc"; "I really am more aware and alert on the field. It helps me stay in the moment"; "I do feel that I have more awareness of my thought[s] and feelings now than before I learned meditation practices. I feel it in football a little but mostly in my life and in how I put things in perspective"; "Yes. When I am mad and take a deep breath and think about what I am about to do before I do"; "Yes. Because it helps me bring my feelings out more and makes me play better"; "Getting along with others."

Asked if they felt they had more control of their thoughts and feelings now, eighteen agreed. Some responses were: "Yes. Such as fighting"; "I'm not sure, but for the most part I have control. I think it made me more patient"; "Yes[,] especially while playing. I am able to control myself and not get [a] stupid penalty"; and "Yes. Concentrating in school."

Most students indicated they felt they knew what it was like to play in the zone since they had been meditating. On a five response-choice scale, ten marked off the highest choice, "a great deal"; nine marked the next choice, "quite a bit." (The first was "not at all," the second, "a little bit," and third, "moderately.") Asked if they felt the meditation helped them find a way to get in the zone, eleven indicated "a great deal," eight, "quite a bit." In describing what it's like to play in the zone students wrote: "You feel no pain. You don't get tired!! Like the [X] game I sprained my ankle and knee but I kept going to get to the playoffs"; "[Playoff game.] Final catch"; "When your [sic] in the zone during the game your [sic] unstoppable and you do everything right. [X and Y game]"; "During the game I don't relize [sic] that I am in the zone [until] I get to the side line and everyone is telling me i [sic] did my job"; "One day in practice one day I was in the zone because no one could stop me."

Helpfulness of discussions. Eighteen students marked one of the two highest responses out of five choices ("quite a bit", "a great deal") when asked if the discussions were helpful, with one student writing in a "six" and marking it. Asked what were the best things they talked about and got out of the discussions, if anything, the most frequently mentioned topic was about teammates and getting along. Four mentioned "life." Some students wrote: "Before games what we should do"; "When the team was not getting along"; "About dissing one another"; "Everything!" "We talked about dealing with everyday life was the best"; "Girls"; "Walk the walk whatever you say prove it"; "family problem, school problem, football problems"; and "meditation."

Scaled responses on helpfulness of meditation and/or discussion. The questionnaire included checking off one of the five scaled choices on items that were organized within five general topics: playing football, relationships with teammates, relationships with young women, relationship with myself, and relationship with a higher power or love. In each section I attempted to sort out whether it was meditation and/or the group discussion that was helpful, if at all.

Playing football. The questions asked about whether during a game the players were better at letting go of thinking about a mistake or bad call and getting back to playing, concentrating more and being less distracted, choking less, and getting into the zone at some point during the season. On all four items, most students (average eighteen) marked the two highest responses with respect to their improvement in playing football. In all cases, meditation was seen by most students to be most helpful; on three items nineteen chose one of the two highest responses. Group discussions were given fewer high responses (9, 11, 13, 13).

Relationships with teammates. Most students (on average about nineteen responses over five items) indicated they were "quite a bit" or "a great deal" better at not crossing the line with hurtful comments, speaking with the person before things build up, making supportive comments, resolving conflicts, and communicating feelings in a respectful way. On all five items, meditation and the group discussions were seen as helping equally and given close to the same value; the mean number of responses for the combined two highest responses was thirteen. In this and the following areas their improvement was attributed less to both meditation and group discussion than in the area of playing football.

Relationships with young women. On the three items, nineteen students marked the two highest responses, "quite a bit" or "a great deal." These questions asked whether they were now more aware of "how I think about and treat young women," "more aware of how being with my homies affects how I behave in front of young women compared to when I am alone with one," and feeling they "now have more compassion and understanding for why some young women feel and act like they do." On the first item, self-awareness around women, thirteen students felt they improved a great deal, one of the highest cluster of responses on any item. On the last item, having more compassion and understanding for women, sixteen indicated they found the group discussion helped quite a bit or a great deal. In terms of helpfulness of group and/or meditation for the other two items, the average number of students who gave one of the two highest responses was lower, both around thirteen.

Relationship with myself. The seven items in this section referred to awareness of bodily feelings, awareness of negative emotions, the ability to sit with and breathe through painful feelings, taking responsibility for one's choices, dealing with authority, letting go of self-concepts, and acceptance of one's self and others. On average, eighteen students felt they had improved in these areas quite a bit or a great deal. For most items, twelve students on average deemed both meditation and the group discussions equally helpful in terms of the two greatest amounts, quite a bit or a great deal. Most significant, for the combined two amounts, seventeen students saw meditation as helping them become more aware of how one's body feels and the ability to breathe and make adjustments to take care of oneself, and nineteen indicated that meditation helped them be "more aware of feelings that come up like worrying, getting down on myself and others, getting angry at myself and others." By contrast, for being more aware that "no one can 'make me' do something, that I can take responsibility for my own choices," sixteen students found the group discussion to be quite a bit or a great deal helpful.

Relationship with a higher power or love. These four questions elicited high degrees of perceived change for an average of twenty students, in large part because three of the items referred to the death of their teammate, MC. They indicated that after his death they "felt a deeper connection to a power bigger than me that is also in me" and that both meditation and group discussion helped. On whether they were able to bring the spirit of MC into their playing with meditative breathing, seventeen responded that meditation helped quite a bit or a great deal. Most (twenty) also said they were better able to handle their feelings about his death by being in this group.

E-mails. Not everyone had an e-mail address during the course of the group. Asked whether the e-mails from me were helpful, all eleven respondents marked "quite a bit" (four) or "a great deal" (seven). Some comments were: "The ones when we were losing 3 games straight and then became a better teammate and self. It brought us all together"; "They gave you inspiration and faith in beating your opponents"; "The one about MC. It helped me go on"; "All of them. After M.C.'s death. Before [three games]"; and "It helped us feel good." Three others said "all."

Visualization. Asked if the visualization practices were helpful, twelve students indicated they helped "a great deal" and six marked "quite a bit." Asked about how specific exercises were helpful, some comments were "Visualizing being one with the ball and scoring a TD"; "About releasing negative energy"; "Visualizing making play on the field"; "Made you get a feel for the game"; "Because I could see what I was going to do beforehand"; "When you make a mistake and improve what you need work in"; "It helped me keep my mind free"; "I was aiming to hit the hole and I did it"; and "By saying we will win this game."

Individual help. On whether there were any things I mentioned individually that were helpful, of nineteen responses, nine marked "a great deal," and eight marked "quite a bit." Some responded: "Concentrating on the ball and not being so tence [sic]"; "About stay [sic] with it and don't give up"; "Getting into the zone and making myself better"; "He said to take your time and visualize"; "To not care what other [sic] think about you. Just handle it the way you want to"; "To stay focused in a game. It made me concentrate more"; "Be calm"; "Playing focus [sic] and being in the zone!!"; "Not to worry about what other people say"; "That we have to stay focused in the game and forget the distractions because it will bring your game down"; "It helped me stay in the zone when I need it the most"; "Don't be intimidated[,] just do your part and help the team out"; "At the [X] game, he reminded me to breathe"; and "Breathe."

What contributed most to playing well. On a list of eleven items that included "other," students ranked how each one contributed to their playing well on a scale from 1 to 5, with 1 not at all, 2 a little bit, 3 moderately, 4 quite a bit, and 5 a great deal. The item that received the highest overall weighted score (5 points for each 5, 4 for each 4, etc.) was "MC's death," followed by "I had something to prove," "practicing hard," "My teammates," and "Getting in touch with my highest (universal) self." "Meditation" ranked sixth. The coaches' knowledge and support, one's family, and the group discussions were clustered together at lower rankings, although nine students ranked the group discussions as contributing "moderately" (3).

Their teammate's unexpected death in the middle of the season was a significant motivator, as was their own need to prove something about themselves. When it came down to having to grind it out on the football field, daily hard work and the encouragement and support of their teammates understandably had more of an impact than the less frequent meditation and group discussions, although getting in touch with one's highest self figured in just one point less than the overall ranking of "teammates."

Finally, all twenty-one who responded to the item on whether or not they would recommend the group to other athletes marked "quite a bit" (9) and "a great deal" (12). Asked why or why not, some said: "It improves your mind"; "helps keep your mind free"; "help [sic] you deal with everyday life"; "gives you confidence"; "helps become a person"; "To get in the zone"; and "So that they can get in touch with there [sic] inner feeling and maby [sic] get into the Zone." In the space for any other comments, some expressed their thanks. One said, "This was a great experience in my life, and I hope others take the same oppurnity [sic]."

Did the Boyz Become Buddhas?

The easy way to answer this question is with the partial truth that there is nothing to become, since everyone already is a Buddha. In the highest sense everyone is fine and wonderful just as they are; it's just a matter of recognizing that. In this sense, if the question means, did they reach that awareness, or enlightenment, as did the Buddha? well, no. However, if it means, are some of the young men developing along a path to becoming more enlightened (mindful) beings? the answer is yes.

In terms of some of the results on the battery of formal tests, it appears that some young men did evolve to more conscious, responsible, and self-reflective levels of awareness. The young men need to continue to develop higher, more autonomous skills and learn to let go of ego attachment; they still feel they have something to prove. That drive is not only appropriate to adolescents but, in particular, to urban African American male teens. Over time it is possible they may transcend their ego and become disidentified with it. As they mature and if they continue to meditate and practice mindfulness, there is no telling how far some may evolve.

The qualitative responses to the survey questionnaire provide some evidence that these young men have become more self-aware in important areas of their lives and have increased the ability to sustain their concentration of the present while playing football. Some of them exhibited growth on items that reflect issues of masculine identity development, such as being more mindful of how one relates to peers in aggressive and defensive ways and how one relates to young women, to one's self, and to something higher than one's own ego. Being mindful of feelings like hurt and anger, of hurtful behaviors, and of the need to take responsibility for one's feelings are crucial aspects of development that these young men demonstrated in both word and deed.

As a group the young men appropriated some of the concepts of meditation into their own language and practice, for example, to be "serious" was to be mindful and not distracted. They were able to think about meditation and breathing and developed a sense of what the zone means while playing football and during other times.

Borough High's winning football season was without doubt a tribute to the coaches' expertise, hard work, and support, and to the players' resolve, perseverance, skill, and effort. The young men's success was also based in part on their improved ability to get along with and communicate their needs to their teammates and coaches, to become more mindful of themselves and their surroundings, to deal with loss of many kinds, and to sustain their focus and concentration under difficult circumstances. More important than their success in winning games, these qualities stand as enduring testimonies to their growth.

Part Three

It Might Be Time to Move On: Integral School Counseling

Chapter Six

Turn the Wheel: Integral School Counseling for Male Teens

So if you think your life is shrinkin
It may be cause you keep thinkin
Not that intellect is wrong
It's just the beginning, it might be time to move on

—KRS-One (2002), "Trust," from *Spiritual Minded*

A Framework and Rationale

Through discussion and meditation, many of the young men in the football group were able to process and integrate their experiences and move on to the next level of awareness. For many, this advance meant becoming more socially responsible and attuned to empathy and interpersonal relations. Some were able to move from conventional thinking to a more conscientious and autonomous level. A few may have experienced the zone, a peak experience that gives one a taste for something higher than everyday consciousness. With respect to working with all male youth in schools, there is a need for an overall approach to the evolution of masculine gender identity that allows for internal development and that integrates early developmental stages into higher ones. What is most important is to honor the intrinsic quality of consciousness, of being present in this very moment, rather than the focus on any external method or analysis. Without recognizing and appreciating this, educators and counselors tend to spin off into external solutions that reproduce the very loss of mindfulness that yields so much unhappiness in the first place.

One recent counseling model that envisions higher development beyond conventional norms is a wisdom-based paradigm (see Hanna, Bemak, & Chung, 1999). Robert J. Sternberg (2002, November 13) argued there is something missing in education: "I believe it is that, for the most part, we are teaching students to be intelligent and knowledgeable, but not how to use their intelligence and their knowledge. Schools need to teach for wisdom, not just for factual recall and superficial levels of analysis" (p. 1). Wisdom differs from intelligence. Intelligence is more narrowly defined, concerns itself with results, and has little patience with ambiguity. Wisdom, by contrast, includes dialectical reasoning, tolerance of ambiguity, perspicacity, and meta-cognition. The wisdom paradigm encourages the counselor and educator to recognize both universal and unique attributes of a person and is morally concerned with the highest good for all. Wisdom is not complete without compassion. It includes qualities such as empathy, self-awareness, and the capacity for both understanding and transcendence of one's self and of others' cultural boundaries.

However, as Sternberg also warned, educators whose power and prestige depend on conventional criteria such as test scores and who work in entrenched educational structures are not going to promote wisdom. Wisdom may be best alluded to and arrived at through higher, more integrative forms of awareness and through contemplative ways of knowing. One way is through an integral counseling approach.

The purpose of integral school counseling is to help a student move toward full development and awareness; this includes the quality of compassion toward oneself and others. It is as necessary for the counselor to engage in this process as it is for the client. Fukuyama and Sevig (1999) believed that in counseling, an appreciation of multicultural perspectives and a spiritual approach that sees universality among all people can inform each other. The call for a higher level of conscious development accords with the emerging trend of positive psychology that focuses on how people cultivate wisdom, happiness, and healthy states of mind (Larson, 2000). Through an integral approach, boys, as well as girls, can learn to become less identified with and less attached to narrow, oppositional definitions of masculinity and femininity and more aware of the self's universal qualities.

An integral counseling model for young males can be represented in the form of a mandala or wheel (Kraft, 1999). The wheel has been used to symbolize evolutionary transformation and to encounter the teaching that leads to this development is a turning of the wheel (Thurman, 1995). One can enter it at any point. It is designed to raise questions and to display elements that are not fixed but are fluid, dynamic, and interrelated.

The wheel of integral counseling (Figure 1) includes three foundational content areas described by Wilber (1998b; 2000). One is personal awareness and exploration of one's inner world and consciousness (I). The second is educational knowledge about the physical and social world (It). The third is social connection, the need for meaningful community, cultural membership, and social justice (We). Each ring consists of these three realms, or their combined variants.

The wheel is structured hierarchically in terms of epistemology, or ways of knowing. Each outer ring is more evolved than and inclusive of the preceding one. The inner ring represents monological knowing. It regards knowledge as an object of study and does not require dialogue with the subject of investigation. The middle ring relies on dialogical approaches. It uses language to interpret and transform the social meaning of symbols and behaviors. The third or outer ring employs transpersonal or contemplative understanding. Through practices such as meditation it provides other ways of knowing information and broadly empirical means of verification that, as Wilber (1998b) argued, are not reducible to the sensory or mental sciences.

An integral model of counseling youth in schools differs from normative (conservative) and critical (liberal) ones. Normative models seek to adjust students to the dominant conventions of school and society; critical models oppose adjustment in favor of pluralist notions of individual or cultural values. An integral model incorporates and transcends the strengths of both. Based on the research of Kohlberg (1984), Loevinger and Wessler (1970), Kegan (1994), and other developmentalists, it takes into account a person's level of development and seeks to facilitate his or her evolution to the next stage of growth. An integral counseling perspective, however, recognizes higher, transpersonal stages of moral and ego development and also employs transpersonal means to promote comprehensive change. In this way, it aims to improve on current counseling approaches to the evolution of masculine identity.

What Is in the Wheel

The following is a sketch of the elements found within the wheel. The wheel consists of the self at the hub and the nine content areas, three in each of the three rings.

The Self

At the hub or core of the wheel is the Self. This Self broadly takes on three different developmental meanings in relation to the various rings: monological, dialogical, and contemplative. Self-development moves from an uncritical egocentric or normative perspective (monological) through a more conscious, authentic Self (dialogical), to an expanded, holistic Self that includes identification with all beings and things (contemplative).

The Inner Ring: Monological Self-Development

Young children display egocentrism through their limited capacity to take on others' perspectives. Conventional masculinity is a predominant cultural form of egocentrism to the extent that it adopts an individualistic orientation toward others and nature and presumes that the male perspective or gaze is normal. A number of the young men in the study were at this preconventional level of self and tended to see things only from their own point of view.

Another aspect of early identity development may occur when the individual has not yet questioned his or her identity and attempts to submerge the self within society. As with the young men in the study, a problem for young males in this culture is that they often feel they are never masculine enough and struggle to prove their masculinity to themselves and others. There is pressure to attain masculinity, to gain social acceptance and approval of one's gender identity, and young men at this stage are eager to buy into conventional versions of manhood. When male adolescents identify with conventional masculinity, and school counselors uncritically seek to adjust them to that norm, the possibility of assuming other perspectives is precluded.

Content area 1: personal. Traditional school counseling works to strengthen ego functioning, reduce illness, and adjust clients emotionally to the dominant norms of society (see Strohl, 1998). Male adolescents need individual help in order to develop self-awareness of their own emotional issues, as well as basic social skills necessary for social adjustment. Some of the young men at Borough High benefited from learning basic personal skills.

The problem of teaching young males ego skills alone is that these may be used to perpetuate competitive and individualistic patterns of behavior that contribute to social and personal problems in the first place. Counseling may

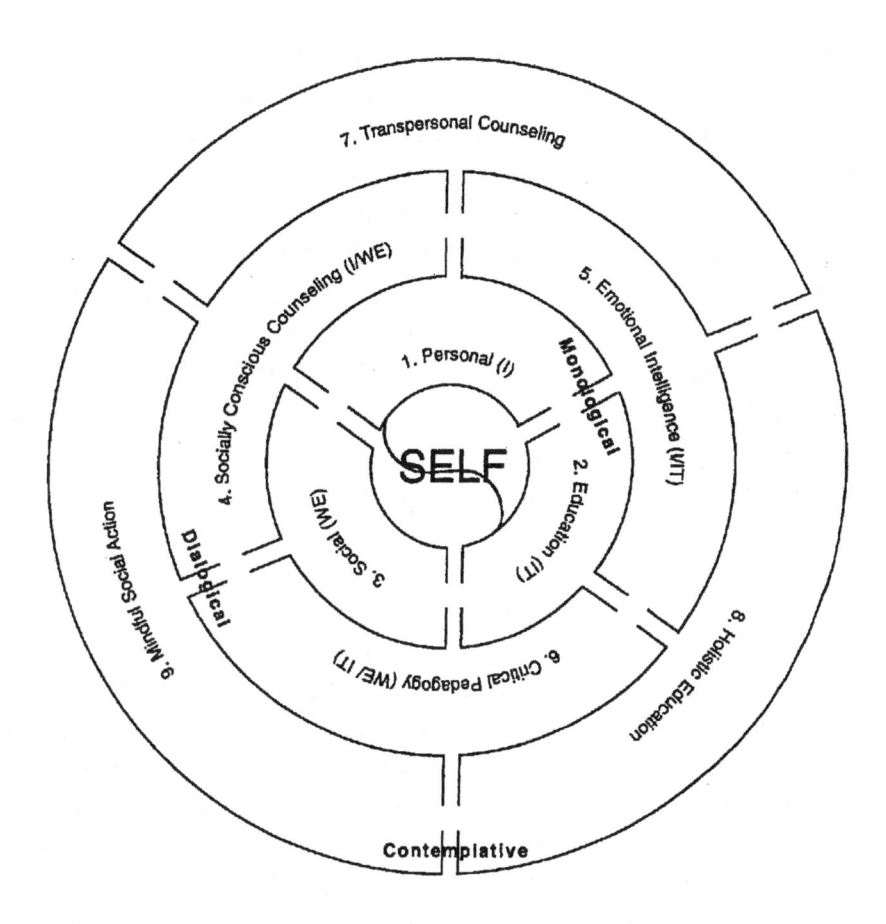

Figure 1. Wheel of Integral Counseling

rely on normative assumptions about what constitutes a functioning male. In one study, adolescent males were counseled in terms of cognitive-behavioral stress management (Hains, 1992). This is a technocratic approach that does not help the subjects question the social sources of their stress or collaborate on addressing them. In another study, adolescents were trained in social skills in order to reduce their depression (Reed, 1994). Reed accepted the conventional notion that a major task for adolescent males is control of the environment through external achievement. He also referred to the need to meet culturally acceptable social goals. These approaches focus on normative standards at the expense of addressing the unique developmental needs of each subject.

Yet humanistic approaches that just promote the self without regard to social context are also inadequate. They tend to decontextualize the self and ignore social inequities. Young males are often already living out the conventional myths of self-contained, autonomous masculinity to which they have been exposed. They need to learn about themselves and about the social contexts and hierarchies that contribute to their own self-formation and that of others.

Content area 2: education. The counselor at this level assists young males in achieving success in education, offers career planning, and provides objective knowledge. The DeWitt Wallace–Reader's Digest Fund (Guerra, 1998) sponsored a professional team to perform a needs assessment of school counselor education. They proposed that counselors should spend less time on students' mental health needs and more time providing students sufficient academic guidance and direction and advocate for them to ensure their success in school.

It is problematic, however, when school counselors accept normative standards of education and are content to play the supporting role of adjusting students to the norms of school success. Who defines educational success, and in what terms? Counseling models that promote reform may still accept the normative educational criterion of school success as a sufficient goal. Part of the difficulties some of the Borough High students experienced were their lack of preparation and connectedness to conventional schooling. The school for the most part was unable and/or unwilling to extend itself to meet their needs.

Adjustment to the standard of school success is an inadequate criterion on educational grounds alone, since much of success is arbitrarily determined and measured by questionable methods such as rote memorization and standardized, multiple-choice tests. With respect to the standards movement, educators have criticized it as elitist, reductionistic, and technocratic and for acting in the service of dominant corporate interests (Gatto, 1991; R. Miller, 1995; Ohanian, 1999).

What is more, the standard of school success is an insufficient criterion for student development. It minimizes other meaningful measures of personal, cognitive, and social growth (Gardner, 1999; Kohn, 2000) and often relies on questionable practices such as assigning excessive amounts of homework that can violate the developmental needs of children (see Crain, 2003). The recent move to revamp school counselor education sponsored by the DeWitt

Wallace–Reader's Digest Fund (Guerra, 1998) preferred school counselors to focus on academic/student achievement rather than mental health. However, this move tends to establish a false dichotomy between mental health and education, subordinate development to measurable achievement, and reduce learning and knowledge to success as narrowly defined by the school.

Young men can learn about the competitive power hierarchy of the educational system and how it encourages some males to oppress others. They can consider alternative, more fulfilling meanings of work and career. Schools need to challenge the narrow range of subjects and curricula that boys perceive as acceptable masculine choices and encourage boys to cross gender boundaries in subject choice (see Gilbert & Gilbert, 1998).

Content area 3: social. School counselors urge awareness of one's social and group memberships, promote social responsibility, and work to change the environments that affect development and mental health, including families, peers, the workplace, school, and community.

Even when school counselors work together with social systems such as child and family welfare, juvenile justice, and managed care (Keys, Bemak, & Lockhart, 1998), a shortcoming occurs when they do not take into account the unequal and undemocratic power relations in those environments. The systems that Keys et al. identified may even contribute to or perpetuate the students' problems; these systems are not necessarily designed to make changes in the environment as they reflect their own bureaucratic or corporate interests.

The report to revamp school counselor education sponsored by the DeWitt Wallace–Reader's Digest Fund (Guerra, 1998) also denied this reality. It recommended counselors work with teachers, parents, and the community to create ways to help all students succeed. It is unlikely that certain powerful social institutions favor every student to succeed in traditional terms, let alone in terms of each student's unique development. What is more, school success alone is not going to change these social inequities; broader changes in the society are needed.

Male youth need to learn about unequal and unjust power relations and the politics of social institutions so that they can help to change them in more democratic ways. They can benefit from genuine community by experiencing their own interdependence and connectedness with all other living beings and nature.

The Middle Ring: Dialogical Self-Development

In the second ring are more dialogical, critical, and dynamic approaches that share and transcend elements of the inner ring. They tend to contextualize counseling and educational practices in terms of social categories such as culture, gender, class, or interpersonal relations in order to promote individual or social change rather than adjustment to conventional norms. The dialogical model acknowledges the social interdependency of the self; it regards the self as a social being and society as comprised of unique individuals. A number of the young men in the group were moving toward this dialogical self and becoming more conscious of their social nature.

An aspect of this social self occurs as self-identity expands to group membership. It is characterized by feelings of excitement and pride and a sense of belonging to a social group (Fukuyama & Sevig, 1999; Myers et al., 1991). This self-identity may regard the celebration of cultural difference and the resistance to oppressive social and political forces to be a self-liberating strategy (for example see Anzaldua, 1990). However, the exclusive focus on group identity difference fails to recognize genuine commonality and universality among others, even one's oppressors and enemies. In school, many boys learn to engage in subcultures of male solidarity that exclude girls and regard them as inferior.

A postmodern version of the dialogical self alludes to a vanishing solid identity. In its place lies a multiplicity of social selves found within oneself or even a multicultural self. This site becomes a hybrid or a crossroads of various selves that allows for contradictory aspects. However, since a number of writers who assume a hybrid, multiplicity of selves regard the world as devoid of transcendence, it is not surprising to find that relativistic networks of selves do not lead to higher self-development. A more radical postmodern claim is that because the self is always part of a network of social relations there is no I at all, only vast networks of intersubjective and linguistic relationships (see Wilber, 1998b, pp. 129–130). All these forms negate any meaning of self-development in favor of the We and deny an essential aspect of human experience.

A higher stage of self-development furthers personal growth by promoting the meaningful subjectivity of all social relations through social justice. This challenges the dominant society through critical reflection and emancipatory practices. Rather than considering a holistic, inclusive self, however, this dialogical perspective still views the self and the world in external terms and mainly in opposition to socially dominant others and forms of meaning (Us versus Them).

One feminist take on this emphasizes the interconnectedness, relational aspects, and permeability of a woman's self. Connection with and care for others is a meaningful value of self-development, for example, as expressed in Gilligan's (1982) second level of moral development. The social capacity for connection is identified as a feminist quality for which most girls and women have been socialized. However, Wilber (1998a) pointed out that this is not the same as having attained a universal level of development, such as Gilligan's highest level, universal care, which is more rare and more difficult to achieve. As Kupers (1993) noted, not all women inherently possess the universal quality of care, nor do all men lack it.

Content area 4: socially conscious counseling (combined personal and social). Counselors at this level enhance students' awareness and acceptance of their own and others' cultural and gender identities and may promote more socially just forms of relations.

However, socially conscious or multicultural counseling can collapse into rigid, intolerant values. For example, Weinrach and Thomas (1998) pointed out that defending diversity-sensitive counseling has led in some cases to harsh criticism, rigid polarization, and doctrinaire rhetoric and behavior. This problem occurs when counseling approaches based on personal experience and social ideologies sacrifice the need for openness to knowledge and learning in the service of unassailable political, ideological, and emotional attachments.

Some socially conscious counseling approaches help boys become compassionate, self-aware men who oppose violence and inequality (e.g., see Kivel, 1999; Men for Change, 1999). However, they do not provide a mindful practice that allows the practitioners to self-reflect on their own assumptions and processes. These methods themselves then often become self-serving, externalized techniques to which the practitioners become overly attached.

Kivel took a social and political tack and urged men to "get together" (ibid., p. 31) with others for the good of all. Yet he does not explain how adults, let alone boys, can manage to do this. What enables adults to help young boys if they themselves are not developing a higher awareness? That is, to extend Kivel's terms, how can adults and young males evolve if they are not working to get *it* (i.e., their own self-development) together?

A number of socially conscious counseling approaches emphasize work with special populations of adolescent males, for example, Hispanic Americans, gays, and teen fathers (Horne & Kiselica, 1999). One problem is that counseling clients from the a priori standpoint of ethnic or other social categories can lead to meaningless, stereotypical generalities (Lee, 1995). A deeper issue is that the sole focus on identity difference obscures genuine commonality among others. Many Borough High students were proud of their cultural heritage but quite a few were unable to see beyond these categories to recognize what they share with everyone.

The issue of development for African American male adolescents is problematic for counselors and educators because of American racism. Schools tend to assume African American male youth must adjust to dominant cultural standards with which many youth are at odds, instead of the school making an effort to meet the cultural, social, and individual needs of the young men (Bass & Coleman, 1997). Many black men encounter negative stereotypes about their masculinity and experience disproportionate rates of low self-esteem, poverty, unemployment, poor health, violence, imprisonment, and school failure (Lee, 1996). As a consequence, Lee argued, many are denied even the chance to succeed at society's version of conventional masculinity, to perform as family caretaker and provider and experience the power and benefits that accompany these roles.

Lee developed educational empowerment programs for African American male youth from what he called an African American cultural perspective. He pointed out that certain expressive patterns of African American male behavior are unique to African American culture and are often misinterpreted and penalized by school officials, teachers, administrators, and counselors. These expressive behaviors, Lee felt, may have arisen as healthy coping mechanisms; rather than risk confronting racism with anger and aggression, black men developed them as a means of survival. For many young African American men who grow up facing poverty, prison, violence, and death, an exaggerated form of masculinity may serve to lessen low self-esteem that stems from racism and the inability to satisfy traditional male role expectations (Franklin,

1987). Ann Ferguson (2000) argued that exaggerated masculinity is in fact a way for young black men to make a name for themselves in a repressive school setting. Through asserting heterosexual power against women and gay men, engaging in disruptive, transgressive behavior, speaking defiantly in black vernacular, and physical fighting, she felt, working class black male youth create a respected masculine identity for themselves. She suggested that even getting into trouble is a way for them to recoup a sense of self as competent and worthy within a racist school system that stigmatizes, punishes, and discourages them from succeeding. This analysis helps explain some of the behavior of the Borough High football players.

While many African American male youth do need empowering interventions such as Lee proposed, Lee did not challenge the privileges of conventional masculinity within his model (nor did Ferguson). Masculinity is not an internal essence that African American males have or lack, but the assumption and possession of a variety of hegemonic privileges that are denied many of them (Segal, 1990). As hooks (1988) and other black feminists have argued, the struggle of African Americans should not be made synonymous with black males' attempts to gain patriarchal power and privilege.

It is indeed necessary to understand how some young African American men construct the meaning of masculinity and come to regard it as a way to assert themselves in the face of dominant and harmful social forces. However, it would be a disservice to stop there and allow this explanation to justify those aspects of masculinity that harm both women and the young men themselves. James Earl Davis (2002, May) urged educators who examine race not to leave out a critique of the restrictive and negative aspects of conventional masculine culture:

> American education cannot afford to give less attention to the role Black boys play in the enforcement and making of normative masculinity at school and the need to broaden the range of masculine behaviors available to Black boys. In the end, the goal is for school to create new images for Black boys that disrupt hegemonic masculinity that privileges certain dispositions and behaviors. (p. 30)

Lee did not question the extent to which some aspects of expressive masculinity, including the cool pose and woofing, also prevalent in some rap music, may now be inadequate coping mechanisms, some of which are harmful to black women and black men themselves. African American male adolescents pay a price for adopting the cool pose (Majors & Billson, 1992), for example, when it impedes emotional intimacy with women and when it leads to mistreatment of self and other African Americans by way of aggression or heavy drinking (see Lazur & Majors, 1998). It may take the form of aggressive pressure placed by some black male students on their uncool, academically successful peers to stop achieving in school, regarded as acting white or gay (Belluck, 1999, July 4; Beymer, 1995; Fordham, 1996; Herbert, 2003, July 10). Adopting a resistant, marginalized posture may also further contribute to some young men moving away from school toward gangs.

This is a crucial issue. Schools must take significant responsibility for allowing meanings and measures of success to be narrowly defined as white, middle-class values that contribute to the alienation of many African Americans and other disenfranchised groups. Similarly, the schools fail to address the emotional vacuum that gangs rush in to fill. While this is a current controversy, the point is that it is necessary to look at both the psychological and cultural realms within black, Latino, and white communities as well as the structural deficits and racist power imbalances of the dominant educational and social institutions.

Young black men lack positive role models, Lee (1996) argued, and although self-aware, culturally informed, white men can help, "Only a Black man can teach a Black boy how to be a man" (p. 77). By asserting that there is a unique African American masculinity and that only black men can teach it, Lee presumed there is but one essential African American masculinity and confined himself to a narrow ethnocentrism that closes itself off to dialogue or shared universal values with others. Black men, along with women and gay men, correctly reject the traditional hierarchy of white masculinity that subordinates them, as they struggle to transform the old power relations of white manhood (Segal, 1990). However, African American men, as well as women, gays, and other self-identified group members, may become truly empowered from a vision found within each respective culture that both incorporates and transcends their own unique identity (hooks, 1988; see also Calhoun, 2003, summer; and Walker, 2003, summer).

Qualities such as empathy and compassion, grace and humor, tolerance of ambiguity, and working for social justice, Fukuyama and Sevig (1999) believed, are values shared by both multicultural and spiritual perspectives and can be cultivated. A meditative stance offers African American male youth a higher way of being than either identification with an ethnocentric form, for example, the cool pose, or with dominant white masculinity. Each can have harmful consequences for a black male adolescent. A mindful way of being allows one to identify with something higher than restrictive social categories of resistance or conformity. Socially conscious counselors need to find mindful ways to help schools, teachers, students, and counselors themselves overcome prejudice, discrimination, racism, and sexism in all its everyday forms. This, too, requires more than what Ann Ferguson (2000) called for, a restructuring of the entire educational system; it means evolving our interior consciousness as well. The black poet Isaac Julien wrote that the most difficult and important realm to work on is the mind, "the last neo-colonialised space to be decolonialised" (Segal, 1990).

Content area 5: emotional intelligence (combined personal and educational). Counselors who promote emotional intelligence (emotional literacy) educate children to become aware of feelings and relationships in order to handle them in satisfying ways (Goleman, 1995). Boys are especially vulnerable to emotional problems because the norm of masculinity discourages them from expressing feelings other than anger and from developing emotional skills such as empathy and the ability to identify their own and others' feelings. A number of school programs aim to teach boys emotional and relationship skills (see Connell, 1996; Men for Change, 1999; Pollack, 1998).

Goleman (1995) pointed out that healthy emotions strengthen the immune system and that the emotional brain can be reeducated. However, Goleman did not integrate emotional illiteracy with political, social, and economic forces that contribute to adolescent problems.

Such problems often are no longer individualistic but are borne by peer groups. Peer behavior assumes an emotional life of its own and counselors also need to work with groups and the family-school as a system. An emotionally troubled boy with a disturbed family history takes on a more dangerous level of problems when he joins up with other troubled peers whose problems no longer can be reduced to lack of individualistic skills (Garbarino, 2000). Nor is it sufficient to address the issue of boys' masculine identity solely on an individualistic basis; for example, boys' sexist pretensions are moderated in mixed groups with assertive girls, and many adults notice the difference between the aggressive actions of male teens in groups and their cooperative and peaceable behaviors when they are alone (Connell, 1996). In the Borough High School football group we discussed this issue and the young men agreed that it occurred when they were not mindful.

Peer groups in turn need to be critically situated within larger social institutions such as the school. School-based emotional intelligence programs can address the issue of cliques, reduce impulsivity, sexual harassment, gay bashing, and date rape, and bully-proof schools (Garbarino, 2000).

It is ironic that Goleman (1988), with a longtime interest in transpersonal psychology, did not refer to meditation as a means to further self-awareness and to handle emotions, let alone as a basis for mindful social change. Instead, he is content to place ultimate faith in school-based education as the primary means to eliminate emotional illiteracy. The schools and educators themselves need to realize a vision of wholeness in order to practice emotional literacy and work to change their own lives in ultimately self-reflective and mindful ways. Without a transcendent vision, teaching emotional intelligence can become another external method, pedagogical technique, or educational fix that educators apply to others and that allows them to avoid examining and changing their own practices.

Skills are not enough. In an interview, Linda Lantieri, an educator in social and emotional learning, traced her evolution in thinking about the limitations of emotional skills teaching:

> I began to see that just teaching skills was not going to be enough. If young people are not connected to the unique meaning and purpose of each person's life, then even if we possess skills, we may or may not have the motivation or even the inspiration to use them...I was realizing that it's not so much about skill development, it's about working with our own character and about connecting up skills with our own inner lives. (Redefining, 2002, p. 12)

Without a transcendent reference point beyond language, that is, without the interior development of wisdom, teaching emotional intelligence can lapse into another objective language game, something that is external to personal meaning. Learning to speak the appropriate language of emotional intelligence becomes an exercise in performance. In their work with violent boys, James Garbarino (2000) and Claire Bedard discovered that unless the boys had internalized the inner meaning of a cognitive-behavioral training program, Anger Replacement Training, they could memorize the list of techniques and concepts and parrot them back but could not apply them in a real-life situation. Garbarino noted that conventional programs may provide necessary psychological and social anchors but "are unlikely to provide the spiritual anchors that are required for success with the most traumatized, troubled, and violent boys" (pp. 215–217).

Without a self-reflective approach such as meditation that connects with the higher wisdom and compassion of their own inner lives, counselors and educators themselves may avoid examining and changing their own practices. As with any dialogical method aimed at changing consciousness, the educators can become attached to the methods themselves as techniques or ideological fixes. This is because the methods are not intrinsically self-reflective, nor do they approach development from a higher, universal point of reference.

Christine Shea (2000) urged critical, constructive, and spiritual educators who attempt to transform or change others to engage in personally transformative processes themselves. She based her recommendation on Anne Schaef's (1988) analysis of our culture, which she argued is an addictive one: everyday addictions shut off awareness of feelings and keep us from recognizing our oneness with all things and our inner relationships with everything on the planet. Shea proposed that educators take steps to recover from the addictive system that has conditioned us. She asked critical pedagogues and educators who espouse spiritual transformation to analyze the addictive patterns of everyday life, to experience living as a process, and to be open to a holistic approach that entails recovery from addictions.

That educators who wish to transform others must themselves recover from the addictive processes of control in which they are engaged is an important and compelling plea. At issue here again are how the recovery occurs and what recovery means. Even in the twelve-step program, which Schaef endorses, as apparently does Shea, people can become addicted to the performed, external, objectified aspects of the program—its language, rituals, and social groups (see Forbes, 1994). The form the recovery itself takes is not a guarantee that recovery from addictive attachments will occur. How does one shed the ego and, in Shea's terms, recognize our inner relationships with everything? There remains a need for a mindful, nonconceptual practice that subjects every activity, including recovery, to higher awareness.

Content area 6: critical pedagogy (combined education and social). Educators committed to critical pedagogy challenge normative models of education that function to maintain the hierarchy of social power relations based on class, gender, and ethnicity. These educators aim to promote critical awareness of how knowledge is socially constructed and how power plays a role in that construction through what Freire (1970) called a problem-posing form of education. Counselors can use methods of critical pedagogy that help students evaluate popular culture and endorse media literacy (McLaren, Hammer, Sholle, & Reilly, 1995). Popular culture contains images and meanings of masculinity that enter school life, such as wrestling and male rappers. The group spent some time looking at male role models in professional sports, music, and popular culture. Another tool of critical pedagogy is autobiographical writing; instead of accepting dominant-defined gender and cultural identities, critical pedagogues encourage students to produce multiple narratives of the self through writing assignments.

Critical pedagogy too comes up against its own foundational shortcomings. The failure to find a way beyond the ambiguities of language and the inevitable social construction of power is evidenced in one critical pedagogical program for young males. A model for enhancing critical consciousness in young African American men by examining popular culture (Watts, Abdul-Adil, & Pratt, 2002) aimed to promote young males' sociopolitical development. The program sought to avoid indoctrination and moralizing; instead, it employed critical interrogation of popular culture such as gangsta rap music in order to generate the positive values of a warrior. According to the authors, warrior values are explicitly not sexist or brutal and instead refer to fighting for higher goals through discipline and in unity with one's community.

Critical consciousness methods and warrior values by themselves, however, are not transcendent or self-reflective in a way that leads to a higher order of development. Without a higher, nondual consciousness there is nothing that enables young males to liberate themselves from the socially constructed dualism of Us versus Them, and from shifting from one socially defined role to another. A pitfall of "fighting fire with fire" (p. 45), of using one masculine image, the warrior, to fight a less valued one, is that the contradictory elements are never transcended, only rearranged, and *warrior* retains an ambiguous meaning. The ultimate goal of the warrior program appears to be the liberation of the oppressed group. In contrast, Trungpa (1988) defined *warrior* in unambiguous, higher developmental terms as anyone who has the courage to examine the nature of all of one's experience in order to establish an enlightened society for everyone. The goals of the critical consciousness program, survival, security, prosperity, community, and unity, by contrast, are not intrinsically higher values. They are so general that even harmful and exclusionary social movements could use them to justify their actions. Without a mindful, more highly self-aware practice, critical consciousness by itself does not lead to higher development.

Critical pedagogy, despite its rhetoric about personal meaning and choice, often does not address personal, relational aspects of the student and teacher and does not critically reflect on its own practices. For example, Locke and Faubert (1999) used Freire's (1970) model of critical consciousness in counselor education but did not spell out any specific method of how the teachers and students actually struggle to carry it out or how they experience the process. Critical pedagogy shows little interest in addressing the internal and emotional development of either the student or teacher. Despite their best intentions to arrive at truth and facilitate political change, Nemiroff (1992) argued, critical pedagogy is not interested in showing how critical thinking is internalized into the psychological landscape of each individual.

Although boys need literacy skills (see Gilbert & Gilbert, 1998), there is a problem with relying on literacy alone to help boys overcome conventional masculinity. Language is subject to endless meaning and interpretation based on social context. Counselors need to help students to link language with their innermost meaningful experience, such as one's interconnectedness with the universe, and not just to regard literacy as a means to change power relations. Some educators—for example, White (1998) and Denborough (1998)—urged students to construct multiple narratives of the self and assumed that there is no true sense of self to attain, only endless self-interpretations. As Gore (1993) pointed out, language becomes subject to endlessly shifting regimes of power, ideology, and gender relations that can be used in turn to dominate others. Without a higher nonconceptual awareness, literacy skills do not help young men transcend conventional concepts of masculinity.

Michael White (1998) attempted to overcome the dominant male culture and contribute to a more satisfying male identity by proposing the need to construct alternative narratives of masculinity. White assumed that "power relations govern the production of truth" (p. 173) and that "an objective knowledge of the world is not possible" (p. 174). He claimed that "all essentialist notions about human nature are actually ruses that disguise what is really taking place" (p. 174). For White, the knowledge and practices of our culture, social structures, and communities "are significantly determining of the very stuff of identity" (p. 174). According to White, men can renegotiate their multiple subjectivities, construct alternative narratives of the self, and resist and dismantle the knowledges and practices of the dominant men's culture.

If, however, there are no objective facts about men, if there is no truth except that governed by power and determined by social relations, then there is no objective matter to interpret in the first place and no greater truth to reach for beyond endless relations of power and the rearrangement of language through narratives. How can one evaluate a narrative except on the basis of truths that stand outside those determined by social power?

White undermines his own statement in the very act of making it, what Wilber (1998b) calls a performative contradiction. He claims there are no truths—except of course this very utterance that he implicitly asserts is true. What is more, he himself is a proponent of alternative narratives that he believes are truer than others, for example, something is "really taking place" and that there is a more authentic way to be a man than what is offered by the dominant men's culture.

From this viewpoint there is nothing to prevent any newly constructed narrative from being governed in turn by unsatisfying power relations, especially given that no one form of identity is more true than any other. For example, Denborough (1998) described a workshop for male adolescents that helped them challenge the conventional male narrative of acting tough and dominating others. He induced the boys to recognize men as the primary participants in societal violence and to name this dominant plot as "being tough" (p. 103). He then invited them to come up with a counterplot to resist being tough, in this case "being yourself" (p. 104), and encouraged them to find ways to then be oneself. Denborough, however, undercut his program by falling back on a social constructionist assumption. He said that while "being yourself" is a common counterplot, "There are, of course, many counterplots, but we are concerned with articulating and strengthening just one for the time being" (p. 104). He implied that this was just one of a number of counterplots and that any one the boys come up with is okay. That is, he was compelled to adhere to his belief that narratives cannot be evaluated, and that if this is one the young men construct then it is acceptable, as are any others. It also happens to be the one of which he approves.

It is not surprising, however, that there is an ambiguity in the language of "being yourself" that also undercuts the sense of whether the young men evolve beyond conventional masculinity. Denborough pointed out that at one school, the students "called the old way of being a man 'cool and tough' and the new way 'a new cool and tough'" (p. 104). It is not surprising that this counterplot still depends on a language of social resistance to the dominant social order; that is, it is still defined in terms of power relations rather than from a perspective that can transcend them.

In fact, Denborough has no faith that the boys can develop a higher consciousness on their own independent of social power relations: "For us to suggest that boys have the power to change their identities and ways of behaving, without support from family, school, and the broader culture, is to do more harm than good" (pp. 106–107). For Denborough, there is no possibility of the development of a higher consciousness that is not dependent on social and cultural constructions. This is not to say that change within the broader cultural and social systems is not necessary for the young men's development. However, this differs from Denborough's assumption that development can only occur based on changing the web of social relations. Without a higher level of awareness, without a notion that some ways are more developmentally advanced than others, the same language of cool and tough in turn is likely to be used to justify another cool and tough version of masculinity and lapse into an endless power struggle with other socially determined conventions.

Can critical knowledge be grounded in nature rather than narrative? Bowers (1993) argued that a higher form of knowledge resides in safeguarding the environment, and he is skeptical of Freire and those who promote critical pedagogy. Their reliance on the autonomous individual guided solely by critical judgment, dialogue, and other rational processes, he felt, are anthropocentric, Western assumptions that have contributed to ecological disasters. For Bowers, promoting the liberation of autonomous, rational individuals above all else severs people from their interdependence with traditional cultural forms of life as well as with the natural environment.

Bowers however took a prerational turn and just reversed Freire's dichotomy by elevating nature over human culture. He saw progress in materialist and survivalist terms and favored an educational thinking that contributes to the "long term sustainability of the ecosystems, and thus to the survival of the culture"(1995, p. 15). O'Sullivan (1999), who also sought a holistic vision of education based on ecology, said, "Before we are humans, we are earthlings" (p. 262). For O'Sullivan as well it appears that the earth and nature are primary, culture is secondary. This is a dualistic model in which human, personal meaning is placed second to survival, mute nature, or existence as the supreme value of education. Bowers harked back to idealized and romantic versions of interdependent forms of life of what he calls primal cultures and presented no future vision of how we can build a harmonious world.

Freire did appear to accept a split between nature and culture. Favoring culture, he then proceeded to emphasize the work of dialogue, critical reflection, and cultural change within this cut-off realm. Rather than adopt a holistic view of the interconnectedness of all beings and things, he preferred to regard change as coming from critical reflection alone. Although Freire at times expressed a desire for total transformation, he and other critical pedagogues overall have regarded the self's liberation from the dominant culture through dialogical and critical knowledge as the highest universal form of consciousness. Their appeal for radical transformation stopped short of considering the possibility of a whole union of mind, body, and spirit (see Fukuyama & Sevig, 1999; hooks, 1994).

The Outer Ring: Contemplative Self-Development

The outer ring represents the transpersonal approach and draws on contemplative knowing. This third, or contemplative, level of self-development furthers individual consciousness, objective knowledge, and social justice by means of an integral, transrational awareness.

Contemplative awareness and the letting go of attachment to one's self cannot be reduced to language, which divides up the world and captures it through categories and concepts. Rather, it must be personally experienced from a more evolved perspective. Contemplative knowledge is not a narrative that would express a conceptually complete set of information about the self, which is impossible, as postmodernists have shown. Instead, by meditating on the nonexistence, or emptiness, of self, the point is

> to develop fully the subject's capacity for non-conceptual clarity, intensity, and expansive, zestful attention. Experience of emptiness requires and strengthens this capacity, until the practitioner becomes capable of resting in this nonconceptual and stable subjective dimension. There is no subjective impulse or objective character by which one is inevitably drawn on to the next incomplete set of details. In this sense, the subject is complete and at rest in ways unimaginable in feminist or other postmodern perspectives. (Klein, 1995, p. 141)

The ego is a temporal construction that is useful in dealing with the world; people and things are recognized as themselves only in relation to other people and things (Thurman, 1995). Yet this is neither relativism, nor an annihilation of difference into some meaningless void, nor an artificial synthesis. The very awareness of otherness, and the contemplative appreciation of difference, or pluralism, can lead to higher development (Simmer-Brown, 1999). To fully engage with the other through commitment to openness and a tolerance for uncertainty, without preconceptions, respects difference and transforms relationship itself. Multicultural growth and spiritual growth are not exclusive; they can promote each other as the self moves toward greater awareness in terms of both inner and outer development (Fukuyama & Sevig, 1999).

In the end the self is important, for developing each person creates a healthy, enlightened society from the bottom up, what Robert Thurman (1998) called a "cool revolution." The self is nondual, experienced through enlightenment as beyond categories of uniqueness and universality. It becomes identified with all beings and things, past, present, and future. Its true nature is revealed to be compassion, or selflessness, the dedication to relieve suffering and promote happiness in all living beings, including one's self.

Content area 7: transpersonal counseling. Transpersonal counselors help clients transcend identification with the ego and point the way to the realization of the interconnectedness of all existence through higher states of consciousness (Strohl, 1998). Such counselors employ meditative practices in order to help the client go beyond the ego as the highest level of human potential, disengage from overattaching oneself to self-constructs, and attend to deeper feelings and emotional states (Epstein, 1995; Vaughan, 1995).

Transpersonal counselors must take into account the student's ego strengths. The type and degree of emotional problems a male adolescent experiences can limit his capacity for emotional and identity development. Rachael Kessler (2000), a holistic educator who has done significant work helping high school teens cultivate their inner lives, argued that mindfulness in the form of meditation dissolves the ego and that that is harmful to teens. She assumed that meditation will destroy any ego and all that will be left is a pathological void or sense of emptiness. However, it is not the ego itself that prevents the ability to develop beyond conventional consciousness; it is the attachment to the ego and belief that the ego is the only reality that gets in the way. Meditation can help male adolescents detach from the ego and learn to look at it as a useful tool rather than a literal picture of their real or whole nature. Contrary to the notion that meditation leaves teens in a pathological state of meaningless or emptiness, meditation along with other integral practices help strengthen ego skills and generate more meaning by allowing for teens to be more aware of what is going on with them and around them (Bogart, 1991).

Therapists like Terrence Real (1997) have worked with men and male youth to help them experience the wounds and emotionally cut-off parts of their childhood in order to reach a higher level of ego integration, so that the man develops a better relationship with himself. Real saw this as a means to transform one's entire way of life. The ability to form a relationship with one's immature parts and to bring to bear one's higher self on everyday living is enhanced by meditative practices (Epstein, 1995; Wellwood, 1985). Teens who meditate reported positive experiences (Bombardieri, 2000, July 17), as did the young men of the Borough High football team.

Some transpersonal counselors such as Epstein (1995) and Strohl (1998) have minimized community and interconnectedness in terms of engagement with the world or nature. Yet meditation can help one expand the meaning of self. In schools, counselors can help young males to disengage from narrow self-constructs of masculinity.

Content area 8: holistic education. Holistic education promotes an integral approach to learning and development within the context of educational institutions. According to Miller (1997), it has emerged as an outcry against educational forms that deny the wholeness of human life and the spiritual unfolding of each individual by commodifying nature (i.e., regarding nature as a commodity for consumption) and reducing the individual to a quantifiable, economic resource. Holistic educators promote higher awareness through creating school conditions that enhance a contemplative approach to learning. These include being open to and attending to the present, taking care, and seeing in each present moment the opportunity for transformation (Glazer, 1999; see Flake, 1993; Lantieri, 2001). This approach allows for both inner development and meaningful social community. Parker Palmer (1998) appealed to educators to be faithful to both the inward teacher and to the community of truth, and to hold to thinking that allows for both/and, not either/or, experience. David Purpel (1989) called for a prophetic education in which educators stand up for social justice and against violence and exploitation and grounds these in a moral and spiritual vision and tradition.

Teachers who use meditation and mindfulness practices in elementary and secondary schools have benefited students in significant ways (Higgins, 2003, June 5; Levete, 1995; Miller, 2000; Rozman, 1994). In one college-level study, relaxation meditation improved the memory of African American college students (Hall, 1999). Meditation can be used to reduce anxiety, frustration, and judgmental reactions in cross-cultural contacts. Rather than relying on cultural-specific knowledge, people were more understanding of others when they became momentarily detached from their own experience, observed others' behaviors and their own reactions, refrained from premature judgments, and were relaxed enough to gain an understanding of why differences were disturbing (Fukuyama & Sevig, 1999). Overall, boys can benefit from exposure to broader, holistic educational and curricular possibilities in terms of career choices and social development.

Some descriptions of holistic educational programs tend to emphasize educational aspects of development at the expense of psychological needs and social engagement. Also, in many holistic education programs, there is no distinction between prerational and transrational development; some glorify children's spirituality without considering its developmental limitations. As it is, Ron Miller (1997) noted that holistic education faces resistance from educators and those in power who consider education primarily as a means to compete and win in the global economy.

Content area 9: mindful social action. Mindful social action stands for spiritually healthy practices and creating a harmonious relationship with the environment and others rather than practices that are acquisitive, competitive, violent, and exploitative ones. Counselors can help young males cultivate and care for community as an antidote to the social forces that contribute to performance-based esteem (Real, 1997) and the pressures to "act like a man" (Kivel, 1999). An enlightened vision is to imagine a day when excessively acquisitive or competitive behavior, regarded as desirable male traits, become socially and personally unacceptable.

Spiritually motivated activists see the means as equal to the ends. The first step to peace is to act mindfully in a peaceful manner; but working for peace may also be necessary in order to have peace in oneself (Nhat Hanh, 1987, 1991; see also Jones, 2003). Learning to work together with others, to practice nondefensiveness, to seek, accept, and provide support, and to allow for differences while striving for genuine unity are all crucial elements of social action (Queen, 2000).

If everyone is already interconnected, how does one counter those who act inhumanely and unjustly? If difference exists and conflict around injustice must occur, how does one see the other's ultimate humanity? Compassion toward enemies does not means that one gives in to the oppression. The prophetic strain (Purpel, 1989) regards love as both compassion and the critical expectation of rightful behavior and self-realization on the part of the beloved. Some transpersonal practices include this need to take an active stand against social injustice and at the same time maintain a vision of interconnectedness. Educators Parker Palmer (1998) and John P. Miller (2000) discussed a personal decision to work for social change based on one's own integrity and refusal to lead a life divided from one's principles or soul. Purpel (1989, 2000) as well urged educators to make their work a prophetic endeavor, one that promotes social justice and compassion for all. An issue here is that a prophetic stance must clearly depend on both a vision and a practice of unity consciousness—the means are the ends. Otherwise, a prophetic approach collapses into moralistic exhortation and judgment—haranguing others to be compassionate on behalf of some external authority.

A mindful, contemplative knowing can inform action for social justice by helping one focus on higher goals while attending to destructive emotions that arise in the mind. These include rage, envy, greed, judgment, competitiveness, and power. By noticing them and watching them come and go one can avoid acting them out in the world. We also can recognize that disliked objects or others do not have to have independent power over us, as they are not ultimately separate from ourselves (Leighton, 2003).

To approach political change this way is to minimize the rigid, dichotomous nature of the self/other relationship by recognizing that the other, although still different, lacks a static identity. A person's conventional role based on occupation or on his or her social position such as a friend or foreigner is not fixed in stone. When we realize this, the person's relative identity and lack of absoluteness become clear and the tendency to rigidity or fanaticism is lessened (see Thurman, 1998). This also becomes true when we consider political belief systems. As the Zen teacher Enkyo O'Hara (2001, fall, winter, p. 4) said, "By not solidifying around our emotions, by not giving them a name and a rationale and an ideology, we refrain from creating 'isms'–racism, nationalism, yes, even Buddhism. The 'isms' become our prisons." In a complementary way, the more one is aware of the fluid and contingent nature of one's identity, the more likely one can work in political coalitions with others. This is because in coalition politics acceptance of incompleteness is crucial (see K. E. Ferguson, 1993).

For Glassman (1998), a Zen Buddhist, social activist, and founder of the Peacemaker Order, to make peace is to bear witness, to attend to the pain and injustice in the world with our entire body and mind. Being in this moment of unknowing leads to loving action and to healing society and ourselves. Bearing witness to one's own and others' pain and trauma brought about by violence is a part of the political process of building community. Through bearing witness private pain is transformed into political or spiritual dignity.

Choosing meaningful work (in Buddhist terms, right livelihood; Whitmyer, 1994) is important for males given that they tend to link identity with work. Counselors can help male youth think about the kind of lives they wish to live, then help them evaluate and fashion career strategies that are in accord with their deepest intentions and that serve others. The capitalist work ethic is often used to justify exploitative work arrangements and emotionally unhealthy relations such as workaholism and harsh competitiveness. In the group we were able to touch on what work meant to the young men in terms of their own values and goals and as men in society.

Because many male youth also identify being a man with being a conspicuous consumer, they can practice mindful consumption (see Badiner, 2002). Mindful consumption depends on feeling whole enough without the compulsive need to validate the self through external commodities or to become overly attached to them. It is linked with awareness of the interdependence of all living things and the need to care for the earth and its precious resources.

Mindful social action must face the limits of a culture that promotes materialistic and individualistic values. What is more, as Boucher (1993) pointed out, exploitative behaviors do not disappear easily, even among those who engage in mindful, socially active practices. Overall, there is a need for an integral approach that keeps the wheel turning.

Chapter Seven

Toward Contemplative Urban Education and School Counseling

If the truth is told, the youth can grow
They learn to survive until they gain control

—Nas (2002), "I Can," from *Gods Son*

Becoming Urban Bodhisattvas

Urban school counseling occurs within a complex matrix of everyday life. Urban life is stressful: struggling to survive with underfunded schools, poverty, violence, and pollution, competing for scarce resources, and trying to get along with many kinds of people. While these pose a challenge to create and sustain a contemplative way of life, finding a mindful way to see things as they are, to be fully in the present, is what is required. Like the Buddhist image of the lotus that emerges out of the fire, highly evolved beings may arise from the concrete.

"Maitreya walks our streets right now," the poet Lew Welch wrote: be on the lookout for all of his or her incarnations, for they will "break America as Christ cracked Rome" (Welch, 1979, pp. 196–198). In Buddhist traditions there are various bodhisattva archetypes, such as Maitreya, that appear in everyday life, wise, enlightened individuals engaged with the world who desire to rid it of suffering, and who represent different aspects of the contemplative realm. Some are more socially and politically engaged; others are more spontaneously compassionate on a personal level, as is Maitreya (Leighton, 2003). As an enlightened being a bodhisattva expresses some or all aspects of the wheel—mindful social action, holistic knowledge of the world, and psychological or inner awareness.

The bodhisattva can inspire a higher order urban school counseling practice. A contemplative practice can in turn promote the emergence of bodhisattvas who partake in postconventional development and beyond. In all cases, one displays mindful presence of being, the intrinsically fulfilling nature of awareness and compassion that is the heart and soul of education and all of life's endeavors. Without this, learning and living, as they often do in this culture, become deadened routines devoid of meaning and beauty.

In Buddhism a bodhisattva desires to awaken to his or her true nature as a fully developing being. He or she aims for a higher consciousness that reflects both the necessity to realize one's self through personal awareness and to transform the world through compassion, the desire to relieve one's own and others' suffering. This development takes on a worldly form that enhances others' lives as well. A bodhisattva is aware of the interdependence of all beings. He or she strives for unity-consciousness and realizes that while dualistic concepts of Self and Other are necessary and useful they do not reflect the nondual nature of reality. A bodhisattva intends to promote both a harmonic awareness of the oneness of life that transcends cultural boundaries and the acceptance of multicultural difference, uniqueness, and diversity, without getting stuck in one or the other (Glassman, 1998).

Bodhisattvas can take on many forms in our own culture in this day and age, including political, creative, artistic, and highly personalized ones. As a guide, we can follow a Zen priest, Taigen Daniel Leighton (2003), who considered the various archetypal ones in the Buddhist tradition and related them to well-known figures in public life. *Maitreya*, alluded to above in Welch's (1979) poem, anticipates a future that will fulfill the potential of our own time or being, that everyone is a future Buddha.

Samantabhadra is engaged in doing good for others and performs deliberate political and social acts of compassion. Leighton suggested that Martin Luther King and the athletes Jackie Robinson and Roberto Clemente were modern-day exemplars, not only for their actions on behalf of social justice but for their dynamic energy. Ken Jones (2003) argued that the bodhisattva vow to liberate all beings today also means working to change the social conditions and institutions that contribute to suffering and alienation.

Avalokiteshvara represents less political, more personal, spontaneous expressions of compassion. Leighton considered Mother Theresa and the Dalai Lama as examples.

Jizo bears witness with total presence and dignity and thereby redeems the personal pain and grief of everyday suffering. A jazz musician such as John Coltrane, Leighton proposed, testified to the presence of the divine heart in his work "A Love Supreme." More recently, one might think of Bruce Springsteen who, in the wake of 9-11, summoned everyone to "come on up for the rising," to lift up the spirit to a higher level. Springsteen said, "I think that fits in with the concept of our band as a group of witnesses. That's one of our functions. We're here to testify to what we have seen" (Tyrangel & Carcaterra, 2002, August 5).

Manjushri could see through ignorance and get to the heart or essence of things through wisdom and insight, often working through language. Leighton considered artists who employ words to get at the underlying clarity of everyday life, such as James Joyce and Bob Dylan, to be examples. Perhaps other recent ones take different forms. KRS-One (2002) encouraged his potential protégés to become mindful artists, to rap for love and not get distracted. In "The Conscious Rapper," from the album *Spiritual Minded*, he asked: "So you wanna be a conscious rapper/Can you handle the press and they negative chatter…Can you rock for the love of the art/Can you drop hit after hit after hit and still don't chart?" On "Know Thyself," from the same album, he encouraged his listeners to enjoy the world but to practice non-attachment to material things: "What does it mean to be in the world but not of it/It means you want the cars the cash the jewels the house but you don't love it."

The *Vimalakarti* archtype is in part a rugged individualist who engages in everyday activities with silence as much as skill, and who liberates us from false notions and attachments through theatrical tricks or displays. As exemplars Leighton suggested the actor/director Clint Eastwood, at least in his later films, and Christopher Reeve, who has shown courage in the face of his paralysis. Athletes like Michael Jordan who strive to master their skills of strength and discipline and who play at a high level of consciousness (in the zone) have bodhisattva qualities; within the everyday they demonstrate beauty and transcendence through creative, playful, and dramatic performance.

Becoming a bodhisattva involves personal self-awareness, higher-order thought processes, and active social compassion. As a model of integrative power, Diana Winston (2002, spring p. 35) asserted, "[I]t means taking our power…and settling for nothing less than full liberation of the personal, relational, social and political realms of existence." Winston (2003) encouraged teens who want to help others to be themselves and find something that makes them happy.

A bodhisattva displays characteristics of postconventional human development. In terms of wisdom (see Hanna, Bemak, & Chung, 1999) these include dialectical reasoning, compassion, and the capacity for both understanding and transcendence of one's self and of others' cultural boundaries.

With respect to moral development such a person operates at the level of both universal justice (Kohlberg, 1984) and universal care (Gilligan, 1982). A highly evolved person has experienced and integrated earlier, self-oriented and conventional moral stages. She or he understands and can draw upon previous levels of moral reasoning from an integral, compassionate perspective.

From the standpoint of ego development an evolved person integrates and transcends his or her own personal history of experiences. This involves the ability to recognize and sit with feelings such as pain, anger, abandonment, anxiety, humiliation, sadness, and fear, and to offer oneself compassion and acceptance. The person then becomes less attached to conditioned responses that for most people represent their ego identity and instead are able to respond to what is happening in the present in a way that transcends the narrow ego. Robert Kegan (1994) described a higher-order level of development in which one sees conflict as a signal of overidentification with a single system or viewpoint and in which one commits to a transformative process rather than to a static identity. Jane Loevinger (Loevinger & Wessler, 1970) considered a high level of ego development to include a unity of the specific and the general and a concern for both inner and outer life. Self-actualizing people (Shostrum, 1996) share similar traits such as a capacity for intimacy and an ability to transcend dichotomies such as masculinity-femininity.

These postconventional, bodhisattva traits are heroic in the most highly developed sense. An educator (Gibbon, 2000, winter) urged us to reconceptualize the hero for today's youth as one who values wisdom over information, and who can be both realistic and affirming. In a more mature society in which we are aware of all the problems and flaws of individuals, the need for heroes recast in more subtle and complex terms would include "a recognition of weaknesses and reversals along with an appreciation of virtues and triumphs. And we need to recognize that an egalitarian multicultural society requires that the pantheon of heroes can be expanded" (p. 47).

Many of the young men on the Borough High football team prefigured bodhisattva qualities. Their compassion, insight, humor, flexibility, courage, honesty, passion, and openness to the world are already in evidence.

With respect to postconventional gender identity, what would a world of male bodhisattvas look like? It includes some characteristics of traditional masculinity that women as well as men admire: courage, strength, endurance, mastery, risk-taking, and taming (but not exploiting or destroying) the forces of nature. For Wilber (2000), gender identity could move toward androgyny and higher levels of awareness beyond the concept of gender itself. Richard Goldstein envisioned a world of conscious males as one in which

> masculinity would be something every male possesses, not a test every boy must take. Gay men would be free to follow their hearts without sacrificing prestige—and so would straights...Homo- and heterosexuality would not cease to exist, but these categories would become far more individualized. Gender would be a journey, not a destination. (2002, July 2, p. 61)

In a world in which competition and domination no longer reign, Kupers asked, "Who would be the oddball, the man who values personal relationships and childrearing responsibilities or the one who ignores family life in order to concentrate on excelling at work and climbing higher in the hierarchy? How would we define power?" (1993, p. 177).

Contemplative Urban School Counseling

A contemplative urban school counseling practice would employ approaches from all three areas, transpersonal counseling, holistic education, and mindful social action. While there are urban school counselors and educators who have begun contemplative practices in their schools, there are few programs that comprehensively address all three on an integral level, let alone as urban school-based programs aimed at male youth.

Nemiroff (1992) described a "critical humanistic" educational model that incorporated affective introspection, intellectual knowledge, and social analysis and action for students. She urged alternative-minded educators to remain open and avoid institutionalization of one's efforts while maintaining integrity and to be "accepting of the outer institution on which you depend for resources without internalizing its values" (p. 184). This dialectical "juggling" act (ibid.) requires a mindful, meditative focus on a stable point beyond the ever-shifting emotional, pedagogical, and social contingencies in order to maintain the posture. A mindful counselor or educator needs to understand and respect the varying developmental levels of consciousness found within a school community and help everyone evolve toward higher, more integrated levels of awareness. Mindful practice in an urban school means being open to the present and being fully present with each task and with each person with whom one encounters.

Some contemplative programs may meet with some resistance from the school. In introducing the program, the counselor distinguishes spirituality, a more commonly shared value, from particular religious beliefs, which, as Myers, Sweeny and Witmer (2000) argued, would be inappropriate. Practicing yoga, for example, is increasingly popular in some schools (see Brown, 2002, March 24; DeChillo, 2002, December 14) but has raised controversies in others. Yoga curricula, however, that eliminated language that can be construed as religious have been successfully implemented in school districts around the nation (Sink, 2003, February 8). Deborah Rozman (1994) suggested that teachers also can refer to meditation as awareness training, concentration, centering, and relaxation, among other alternative terms, when bringing a program to members of the school community.

An integral program for male youth would address all aspects of growth. Its purpose is for young men to increase their critical and emotional awareness of the traditional norm of masculinity, to learn new emotional skills, to gain knowledge of broader psychological, social, and political issues, and to serve as potential leaders among other young men in the community as they heal their own wounds and engage in caring, democratic practices. The young men's level of development could be assessed along various lines such as self-identity, moral reasoning, ego development, interpersonal skills, self-actualization, and gender identity. The aim would be to continue to move the students' level of self-development toward higher and more integrative realms.

An integral practice distinguishes between gender-specific and gender-relevant programs (Connell, 1996). While the program begins with young men (gender-specific), at a later time it evolves to include young women as well.

There is no justification to maintain perpetual gender segregation given the ultimate principles of commonality and respect for difference. The following are possible components of a contemplative practice in urban schools, which are interlinked.

Psychological

As with the football players at Borough High, the counseling component takes the form of an experiential group based on group counseling principles and committed to mindful practice. In general, it would convene at a separate time than a pedagogical class. Through discussing ground rules, including the need to be mindful of feelings, respect, and confidentiality, participating in warm-up exercises, and establishing purpose, the group develops a sense of trust and safety. It then works on various problem-solving issues, including the meaning of masculinity. The members may deal with grieving and healing around trauma, loss, and family issues, and insights and personal explorations regarding self-awareness and development, health and care of one's body, sexuality, substance abuse, family, women, peers, homophobia, racism, media, materialist values, violence and conflict resolution, and fathers and fatherhood. All of these issues came up in our group. The group provides a safe space for young men to bear witness to each other's lives, to explore vulnerable feelings, to reflect on larger values and meanings, and to experience meditation and mindful everyday practice within the group itself.

One aim is to increase mindful awareness around issues such as self-respect and assertiveness and to enable the students to work through unresolved emotional issues with others. As in our group, young men would be supported to express vulnerable feelings and learn to deal with them. Counseling would emphasize developing affective qualities such as empathy, caring, connectedness, the capacity to experience a more meaningful sense of pleasure, and mindfulness, as the youth develop a higher sense of purpose and self.

Young men can learn that being a functioning person is not enough, that there is a deeper level of self that gets covered up by social norms and that can be experienced directly (see Rowan, 1997). They also can learn emotionally acceptable ways to experience vulnerability, to question the need for control, and to become aware of a different form of power other than power over women and other men as a consequence of conventional masculinity. Through developing empathic skills they can see the world from the standpoint of the Other, including other masculinities, and even "learn to be the opposite sex" (Sapon-Shevin & Goodman, 1992; Connell, 1996).

Educational

Holistic education is both experiential and formal. In contemplative classrooms there is a conscious commitment to mutual respect, openness to others based on mindfulness of preconceived judgments and categories, and a practice of attending to the present moment. The process of learning is psychologically and politically self-reflective and encourages personally meaningful practices.

Teachers in contemplative classrooms practice holistic, whole-bodied, learning. This can mean discussions stemming from reading articles, books, and poems, studying films and popular culture productions, and writing position papers, poetry, and journals. The class would engage in role-playing, drama, yoga, visualization, artwork, and rapping and other music forms, set up group projects on the community and the natural world, invite guest speakers such as spiritually evolved adult males, and take field trips. Students would reflect on these activities through writing, reading, video production, and research skills. They would be aware of and focused on multicultural patterns, traditions, and cultural border crossings when they are relevant and enlightening. The class might make use of narratives learned through oral history and interviews with members of the community.

The curriculum to some extent would be built around the students' interests within a range of topics. Students learn about social power hierarchies and their current place within them. They explore the problematic social and psychological aspects of masculinity within areas such as violence and bullying, youth gangs, substance abuse, the family, parenting, health and mind-body connections, schooling, sports, environmental concerns, gender and peer relations, gays and homophobia, critical media literacy and popular culture, corporations, work and the workplace, and local communities and neighborhoods. They learn the rationale for transpersonal activities such as meditation and yoga.

An aim is to increase students' higher-order cognitive abilities that generate wisdom, such as dialectical thinking, tolerance of ambiguity, perspicacity, problem finding and solving, and meta-cognition. These cannot be separated from affective issues and go hand in hand with the cultivation of compassion. Beginning the day with meditation creates a more calm, relaxed, and respectful classroom that is conducive to learning (Rozman, 1994).

Social Action

The social action component might consist of mindfully working on a community peace-making group project. Students could visit centers where people are working toward social justice or conflict resolution on local and global levels. Kupers (1993) suggested that young men might work on projects that enhance gender relations, such as those that help women take back the night, stop date rape, challenge sexual harassment, promote more good quality child care, or end domestic violence, or join gays and people of color in fighting AIDS and fighting discrimination. Students can serve as mentors and tutors to younger male students in an after-school program. They could work on local and global peace or environmental issues and link them with school curricula, research projects, and personal, spiritual, and vocational interests.

The aim is to engender compassion and empathy as social skills and to employ them in an active fashion with others in a practical, mindful way. Another aim is to increase the students' capacity for accepting difference and for both understanding and transcending one's self and others' cultural boundaries. The students' moral and personal values may evolve from a self-centered or conventional level to one concerned with universal values of care and democracy. They may gain a greater vision of alternative means to resolve conflict and to promote peaceful solutions to interpersonal and societal conflict. The expectation is that they would experience a broader sense of community that is essential for full growth.

The School Itself

The purpose of education is not the accumulation of information in order to compete for success. Education is the experience of being fully present to oneself and the world; it is transformation toward wholeness. A contemplative urban educator such as a counselor is committed to the happiness, well-being and full development of the entire school community (see Forbes, 2004). He or she encourages a mindful practice among all members of the school in order to help make the school a joyous, caring, emotionally and physically safe place or sanctuary (Bloom, 1997; Noddings, 1992). The contemplative urban educator helps people consider their attachments to their bureaucratically or professionally defined roles in the system. He or she promotes flexibility, creativity, respect for individual styles and interests, meaningful learning, and cooperative, participatory, and self-aware approaches to knowledge and growth.

A mindful approach generates more advocacy and collaboration within the school and the broader community. Mindful practice fosters openness and fluidity in terms of acknowledgment of difference without becoming overly attached to one's own ethnic, gender, and class identities and the fixed perception of them in others. It allows for genuine attachments, which provide a climate for emotional safety that promotes real fulfillment and happiness for everyone.

Prove It

A growing body of evidence shows meditation is beneficial to people in terms of health issues such as high blood pressure, pain, and stress-related illnesses (Hall, 2003, September 14; Goleman, 2003). Research can and should demonstrate the usefulness of meditation in terms of psychological well-being and educational development as well. For example, with respect to ego development, some research suggests that meditation improved cognitive development as measured by Loevinger's sentence completion test (Alexander & Langer, 1990). In schools, counselors can assess meditation programs for masculine gender identity development by way of action-oriented research (Allen, 1992) or quasi-experimental methods in order for counselors to demonstrate the credibility and value of the program to the community. They can assess goals shared by the school community such as character development, conflict resolution skills, and improved academic performance. They can do so through self-reports, observations, and pre- and post-questionnaires on development, as did this pilot project.

Children Are Our Present

We often hear that children are our future. The problem with this cliché is that educators, parents, and even students often ignore the present moment. Young people today experience considerable pressure to succeed within some future that never arrives. We tend to live in an imaginary tomorrow—grooming the child for a better grade, test score, or school—to the point where the child and the adult are no longer present with each other or with themselves. When that day does arrive, one spends it anticipating yet another future time. We go about trying to reform the structure of the schools, as if that guarantees the consciousness of the people inside them will also change. We ignore what is happening now and swing from one non-present moment to the next, between ruminating about the past and obsessing about what might occur. Educators, parents, and children suffer when we cling to notions and things we think will keep us safe and happy forever after, such as social status, material possessions, or unchanging beliefs about the world and ourselves. Because these things are by nature temporal and short lasting, we remain unhappy.

We live in a time of urgency when life and life-threatening forces hang in the balance. People in power attach themselves to and act on outmoded assumptions about masculinity they mistakenly believe will keep them secure. For example, you must maintain power over women, gays, and people deemed weaker than you; you will lose your privilege if you give full awareness to human feelings; fear and control comprise the basis of personal and political relationships. Many of us succumb to mindless thinking and acting that perpetuate this kind of existence: becoming attached to material consumption, status seeking, and delusions about others and ourselves. By doing so we give away our true power, thwart our higher nature, and subvert our peace of mind.

At the same time the world has given rise to life-sustaining awareness. Since 9-11, many have come to realize that permanent security through conventional means is an illusion. We require a higher level of awareness, because the things we thought would give us safety and security do not last. Global consciousness recognizes the interdependency of every person, even all beings, in every part of the world. Optimal human development means that all children everywhere require the same things: healthy attachments, emotional literacy, a sense of meaning and purpose, the time to grow at one's own pace, and caring communities. Recent scientific evidence shows that mindful practice has an effect on the brain and allows human development to extend beyond conventional awareness. When this occurs, the ordinary world becomes a timeless realm of extraordinary beauty, compassion, and joy.

For the young men of Borough High, football was a good place to initiate their quest for the zone. They learned to be mindful of what was going on with themselves and to attend to the moment. They began to see how the mind works and how it can evolve. They found some peace of mind and a sense of mastery when they let themselves be. For the rest of us, everything can begin now, by attending to the next breath. In that awakening is the awareness that we already dwell in the zone.

Bibliography

Addis, M. E., & Mahalik, J. R. (2003, January). Men, masculinity, and the contexts of help seeking. *American Psychologist, 58*, 5–14.

After school advancement program (2000). TASC application I.D. # 53009. Brooklyn College Community Partnership for Research and Learning.

Alexander, C., & Langer, E. (Eds.). (1990). *Higher stages of human development: Perspectives on adult growth.* New York: Oxford.

Allen, J. M. (1992). Action-oriented research: Promoting school counselor advocacy and accountability. Ann Arbor, MI: ERIC Counseling and Personnel Services. (ERIC Document Reproduction Service No. 347477).

Anderson, D. (2003, March 23). It is time to clean up the war vocabulary in sports. *New York Times*, p. sp11.

Anselmi, D. L., & Law, A. L. (1998). Introduction: Gender, cognition, and education. In D. L. Anselmi & A. L. Law (Eds.), *Questions of gender: Perspectives and paradoxes* (pp. 419–435). Boston: McGraw-Hill.

Anzaldua, G. (1990). La consciencia de la mestiza: Towards a new consciousness. In G. Anzaldua (Ed.), *Making face, making soul: Creative and critical perspectives by women of color* (pp. 377–389). San Francisco: Aunt Lute.

Araton, H. (2003, July 20). An accuser has no fans or voice. *New York Times*, pp. sp1, 6.

Arenson, K. W. (2003, September 15). Study of elite colleges finds athletes are isolated from classmates. *New York Times*, p. A12.

Badiner, A. H. (Ed.). (2002). *Mindfulness in the marketplace: Compassionate responses to consumerism.* Berkeley, CA: Parallax.

Bailey, S. M. (1998). The current status of gender equity research in American schools. In D. L. Anselmi & A. L. Law (Eds.), *Questions of gender: Perspectives and paradoxes* (pp.461–472). Boston: McGraw-Hill.

Bankart, C. P. (2002). Mindfulness as a useful therapeutic adjunct with men. *SPSMM Bulletin, 7*(4), pp. 5–7.

Barra, A. (2002, September 29). Talk about fan-unfriendly. *New York Times*, p. wk 7.

Bass, C. K., & Coleman, H. L. K. (1997). Enhancing the cultural identity of early adolescent male African Americans. *Professional School Counseling, 1*, 48–51.

Battista, J. (2002, December 13). For Jets, a little too much spirit. *New York Times*, pp. D1, 2.

Beale, L. (2001, September 16). Watching a game rule a town. *New York Times*, p. AR17.

Beck, D. E. (1998, November 19). Friday night without high school football? Thinkable. Retrieved June 7, 2003, from http://www.spiraldynamics.com/archive/Beck/columns/X981119.htm

Beck, D. E., & Cowan, C. C. (2002). *Spiral dynamics: Mastering values, leadership, and change*. Oxford, UK: Blackwell.

Belluck, P. (1999, July 4). Reason is sought for lag by blacks in school effort. *New York Times*, pp.1, 15.

Bem, S. L. (1974). The measurement of psychological androgyny. *Journal of Consulting and Clinical Psychology, 42*, 155–162.

Berger, J. (2002, September 17). Well, the ices are still Italian; immigration patterns shift, altering the old neighborhood. *New York Times*, p. B1.

Berkow, I. (2001, August 5). In plain talk, there is an explanation for Stringer's death. *New York Times*, p. sp13.

Bernstein, V. (2002, December 31). Attention shadows high school star. *New York Times*, p. D5.

Betts, K. (2002, December 15). Yoga, unlike fashion, is deep. Right? *New York Times*, pp. st.1, 6.

Beymer, L. (1995). *Meeting the guidance and counseling needs of boys*. Alexandria, VA: American Counseling Association.

Bissinger, H. G. (1990). *Friday night lights: A town, a team, and a dream*. Reading, MA: Addison-Wesley.

Bloom, S. L. (1997). *Creating sanctuary: Toward the evolution of sane societies*. New York: Routledge.

Bly, R. (1990). *Iron John: A book about men*. Reading, MA: Addison-Wesley.

Bogart, G. (1991). The use of meditation and psychotherapy: A review of the literature. *American Journal of Psychotherapy, 45*, 383–412. Retrieved February 8, 2001, from http://jps.net/gbogart/med_article.html

Bombardieri, M. (2000, July 17). Meditation program is aimed at teens. *Boston Globe*. Retrieved October 12, 2001, from http://about.beliefnet.com/story/33/story_3324.html

Bordo, S. (2000). *The male body: A new look at men in public and in private.* New York: Farrar, Straus & Giroux.

Boucher, S. (1993). *Turning the wheel: American women creating the new Buddhism.* Boston: Beacon.

Bowers, C. A. (1993). *Education, cultural myths, and the ecological crisis: Toward deep changes.* Albany: SUNY Press.

Bowers, C. A. (1995*). Educating for an ecologically sustainable culture: Rethinking moral education, creativity, intelligence, and other modern orthodoxies.* Albany: SUNY Press.

Boyd-Franklin, N., & Franklin, A. J. (2000). *Boys into men: Raising our African American teenage sons.* New York: Dutton.

Brooks, G. R., & Silverstein, L. B. (1995). Understanding the dark side of masculinity: An interactive systems model. In R. F. Levant & W. Pollack (Eds.), *A new psychology of man* (pp. 280–336). New York: Basic Books.

Brown, P. L. (2002, March 24). Latest way to cut grade school stress: Yoga. *New York Times,* p. 33.

Brown, P. L. (2003, February 8). Among California's S.U.V. owners, only a bit of guilt in a new "anti" effort. *New York Times,* p. A15.

Brown, K.W. & Ryan, K.M. (2003). Benefits of being present: Mindfulness and its role in psychological well-being. *Journal of Personality and Social Psychology, 84,* 822–848.

Burke, M. T., Hackney, H., Hudson, P., Miranti, J., Watts, G. A., & Epp, L. (1999). Spirituality, religion, and CACREP curriculum standards. *Journal of Counseling & Development, 77,* 251–257.

Busch, C. M. (2003, July/August). It's cool to be grounded. *Yoga Journal,* 94–99, 154–156.

Butler, K. (2003, summer). Eye on the ball. *Tricycle,* 53–57, 101–104.

Calhoun, R. (2003, summer). Inside a triple parentheses: Being a black Buddhist in the U.S. *Turning Wheel: The Journal of Socially Engaged Buddhism,* 39–42.

Capuzzi, D., & Gross, D. R. (Eds.). (1999). *Youth at risk: A prevention resource for counselors, teachers and parents.* Washington, DC: American Counseling Association.

Chass, M. (2003, February 19). Varied factors caused pitcher's death. *New York*

Times, p. D1.

Chesler, P. (2002). *Woman's inhumanity to woman.* New York: Thunder's Mouth/Nation.

Common (2000). Geto Heaven, part 2. On *Like water for chocolate* [CD]. Los Angeles: MCA.

Connell, R. W. (1995). *Masculinities.* Berkeley: University of California Press.

Connell, R. W. (1996). Teaching the boys: New research on masculinity, and gender strategies for schools. *Teachers College Record, 98,* 206–235.

Conniff, R. (2003, March 24). Title IX: Political football. *Nation,* 19–21.

Cooper, A. (1998). *Playing in the zone: Exploring the spiritual dimensions of sports.* Boston: Shambhala.

Courtenay, W. H. (2000). Behavioral factors associated with disease, injury, and death among men: Evidence and implications for prevention. *Journal of Men's Studies, 9*(1), 81–142.

Crain, W. (2003). *Reclaiming our childhood: Letting children be children in our achievement-oriented society.* New York: Times.

Csikszentmihalyi, M. (1990). *Flow: The psychology of optimal experience.* New York: Harper & Row.

Cummins, H. J. (2002, December 13). "Gaybashing" is most common bullying in schools. Retrieved December 21, 2002, from http://www.startribune.com/viewers/story/php?template =print_a&story =3528825.

D'Andrea, M., & Arredondo, P. (2003, July). Getting in the zone: Using Zen philosophy to promote human development and multicultural understanding. *Counseling Today,* 26–27.

Davis, J. E. (2002, May). Race, gender, and sexuality: (Un)doing identity categories in educational research. *Educational Researcher, 31*(4), 29–32.

Dead Prez (1999). Score. On *Soul in the hole* soundtrack [CD]. New York: Relativity.

DeAngelis, T. (2001, March). What makes a good afterschool program? *Monitor on Psychology, 32,* 60–62.

DeChillo, S. (2002, December 14). Stretch. Pose. Rest. It's kindergarten yoga. *New York Times,* B1.

Denborough, D. (1998). Step by step: Developing respectful and effective ways of working with young men to reduce violence. In C. McLean, M. Carey,

& C. White (Eds.), *Men's ways of being* (pp. 91–115). Boulder, CO: Westview.

Derezotes, D. (2000). Evaluation of yoga and meditation trainings with adolescent sex offenders. *Child and Adolescent Social Work Journal, 17*, 97–112.

DMX (1998). Look through my eyes. On *Its dark and hell is hot* [CD]. New York: Def Jam.

Dolby, N. (2002). Youth, culture, and identity: Ethnographic explorations. *Educational Researcher, 31*(8), 37–42.

Dubner, S. J. (2002, August 18). Life is a contact sport: Where N.F.L. rookies learn the facts of life. *New York Times Magazine* pp. 23ff. Retrieved July 29, 2003, from http://stephenjdubner.com/journalism/091802.html

Eccles, J. S., & Templeton, J. (2002). Extracurricular and other after-school activities for youth. In W. G. Secada (Ed.), *Review of Research in Education, 26* (pp. 113–180). Washington: AERA.

Edmundson, M. (2000, October 9). Bad boys, whatcha gonna do… [Review of the book *The war against boys*]. *Nation*, 39–43.

Edwards, H. (1983). Educating black athletes. *Atlantic Monthly, 252* (2), 31–38.

Edwards, H. (1984). The black "dumb jock": An American sports tragedy. *College Board Review, 131*, 8–13.

Egan, T. (2002, November 22). Body-conscious boys adopt athletes' taste for steroids. *New York Times*, p. A1.

Eisler, R. M., & Skidmore, J. (1987). Masculine gender role stress: Scale development and component factors in the appraisal of stressful situations. *Behavior Modification, 11*, 123–136.

Epstein, M. (1995). *Thoughts without a thinker: Psychotherapy from a Buddhist perspective.* New York: HarperCollins.

Epstein, M. (1999). *Going to pieces without falling apart: A Buddhist perspective on wholeness.* New York: Broadway.

Faludi, S. (1991). *Backlash: The undeclared war against American women.* New York: Anchor.

Faludi, S. (1999). *Stiffed: The betrayal of the American man.* New York: William Morrow.

Fender-Scarr, L. K. (2001). Conceptualizing eating pathology in athletes from a cognitive-behavioral perspective. *Journal for the Professional Counselor,* 16(2), 13–22.

Ferguson, A. A. (2000). *Bad boys: Public schools in the making of black masculinity.* Ann Arbor: University of Michigan Press.

Ferguson, K. E. (1993). *The man question: Visions of subjectivity in feminist theory.* Berkeley: University of California Press.

Flaherty, J. (2000, December 12). Experiment aims to get real men to go to the doctor. *New York Times,* p. F6.

Flake, C. (Ed.). (1993). *Holistic education: Principles, perspectives, and practices.* Brandon, VT: Holistic Education Press.

Fontana, D., & Slack, I. (1997). *Teaching meditation to children: Simple steps to relaxation and well-being.* London: Thorsons/HarperCollins.

Forbes, D. (1994). *False fixes: The cultural politics of drugs, alcohol, and addictive relations.* Albany: SUNY Press.

Forbes, D. (2004). What is the role of counseling in urban schools? In S. R. Steinberg & J. L. Kincheloe (Eds.), *19 urban questions: Teaching in the city* (pp 69–83). New York: Peter Lang.

Fordham, S. (1996). *Blacked out: Dilemmas of race, identity, and success at Capital High.* Chicago: University of Chicago Press.

Franklin, C. (1987). Surviving the institutional decimation of black males: Causes, consequences and intervention. In H. Brod (Ed.), *The making of masculinities: The new men's studies* (pp.155–170). Boston: Allen & Unwin.

Freeman, M. (2001, June 3). Retired at 30 from Vikings, Smith seeks different goals. *New York Times,* section 8, p. 9.

Freeman, M. (2002, January 31). Painkillers a quiet fact of life in the N.F.L. *New York Times,* pp. D1, D3.

Freeman, M. (2002, November 1). N.F.L. needs to crack down on potentially lethal hits. *New York Times,* p. D1.

Freeman, M. (2003, July 13). When values collide: Clarett got unusual aid in Ohio State class. *New York Times,* section 8, pp. 1,4.

Freeman, M., & Villarosa, L. (2002, September 26). The perils of pro football follow some into retirement. *New York Times,* D1.

Freire, P. (1970). *Pedagogy of the oppressed.* New York: Seabury.

Fuchs, C. (1996). "Beat me outta me": Alternative masculinities. In P. Smith (Ed.), *Boys: Masculinities in contemporary culture* (pp. 171–197). Boulder, CO: Westview.

Fukuyama, M. A., & Sevig, T. D. (1999). *Integrating spirituality into multicultural counseling.* Thousand Oaks, CA: Sage.

Galinsky, E., & Salmond, K. (2002). Youth and violence summary and discussion guide. Retrieved October 1, 2003, from: http://www.familieandwork.org/summary/yandv/pdf

Gano-Overway, L. (1999, May 3). Education World Curriculum: Emphasizing sportsmanship in youth sports. Retrieved October 1, 2003, from http://www.education-world.com/a_curr/currl37.shtml

Garbarino, J. (2000). *Lost boys: Why our sons turn violent and how we can save them.* New York: Anchor.

Gardner, H. (1999). *The disciplined mind: What all students should understand.* New York: Simon & Schuster.

Gatto, J. T. (1991). *Dumbing us down: The hidden curriculum of compulsory schooling.* Gabriola Island, BC: New Society.

George, T. (2001, August 15). Taking back their bodies. *New York Times*, pp. 15,16.

Gergen, K. J. (2001). Psychological science in a postmodern context. *American Psychologist, 56,* 803–813.

Getz, A., & Gordhamer, S. (n.d.). Interview on mindfulness and violent youth. Retrieved November 4, 2003, from http://www.youthhorizons.org/interview/James/html

Gibbon, P. H. (2000, winter). Heroes for our age: How heroes can elevate students' lives. *American Educator,* 8–15, 46–48.

Gigantosauruses on the field. (2002, September 29). *New York Times*, p. wk.12.

Gilbert, R., & Gilbert, P. (1998). *Masculinity goes to school.* New York: Routledge.

Gilligan, C. (1982). *In a different voice: Psychological theory and women's development.* Cambridge, MA: Harvard University Press.

Gilmore, D. (1990). *Man in the making: Cultural concepts of masculinity.* New Haven, CT: Yale University Press.

Gladwell, M. (2000). *The tipping point: How little things can make a big differ-*

ence. Boston: Little Brown.

Glassman, B. (1998). *Bearing witness: A Zen master's lessons in making peace*. New York: Bell Tower.

Glazer, S. (1999). Conclusion: The heart of learning. In S. Glazer (Ed.), *The heart of learning: Spirituality in education* (pp. 247–250). New York: Tarcher.

Glickman, C. D. (2003). *Holding sacred ground: Courageous leadership for democratic schools*. San Francisco: Jossey-Bass.

Goldstein, R. (2002, July 2). The myth of gay macho. *Village Voice*, 59, 61.

Goldstein, R. (2003, March 24). Neo-macho man: Pop culture and post-9/11 politics. *Nation*, 16–19.

Goldstein, R. (2003, May 21–27). Bush's basket: Why the president had to show his balls. *Village Voice*, 48.

Goleman, D. (1988). *The meditative mind: The varieties of meditative experience*. New York: Putnam.

Goleman, D. (1995). *Emotional intelligence: Why it can matter more than IQ*. New York: Bantam.

Goleman, D. (2003). *Destructive emotions: A scientific dialogue with the Dalai Lama*. New York: Bantam.

Goode, E. (2001, April 25). School bullying is common, mostly by boys, study finds. *New York Times*, p. A17.

Gordhamer, S. (2000, fall). In the zone: An interview with George Mumford. *Sowing the Seeds: Newsletter of the Lineage Project East*, pp. 1,4, 5. Also available at http://www.youthhorizons.org/interview/george.html

Gordhamer, S. (2001). *Just say om! A teenager's guide*. Avon, MA: Adams.

Gore, J. M. (1993). *The struggle for pedagogies: Critical and feminist discourses as regimes of truth*. New York: Routledge.

Guerra, P. (1998). Revamping school counselor education: The DeWitt Wallace-Reader's Digest Fund. *CTOnline: The online news source for professional counselors*. Retrieved October 12, 2001, from http://www.couseling.org/ctonline/archives/ct0298/revamping.htm

Hains, A. A. (1992). Comparison of cognitive-behavioral stress management techniques with adolescent boys. *Journal of Counseling and Development, 70*, 600–605.

Halford, J. M. (1998, December). The spirit of education: Longing for the sacred in schools: A conversation with Nel Noddings. *Educational Leadership, 56*(4). Retrieved October 1, 2003, from http://www.ascd.org/readingroom/edlead/9812/halford.html

Hall, P. D. (1999). The effects of meditation on the academic performance of African American college students. *Journal of Black Studies, 29*(3), 408–415.

Hall, S. S. (1999, August 22). Bully in the mirror. *New York Times Magazine,* pp. 31–35, 58, 60, 62.

Hall, S. S. (2003, September 14). Is Buddhism good for your health? *New York Times Magazine,* pp. 46–49.

Hanna, F. J., Bemak, F., & Chung, R. C. (1999). Toward a new paradigm for multicultural counseling. *Journal of Counseling & Development, 77* 125–134.

Harrison, J. (1978). Warning: The male sex role may be hazardous to your health. *Journal of Social Issues, 32,* 65–86.

Hayes, L. (2002, April). Sports therapy may aid many high school girls. *Counseling Today,* 1, 20, 22, 24.

Herbert, B. (2003, July 10). Breaking away. *New York Times,* p. A23.

Higgins, L. (2003, June 5). Meditation key to education, say school officials. *Detroit Free Press.* Retrieved October 4, 2003, from http://www.freep.com/news/education/tm5_20030605.htm

Hodges, S. (2000, February). Review of *Integrating spirituality into multicultural counseling. Counseling Today,* 32.

hooks, b. (1988). *Talking back: Thinking feminist, thinking black.* Boston: South End.

hooks, b. (1994). *Teaching to transgress: Education as the practice of freedom.* New York: Routledge.

Horne, A. M., & Kiselica, M. S. (1999). Preface: For the sake of our nation's sons. In A. M. Horne & M. S. Kiselica (Eds.), *Handbook of counseling boys and adolescent males: A practitioners' guide* (pp. xv–xx). Thousand Oaks, CA: Sage.

Hughes, R., & Coakley, J. (1991). Positive deviance among athletes: The implications of overconformity to the sport ethic. *Sociology of Sport Journal, 8,* 307–325.

Indicators of school crime and safety (2001). Executive summary. National Center for Education Statistics. Retrieved March 16, 2002, from http://www.nces.ed.gov/pubs2002/crime2001/

Jackson, S. A., & Csikszentmihalyi, M. (1999). *Flow in sports: The keys to optimal experiences and performances.* Champaign, IL: Human Kinetics.

Jolliff, D., & Horne, A. M. (1999). Growing up male: The development of mature masculinity. In A. M. Horne & M. S. Kiselica (Eds.), *Handbook of counseling boys and adolescent males: A practitioner's guide* (pp. 3–23). Thousand Oaks, CA: Sage.

Jones, K. (2003). *The new social face of Buddhism: A call to action.* Somerville, MA: Wisdom.

Jordan, J. M., & Denson, E. L. (1990). Student services for athletes: A model for enhancing the student athlete experience. *Journal of Counseling & Development, 69,* 95–97.

Julien, A. (2002, December 15). The kids are hurting. *Hartford Courant.* Retrieved January 12, 2003, from http://www.ctnow.com/templates/misc/printstory.jsp?slug=hc%Dgenstressday1dec15

Kabatznick, R. (1998). *The Zen of eating: Ancient answers to modern weight problems.* New York: Perigee.

Kaufman, M. (1993). *Cracking the armour: Power, pain and the lives of men.* Toronto: Viking.

Kegan, R. (1994). *In over our heads: The mental demands of modern life.* Cambridge, MA: Harvard University Press.

Kessler, R. (2000). *The soul of education: Helping students find connection, compassion, and character at school.* Alexandria, VA: ASCD.

Keys S. G., Bemak, F., & Lockhart, E. J. (1998). Transforming school counseling to serve the mental health needs of at-risk youth. *Journal of Counseling & Development, 76,* 381–388.

Kimmel, M. S., & Kaufman, M. (1994). Weekend warriors: The new men's movement. In H. Brod & M. Kaufman (Eds.), *Theorizing masculinities* (pp. 259–288). Thousand Oaks, CA: Sage.

Kindlon, D., & Thompson, M. (2000). *Raising Cain: Protecting the emotional life of boys.* New York: Ballantine.

Kipnis, A. (1991). *Knights without armour: A practical guide for men in quest of masculine soul*. Los Angeles: Tarcher.

Kivel, P. (1999). *Boys will be men: Raising our sons for courage, caring and community*. Gabriola Island, BC: New Society.

Klein, A. C. (1995). *Meeting the great bliss queen: Buddhists, feminists, and the art of the self*. Boston: Beacon.

Kogan, M. J. (2000). Men's mental health needs often misunderstood. *Monitor on Psychology 31*, 64.

Kohlberg, L. (1984). *The psychology of moral development: The nature and validity of moral stages*. San Francisco: Harper & Row.

Kohn, A. (2000). *The case against standardized testing: Raising the scores, ruining the schools*. Westport, CT: Heinemann.

Kolata, G., & Bogdanich, W. (2003, February 20). Despite the danger warnings, Ephedra sells. *New York Times*, pp. A1, D3.

Kornfield, J. (Speaker). (1996). *Meditation for beginners* (cassette recording #A395). Boulder, CO: Sounds True.

Kraft, K. (1999). *The wheel of engaged Buddhism: A new map of the path*. New York: Weatherill.

Kralovec, E. (2003). *Schools that do too much: Wasting time and money in schools and what we can all do about it*. Boston: Beacon.

KRS-One (2002). The conscious rapper. On *Spiritual minded* [CD]. New York: Koch Records.

KRS-One (2002). Good bye. On *Spiritual minded* [CD]. New York: Koch Records.

KRS-One (2002). Know thyself. On *Spiritual minded* [CD]. New York: Koch Records.

KRS-One (2002). Trust. On *Spiritual minded* [CD]. New York: Koch Records.

Kupers, T. A. (1993). *Revisioning men's lives: Gender, intimacy, and power*. New York: Guilford.

Kweli, T. (2002). Get by. On *Quality* [CD]. Los Angeles: Rawkus/MCA.

La Ferla, R. (2002, December 15). Yoga wear, not yoga, is the mantra, *New York Times*, p. St. 6.

Lantieri, L. (2001). *Schools with spirit: Nurturing the inner lives of children and teachers*. Boston: Beacon.

Larson, R. W. (2000). Toward a psychology of positive youth development.

American Psychologist, 55, 170–183.

Laselle, K. M., & Russell, T. T. (1993). To what extent are school counselors using meditation and relaxation techniques? *The School Counselor, 40,* 178–183.

Lazur, R. F., & Majors R. (1998). Men of color: Ethnocultural variations of male gender role strain. In D. L. Anselmi & A. L. Law (Eds.), *Questions of gender: Perspectives and paradoxes* (pp. 179–193). Boston: McGraw-Hill.

Lee, C. C. (1995). Reflections of a multi-cultural road warrior: A response to Smart & Smart; Chambers, Lewis & Kerzsi; & Ho. *Counseling Psychologist, 23,* 79–81.

Lee, C. C. (1996). *Saving the native son: Empowerment strategies for young black males.* Greensboro, NC: ERIC Counseling and Student Services Clearinghouse.

Lee, L. (2002, December 29). Another dad flick, and guys are crying. *New York Times,* section 9, pp. 1, 2.

Lee, W. P. (n.d.). Black on black on Buddhism: Interview with George Mumford. Retrieved March 20, 2002, from http://www.spiritrock.org/html/diversity_blackonblack_Mumford.html

Lefkowitz, B. (1998). *Our guys: The Glen Ridge rape and the secret life of the perfect suburb.* New York: Vintage.

Leighton, T. D. (2003). *Faces of compassion: Classic Buddhist archetypes and their modern expression.* Somerville, MA: Wisdom.

Leland, J. (2001, April 8). Zero tolerance changes life at one school. *New York Times,* section 9, pp. 1, 9.

Lemann, N. (2000, July 10). The battle over boys: Will feminists or their foes win the teen-age soul? *New Yorker,* 79–83.

Lepuschitz, J. K., & Hartman, V. L. (1996). Meditation and psychosocial adaptation: An exploratory study. *Current Psychology, 15,* 215–222.

Levant, R. F. (1995) Toward the reconstruction of masculinity. In R. F. Levant & W. S. Pollack (Eds.), *A new psychology of man* (pp. 229–251). New York: Basic.

Levete, G. (1995). *Presenting the case for meditation in primary and secondary schools.* London: The Interlink Trust.

Ligos, M. (2000, May 31). The fear of taking paternity leave. *New York Times,*

p. G1.

Lipsyte, R. (1999, May 9). The jock culture: Time to debate the questions. *New York Times*, p. sp11.

Lipsyte, R. (2002, October 27). Toughest play for veteran of N.F.L. trench warfare. *New York Times*, p. sp11.

Lipsyte, R. (2002, December 15). Economics remain no.1 in the business of college sports. *New York Times*, p. sp11.

Lipsyte, R. (2002, December 22). Conditions favorable for point shaving. *New York Times*, p. sp11.

Locke, D. C., & Faubert, M. (1999). Innovative pedagogy for critical consciousness in counselor education. In M. S. Kiselica (Ed.), *Confronting prejudice and racism during multicultural training* (pp. 43–58). Alexandria, VA: American Counseling Association.

Loevinger, J., & Wessler, R. (1970). *Measuring ego development* (Vols. 1 & 2). San Francisco: Jossey-Bass.

Longman, J., & Fountain, J. (2003, February 8). Phenom's school tries to avoid getting caught up in the game. *New York Times*, pp. D1, 5.

Mahalik, J. R., & Lagan, H. D. (2001). Examining masculine gender role conflict and stress in relation to religious orientation and spiritual well-being. *Psychology of Men & Masculinity, 2*, 24–33.

Majors, R., & Billson, J. M. (1992). *Cool pose: The dilemmas of black manhood in America.* New York: Simon and Schuster.

Mancuso, S. I. (2001, December 21). Branding high school sports. *Philadelphia Inquirer*. Retrieved January 5, 2002, from http://inq.philly.com/content/inquirer/2001/12/21/local_news/JSPORTS21.htm template=aprint.htm

McCreary, D. (2001). Men's drive for muscularity. *SPSMM Bulletin, 6*(4), 7.

McLaren, P., Hammer, R., Sholle, D., & Reilly, S. (1995). *Rethinking media literacy: A critical pedagogy of reproduction.* New York: Peter Lang.

McLean, C. (1998). Boys and education in Australia. In C. McLean, M. Carey, & C. White (Eds.), *Men's ways of being* (pp. 65–83). Boulder, CO: Westview.

Meditation benefits abound for schoolchildren, study finds (2003, January 21). Medical College of Georgia. Retrieved July 26, 2003, from http://www.mcg.edu/news/2003

Meggyesy, D. (1970). *Out of their league.* Berkeley, CA: Ramparts.
Men for Change (1999). *Healthy relationships: A violence-prevention curriculum.* Halifax, NS: Author.
Messner, M. A. (1994). When bodies are weapons. In M. A. Messner & D. F. Sabo, *Sex, violence and power in sports: Rethinking masculinity* (pp. 89–98). Freedom, CA: Crossing.
Messner, M. A., & Sabo, D. F. (Eds.). (1990). *Sport, men, and the gender order: Critical feminist perspectives.* Champaign, IL: Human Kinetics.
Messner, M. A., & Sabo, D. F. (1994). *Sex, violence and power in sports: Rethinking masculinity.* Freedom, CA: Crossing.
Mickens, S. (2003, April 19). No child left maligned. *Teachers' College Record*, ID Number 11152. Retrieved April 28, 2003, from http://www.tcrecord.org/PrintContent.asp?ContentID=11152
Miller, J. P. (2000). *Education and the soul: Toward a spiritual curriculum.* Albany: SUNY Press.
Miller, R. (Ed.). (1995). *Educational freedom for a democratic society: Critique of national educational goals, standards, and curriculum.* Brandon, VT: Holistic Education.
Miller, R. (1997). *What are schools for? Holistic education in American culture.* Brandon, VT: Holistic Education.
Milller, W. R. & Thoresen, C. E. (2003, January). Spirituality, religion and health: An emerging research field. *American Psychologist, 58*, 24–35.
Mims, B. (2001, August 25). Zen: Successful pro athletes know well the state of keen awareness and peak performance. *Salt Lake Tribune.* Retrieved June 7, 2003, from http://www.zencenterutah.org/trib0801.htm
Miracle, A. W., & Rees, R. C. (1994). *Lessons of the locker room: The myth of school sports.* Amherst, NY: Prometheus.
Moore, R., & Gillette, D. (1990). *King Warrior Magician Lover: Rediscovering the archetypes of the mature masculine.* San Francisco: Harper.
Mos Def. (1999). Brooklyn. On *Black on both sides* [CD]. Los Angeles: Priority/Rawkus.
Mulvey, E. P., & Cauffman, E. (2001). The inherent limits of predicting school violence. *American Psychologist, 56,* 797–802.
Murphy, M., & White, R. A. (1995). *In the zone: Transcendent experience in*

sports. New York: Penguin.

Murphy, M., Donovan, S., & Taylor, E. (1997). *The physical and psychological effects of meditation: A review of contemporary research with a comprehensive bibliography 1931–1996*. Sausalito, CA: Institute of Noetic Sciences.

Murphy, S. (1999). *The cheers and tears: A healthy alternative to the dark side of youth sports today*. New York: John Wiley & Sons.

Myers, G. (2002, November 21). Sehorn rips NFL drug rules. *New York Daily News*, pp. 78–79.

Myers, J. E., Sweeney, T. J., & Witmer, J. M. (2000). The wheel of wellness counseling for wellness: A holistic model for treatment planning. *Journal of Counseling & Development, 78*, 251–266.

Myers, L. J., Speight, S. L., Highlen, P. S., Cox, C. I., Reynolds, A. L., Adams, E. M., et al. (1991). Identity development and worldview: Toward an optimal conceptualization. *Journal of Counseling and Development, 70*, 54–63.

Nack, W. (2001, May 7). The wrecking yard: Post-NFL pain. *Sports Illustrated*, 58–75.

Nas (2002). I can. On *Gods son* [CD]. New York: Sony.

Nemiroff, G. H. (1992). *Reconstructing education: Toward a pedagogy of critical humanism*. New York: Bergin & Garvey.

Newell, W. (Ed.). (2000). *What is a man: 3000 years of wisdom on the art of manly virtue*. New York: HarperCollins.

Nhat Hanh, T. (1987). *Being peace*. Berkeley, CA: Parallax.

Nhat Hanh, T. (1991). *Peace is every step: The path of mindfulness in everyday life*. New York: Bantam.

Nideffer, R. M. (n.d.). Calming the mind so the body can perform. Retrieved June 7, 2003, from http://www.enhanced-performance.com/nideffer/articles//article19.html

Nideffer, R. M. (1995). Preventing choking and downward performance cycles. Retrieved June 7, 2003, from http://www.enhanced-performance.com/nideffer/articles//article2.html

Noam, G. G. (2002, November/December). Afterschool education: A new ally for education reform. *Harvard Education Letter Research Online*. Retrieved from http://www.edletter.org/past/issues/2002–nd/afterschool

.shtml

Noddings, N. (1992). *The challenge to care in schools: An alternative approach to education.* New York: Teachers College.

Noguera, P. A., and Akom, A. (2000, June 5). Disparities demystified: Causes of the racial achievement gap all derive from unequal treatment. *Nation,* 29–31.

Ohanian, S. (1999). *One size fits few: The folly of educational standards.* Portsmouth, NH: Heinemann.

O'Hara, E. (2001, fall, winter). Teisho: The teaching of the World Trade Center destruction. *The Village Zendo Newsletter* (New York), 3–4.

O'Neil, J. M. (1982). Gender-role conflict and strains in men's lives. In K. Solomon and N. B. Levy (Eds.), *Men in transition: Changing male roles, theory, and therapy* (pp. 5–44). New York: Plenum.

Oriard, M. (2001, December 23). Football glory and education are a team no more. *New York Times,* section 8, p. 11.

O'Sullivan, E. (1999). *Transformative learning: Educational vision for the 21st century.* Toronto: University of Toronto Press.

Palmer, P. (1998). *The courage to teach: Exploring the inner landscape of a teacher's life.* San Francisco: Jossey-Bass.

Peak performance: Sports and the mind. Hardwood warriors Phil Jackson and George Mumford (n.d.). Retrieved October 1, 2003, from http://www.pbs.org/bodyandsoul/206/jackson.htm

Play it smart (n.d.). Retrieved July 29, 2003, from http://footballfoundationocsn.com

Pleck, J. H. (1980). Men's power with women, other men, and society: A men's movement analysis. In E. Pleck & J. Pleck (Eds.), *The American Man* (pp. 417–433). Englewood Cliffs, NJ: Prentice Hall.

Pleck, J. H. (1995). The gender role strain paradigm: An update. In W. S. Pollack & R. F. Levant (Eds.), *A new psychology of men* (pp. 1–32). New York: Basic Books.

Pollack, W. (1998). *Real boys: Rescuing our sons from the myths of boyhood.* New York: Random House.

Pollack, W. S., & Levant, R. F. (1995). Coda: A new psychology of men: Where have we been? Where are we going? In R. F. Levant & W. S. Pollack

(Eds.), *A new psychology of men* (pp. 383–387). New York: Basic Books.

Pollitt, K. (2003, March 24). Phallic balloons against the war. *Nation*, 9.

Purpel, D. E. (1989). *The moral and spiritual crisis in education: A curriculum for justice and compassion in education.* Granby, MA: Bergin and Garvey.

Purpel, D. E. (2000). *Moral outrage in education.* New York: Peter Lang.

Queen, C. S. (Ed.). (2000). *Engaged Buddhism in the west.* Somerville, MA: Wisdom.

Real, T. (1997). *I don't want to talk about it: Overcoming the secret legacy of male depression.* New York: Fireside.

Real, T. (2002). The awful truth. *Psychotherapy Networker, 26*(6), 34–43, 58.

Redefining the purpose of education with Linda Lantieri. (2002, spring/summer). *Boston Research Center for the 21st Century Newsletter, 19,* 6, 7, 12, 13.

Reed, M. K. (1994). Social skills training to reduce depression in adolescents. *Adolescence, 29,* 293–302.

Rhoden, W. C. (2002, November 16). Faustian pact: Performance for health. *New York Times*, p. D1.

Rhoden, W. C. (2002, November 30). Violent sport must control the violence. *New York Times*, p. D1.

Rhoden, W. C. (2003, February 3). For old-school coaches, the troubling world of a new era's stars. *New York Times*, p. D4.

Rich, F. (2002, November 2). Mr. Ambassador. *New York Times Magazine*, pp. 52–57.

Riethmayer, J. (2001, Spring.) What kids really need. *Professional issues in counseling.* Retrieved August 2, 2001, from http://www.shsu.edu/~piic/spring2001/riethmayer.htm

Roberts, S. (2002, December 22). Web reshapes the pressures of high school. *New York Times*, p. sp.11.

Roberts, S. (2003, September 28). The code of silence corrupts the young. *New York Times*, pp. sp. 1, 9.

Rohde, D. (2001, September 6). Refereeing grown-ups who meddle in child's play. *New York Times*, p. B2.

Rowan, J. (1997). *Healing the male psyche: Therapy as initiation.* New York:

Routledge.

Rozman, D. (1994). *Meditating with children: The art of concentration and centering.* Boulder Creek, CA: Planetary.

Sapolsky, R. M. (1998). *The trouble with testosterone and other essays on the biology of the human predicament.* New York: Touchstone.

Sapon-Shevin, M., & Goodman, J. (1992). Learning to be the opposite sex: Sexuality education and sexual scripting in early adolescence. In J. T. Sears (Ed.), *Sexuality and the curriculum* (pp. 89–105). New York: Teachers College.

Savran, D. (1998). *Taking it like a man: White masculinity, masochism, and contemporary American culture.* Princeton, NJ: Princeton University Press.

Scarsdale school suspends 28 students for drunkenness (2002, September 27). *New York Times,* p. B6.

Schaef, A. W. (1988). *When society becomes an addict.* San Francisco: HarperCollins.

School Administrator (2002, September). Spirituality in leadership. Retrieved September 20, 2002, from http://www.aasa.org/publications/sa/2002_09

Schulte, D. L., Skinner, T. A., & Claiborn, C. D. (2002). Religious and spiritual issues in counseling psychology training. *The Counseling Psychologist, 30,* 118–134.

Seeman, T. E., Duban, L. F., & Seeman, M. (2003, January). Religiosity/spirituality and health: A critical review of the evidence for biological pathways. *American Psychologist, 58,* 53–63.

Segal, L. (1990). *Slow motion: Changing masculinities, changing men.* London: Virago.

Shea, C. M. (2000). De-scribing the discourse of "transformative praxis": Learning from models of holistic mental health. *Encounter, 13*(1), 40–48.

Shockey on radio: I wouldn't stand for gay teammates (2002, September 27). Retrieved July 30, 2003, from http://msn.espn.go.com/nfl/news/2002/0927/1437486.html

Shostrum, E. L. (1996). *Personal orientation inventory.* San Diego: EdITS/Educational and industrial testing service.

Shugar, P. (2001, October 30). Ohio psyched this season. *The Post* (Ohio University). Retrieved March 28, 2002, from http://thepost.baker.ohiou

.edu/archives3/oct01/103001/sl.html

Shulman, J. L., & Bowen, W. G. (2001). *The game of life: College sports and educational values.* Princeton, NJ: Princeton University Press.

Silverstein, O., & Rashbaum B. (1994). *The courage to raise good men.* New York: Penguin.

Simmer-Brown, J. (1999). Commitment and openness: A contemplative approach to pluralism. In S. Glazer (Ed.), *The heart of learning: Spirituality in education* (pp. 97–112). New York: Tarcher.

Sink, M. (2003, February 8). Yoga in Aspen public schools draws opposition. *New York Times,* p. 36.

Skee-Lo (1995). Never crossed my mind. On *I wish* [CD]. Santa Monica, CA: Scotti Brothers.

Smith, D. (2001, July/August). Fostering family health: Prevention and intervention programs for teens require family involvement, says William Pollack. *Monitor on Psychology,* 90, 91.

Sokolove, M. (2002, December 22). Football is a sucker's game. *New York Times Magazine,* pp. 36–41, 64, 68, 70, 71.

Solomon, B., & Gardner, H. (2000). The origins of good work: Getting kids, parents, and coaches on the same page. *Community Youth Development Journal, 1*(3), 36–41.

Sommers, C. H. (2000). *The war against boys: How misguided feminism is harming our young men.* New York: Simon & Schuster.

Spence, C. M. (2000). *The skin I'm in: Racism, sports and education.* New York: Zed.

Spielberg, W. (1999). A cultural critique of current practices of male adolescent identity formation. In A. M. Horne & M. S. Kiselica (Eds.), *Handbook of counseling boys and adolescent males: A practitioners' guide* (pp. 25–34). Thousand Oaks, CA: Sage.

Steigmeier, C. (2001). Men and Work, *SPSMM Bulletin, 6*(1), 7.

Sternberg, R. J. (2002, November 13). Teaching wisdom in our schools. *Education Week.* Retrieved October 1, 2003, from http://www.edweek.com/ew/ew_printstory.cfm?slug=11sternberg.h22

St. Louis, C. (2002, November 10). What they were thinking: Interview with Jeff Rocco. *New York Times Magazine,* p. 36.

Stoltenberg, J. (1990). *Refusing to be a man: Essays on sex and justice.* New York: Meridian.

Strohl, J. E. (1998). Transpersonalism: Ego meets soul. *Journal of Counseling & Development, 76,* 397–403.

Sumedho, A. (2001). *The way it is.* Hertfordshire, UK: Amaravati.

Summit results in formation of spirituality competencies. (1995, December). *Counseling Today,* 30.

Talbot, M. (2003, September 21). Why, isn't he just the cutest brand-image enhancer you've ever seen? *New York Times Magazine,* pp. 31–35, 52, 64, 82–84.

Teachout, T. (2002, September 15). Is Tony Soprano today's Ward Cleaver? *New York Times,* p. wk3.

Thurman, R. A. F. (1994). Meditation and education: Buddhist India, Tibet and modernist America. Retrieved October 1, 2003, from http://www.contemplativemind.org/resources/pubs/thurman.html

Thurman, R. A. F. (1995). *Inside Tibetan Buddhism/Rituals and symbols revealed.* San Francisco: Collins.

Thurman, R. A. F. (1998). *The inner revolution: Life, liberty, and the pursuit of real happiness.* New York: Riverhead.

Trulson, M. E. (1986). Martial arts training: A novel "cure" for juvenile delinquency. *Human Relations, 39,* 1131–1140.

Trungpa, C. (1988). *Shambhala: The sacred path of the warrior.* Boston: Shambhala.

Tyrangel, J., & Carcaterra, K. (2002, August 5). Bruce rising. *Time Magazine,* p. 59.

Van Hyfte, G., & Tejirian, E. (2002). Editor talk: Psychology, identity, and voicing subjectivity in masculinity theory and research. *SPSMM Bulletin, 7,* (3), 11–13.

Vaughan, F. (1995). *The inward arc: Healing in psychotherapy and spirituality.* Nevada City, CA: Blue Dolphin.

Vecsey, G. (2002, September 27). Defining fair play is tricky. *New York Times,* p. D1.

Vecsey, G. (2003, February 19). Baseball has failed to confront drugs. *New York Times,* p. D1.

Villarosa, L. (2002, September 23). As black men move into middle age, dangers rise. *New York Times,* pp. F1, 8.

Vondracek, F. W., & Porfeli, E. J. (2002). Counseling psychologists and schools: Toward a sharper conceptual focus. *Counseling Psychologist, 30,* 749–756.

Walker, R. (2003, summer). Black Buddha: Bringing the tradition home. An interview with Choyin Rangdrol. *Turning Wheel: The Journal of Socially Engaged Buddhism,* 23–25.

Watts, R. J., Abdul-Adil, J. K., & Pratt, T. (2002). Enhancing critical consciousness in young African American men: A psychoeducational approach. *Psychology of Men & Masculinity, 3,* 41–50.

Weaver II, R. L., & Cotrell, H. W. (1992). A non-religious spirituality that causes students to clarify their values and to respond with passion. *Education, 112*(3), 426–435.

Weaver-Hightower, M. (2002). The gender of terror and heroes? What educators might teach about men and masculinity after September 11, 2001. *Teachers' College Record.* Retrieved September 20, 2002, from http://www.tcrecord.org/PrintContent.asp?ContentID=11012

Weinrach, S. G. (2002). The counseling profession's relationship to Jews and the issues that concern them: More than a case of selective awareness. *Journal of Counseling & Development, 80,* 300–314.

Weinrach, S. G., & Thomas, K. R. (1998). Diversity-sensitive counseling today: A postmodern clash of values. *Journal of Counseling & Development, 76,* 115–122.

Welch, L. (1979). Maitreya Poem. *Ring of bone: Collected poems 1950–1971.* Bolinas, CA: Grey Fox Press, pp. 196–198.

Welch, S. D. (1999). *Sweet dreams in America: Making ethics and spirituality work.* New York: Routledge.

Wellwood, J. (Ed.). (1985). *Awakening the heart: East/West approaches to psychotherapy and the healing relationship.* Boston: Shambhala.

Wexler, P. (2000). *Mystical society: An emerging social vision.* Boulder, CO: Westview.

White, M. (1998). Men's culture, the men's movement, and the constitution of men's lives. In C. McLean, M. Carey, & C. White (Eds.), *Men's ways of being* (pp. 163–193). Boulder, CO: Westview.

Whitmyer, C. (Ed.). (1994). *Mindfulness and meaningful work: Explorations in right livelihood.* Berkeley, CA: Parallax.

Wilber, K. (1998a). Ken Wilber responds. In D. Rothberg & S. Kelly (Eds.), *Ken Wilber in dialogue: Conversations with leading transpersonal thinkers* (pp. 306–367). Wheaton, IL: Quest.

Wilber, K. (1998b). *The marriage of sense and soul: Integrating science and religion.* New York: Broadway.

Wilber, K. (2000). *Integral psychology: Consciousness, spirit, psychology, therapy.* Boston: Shambhala.

Williams, L. (2001, June 3). Taking a big breath, N.F.L. tackles yoga. *New York Times*, p. sp.9.

Williams, L. (2002, December 10). Fans in college more likely to binge drink, study says. *New York Times*, p. D2.

Willis, E. (1999, December 13). How now, Iron Johns? (Review of *Stiffed: The betrayal of the American man*). *Nation*, 18–22.

Winston, D. (2002, spring). You too can be a bodhisattva. *Turning Wheel: The Journal of Socially Engaged Buddhism*, 35–37.

Winston, D. (2003). *Wide awake: A Buddhist guide for teens.* New York: Perigee.

Witt, S. (2002, September 23). Utes christen new gridiron with a victory over South Shore. *Bay News* (Brooklyn, NY), pp. 4, 45.

Wong, E. (2001, December 23). Athletes take entitlement out of bounds: Some colleges fail to prevent bad behavior. *New York Times*, pp. sp. 1, 10.

Index

addiction, 18-19, 75–76, 78, 80, 181–182
Afghanistan, 124
African American men, 1, 9, 19, 38, 46, 47, 48, 60, 63, 70, 73–74, 77, 81, 99, 129, 164, 176–79, 182
after–school program, 89–90
aggression, 9, 15, 16, 38, 60
Aitken, Robert, 5
Ali, Muhammed, 112
androgyny, 31, 51, 154, 197
anger, 117–120
Arab American, 1, 124, 126
athletes
    African American, 48
    and pain, 49
    parents of, 60
    Avalokiteshvara, 194

Baltimore Orioles, 80
Baltimore Ravens, 49
Bankart, Peter 89
Bem, Sandra, 153
Bemak, Fred, 38, 173
Bechler, Steve, 80
Bedard, Claire, 180–181
Bettis, Jerome, 49
Bin Laden, Osama, 15
Bissinger, H.G., 69
Bly, Robert, 23, 24
body image, 59, 80–81
Bordo, Susan, 16

bodhisattva, 193–97
Borough High School, 62–66
Bowers, C.A., 185–86
Boucher, Sandy, 192
Boy Code, 11, 20
Brazier, David, 4
breath, breathing, 100, 102, 107, 133, 141, 144, 162
Brodie, John, 86
Brooks, Gary R., 21, 26, 30
Brooklyn, 6, 60–62, 135, 137
Brooklyn College, 89
Bryant, Kobe, 82
Buddha, 163
Buddhism; Buddhists, 3, 4, 93, 193, 194
bullying, 16, 17, 200
Bush, George W., 12, 13, 15, 124–34

Capuzzi, David, 40
Center for Sport, Character, and Culture, 71
Chesler, Phyllis, 22, 26
Chicago Bulls, 93
choke, choking, 52, 87, 103
class, 12, 38, 62, 66, 109
Clemente, Roberto, 112, 194
Close, Ellis, 19
coach, coaches, 60, 81, 83, 92–93, 95, 110–13, 130, 133, 134, 135, 136, 137, 138, 139, 141, 142, 145, 164
Coakley, Jay, 74

Coltrane, John, 195
Common, 29
Connell, R.W., 12, 18, 24, 27, 39, 40
conservatives, 16, 23
contemplative counseling, 186–192, 197–202
conventional masculinity, 2, 3, 10–21, 50, 88
Cooper, Andrew, 3, 84, 85
Cornelius, Randolph R., 14
counseling
   integral, 5–6, 10, 28, 31–32, 34, 45, 60, 168–69
      school, 5, 38–39, 170, 172, 173
      socially conscious, 175–79
      and spirituality, 40– 42
      transpersonal, 180, 187
critical pedagogy, 182–86
Csikszentmihalyi, Mihaly, 3
culture, 30, 32, 186
   popular, 3, 33, 182, 200
Culture of Cruelty, 11, 16, 99, 124, 125
Curry, Tim, 74

Dalai Lama, 194
Davis, James Earl, 177
death of teammate, 139–41, 144, 163
Denborough, David, 183, 184–85
De Niro, Robert, 13
development
   ego, 36, 46, 88
   gender identity, 31, 34–37, 88
   moral, 59, 88, 113, 123, 196
Developmental–Contextualism, 31–32
DeWitt Wallace–Reader's Digest Fund, 172–73, [173]
dissing, 96, 99–100, 126, 128, 134
DMX, 9
dualism, 42
Dylan, Bob, 195

Eastwood, Clint, 195
eating, 97, 98–99, 101
Edmundson, Mark, 24
education, holistic, 4, 188, 188–90, 200–201
ego development, 36, 46, 53, 170, 187, 188, 196
egocentric, 46, 52, 87, 88, 104, 107–8, 113, 127, 170
Eminem, 83
emotional intelligence, 179–81
empathy, 51, 117, 119, 129, 167, 168, 199, 200, 201
Ephedra, 79–80
Epstein, Mark, 5, 103, 188
ESPN.com, 71
essentialist view, 22–24, 30

Faludi, Susan, 14, 24
family, 107–8, 109
fathers, 14–15, 109–10, 113
Faubert, Marie, 183

Faulk, Marshall, 112
Favre, Bret, 78
feminism, 10, 13, 18,19, 25, 26, 175
femininity, 29–30
Ferguson, Ann, 38, 177, 179
flow, 85–86
football
    and body image, 80–81
    college, 72, 75
    dangers of, 68–69
    and health, 78–81
    high school, 6, 66–68, 69–70, 71, 72, 128
    and homophobia, 82–84
    and the media, 68, 69, 71
    and meditation, 1, 102–108, 160
    and misbehavior, 69, 74–75, 75–78
    professional, 67, 71, 77, 125
    and racism, 73, 76
    and sexism, 81–82
    and violence, 81, 84
    and the zone, 85–88, 152, 158–59
Freire, Paulo, 182, 183, 185, 186
Fukuyama, Mary, 5, 178–79

Garbarino, James, 2, 5, 17, 46, 47, 88, 113, 120, 129, 133, 180–81
gays, 11, 16, 177, 200
gender identity, 31
gender role identity, 21
gender role stress, 11, 21–22, 25
Gergen, Kenneth, 43–44
Gilligan, Carol, 22, 175
Gilmore, David D., 30
girls, young women, 22, 124
Gladwell, Malcom, 92
Glassman, Bernie, 5, 191
Glen Ridge, New Jersey, 68, 70
Goldstein, Richard, 14, 16, 197
Goleman, Daniel, 179–80
Gordhamer, Soren, 127
Gore, Jennifer, 183
Green Bay Packers, 78
Gross, Douglas R., 40

heroism, 196–97
holistic education, 4, 188, 188–90, 200–201
homophobia, 11, 82–84, 200
hooks, bell, 177
Horne, Arthur M. 20, 35
Hughes, Robert, 74

integral counseling, 5–6,10, 28, 31–32, 34, 45, 60, 168–69, 198–99
inter–being, 43
Internet, 121
Italian American, 1, 123

Jackson, Phil, 93
James, LeBron, 71–72
Jews, 41, 124

Jizo, 195
Jolliff, David, 35
Jones, Ken, 5, 53, 194
Jordan, Michael, 3, 86, 93, 112, 136, 195
Joyce, James, 195
Julien Isaac, 179

Kabat–Zinn, Jon, 4
Kegan, Robert, 5, 48, 169, 196
Kessler, Rachael, 5, 188
Keys, Susan G., 38, 173
Kindlon, Daniel, 2, 10, 16, 29–30, 99, 124
King, Martin Luther, Jr., 110, 194
Kiselica, Mark S., 20
Kivel, Paul, 2, 97, 108, 175–76
Klein, Anne, 4
Knight, Bobby, 111, 112
Kohlberg, Lawrence, 111, 147, 148–50, 153–54, 154–55, 169
Kopay, David, 82–83
Kornfield, Jack, 4, 100, 105
Kraft, Kenneth, 5
Kralovec, Etta, 67
KRS–One, 57, 167, 195
Kupers, Terry, 12, 21, 23, 25, 36, 49, 175, 197
Kweli, Talib, 147

Lagan, Hugh D., 40
Lantieri, Linda, 180
Larson, Reed

Latinos, 1, 9, 38, 63
leaders, leadership, 92, 134
Lee, Courtland, 91, 176–78
Lefkowitz, Bernard, 70
Leighton, Taigen Daniel, 194, 195
Levant, Robert, 49
Levine, Stephen, 4
Levine, Susan Braun, 20
Lipsyte, Robert, 82
Literacy, 183
Littleton, Colorado, 2, 9, 70, 109
Locke, Don C., 183
Lockhart, Estes J., 38, 173
Loevinger, Jane, 5, 48, 147, 150–51, 153–54, 155–57, 169, 196, 202
Los Angeles Lakers, 93
losing, loss, 104, 199

Macy, Joanna, 5
Mahalik, James R., 40
Manjushri, 195
Maitreya, 193, 194
Maryland, University of, 75
masculine gender identity development, 10, 167, 202
Masculine Gender Response Stress, 147
masculinity, 9, 11, 16, 27, 29–30
  conventional, 2, 3, 5–6, 10–21, 50, 88, 128, 170, 172, 183
  essentialist, 21–24, 30, 177
Massillon, Ohio, 68
mastery, 36, 51–52, 60, 84, 97, 104,

136
Matrix, The, 143, 144
McLean, Christopher, 27
media, 9, 68, 69, 71, 91, 115, 137
meditation
    insight (vipassana), 3–4, 48, 91–92, 97–98, 100, 136, 137, 138, 142, 201
    and male adolescents, 1, 5, 5–6, 46–53, 88, 152–53, 158–59, 179, 188, 200
    and pain, 79, 89
Meggyesy, Dave, 83, 86
men's movement, 23, 25
Messner, Michael A., 81
Miller, John P., 5, 190
Miller, Ron, 5, 42, 189, 189–90
Million Man March, 23
mindful social action, 190–92, 201
mindfulness, 6, 34, 46–53, 97–98, 132, 164, 179, 182
Minnesota Vikings, 77
Miracle, Andrew W. 66, 75
moral reasoning, 51, 91, 111–12, 118–21, 127, 148–50, 196
Mos Def, 60
mothers, 15, 109–10
Mother Theresa, 194
Multiculturalism, 168,
Mumford, George, 92–93
Murphy, Michael, 3, 51, 86
Murphy, Shane, 52
Myers, Jane E., 198

Nation, 69
National Collegiate Athletic Association (NCAA), 76
National Football Foundation, 68
National Football League (NFL), 67, 68, 77, 78, 79, 81, 82, 83
National Mental Health Association, 83
National Organization of Men vs. Sexism (NOMAS), 25
nature, 18, 21, 42, 186, 188
Nemiroff, Greta Hofmann, 183, 197–98
Newell, Waller, 24
New England Patriots, 78
Newsday, 143
New York Giants, 79, 83, 93, 108
New York Jets, 77
New York Post, 139, 144
New York Times, 80
Nhat Hanh, Thich, 4, 5
Nideffer, Robert, 103
9–11. See September 11, 2001
Noddings, Nel, 41
nurture, 21, 26

O'Hara, Pat Enkyo, 5, 191
Oriard, Michael, 72
O'Sullivan, Edmund, 186

pain, 49, 50, 52, 89, 106, 191
painkillers
Palmer, Parker, 5, 189

peer groups, 179–80
Personal Orientation Inventory, 153, 158
Philadelphia Eagles, 49
Pittsburgh Steelers, 49, 80
Play It Smart, 68
Pleck, Joseph, 11
Pollack, William, 2, 20
Pollitt, Katha, 22, 26
postconventional development, 34–37, 45
positive psychology, 168
postmodernism, 3, 43–44, 174, 187
power, 12, 25–27, 36–37, 110, 128, 132, 173, 199–200
pre/trans fallacy, 43, 44, 189
Promise Keepers, 23
prophetic education, 189, 190
Purpel, David, 5, 189, 190

race, racism, 64–65, 109, 121–24, 134, 138, 139
Rashbaum, Beth, 15
Rather, Dan, 12, 13
Real, Terrence, 2, 17, 19, 24, 188
Reed, Michael K., 171
Rees, C. Roger, 66, 75
Reeve, Christopher, 195
relationships, 97, 111, 160–62
Robinson, Jackie, 112, 194
Rowan, John, 36
Rozman, Deborah, 198
sacred space, 52–53

Samantabhadra, 194
school counselors; school counseling 38–39
schools, 9–10, 27.
    and male youth, 37–40, 128, 132.
Schaef, Anne Wilson, 18, 181.
Schwarzenegger, Arnold, 13.
Sehorn, Jason, 79–80.
self
    development
    monological, 170
    dialogical, 170, 174–175
    contemplative, 170, 186–92
Semoi, 29, 30
September 11, 2001(9–11), 13, 14, 27, 61, 124, 203
service project, 129. See also mindful social action
Sevig, Todd, 5, 178–79
Sex Role Inventory, 153, 154
sexism, 23, 26, 81–82, 179–80
sexuality, 97, 113–16
Shea, Christine, 181
Shiva, 29
Shockey, Jeremy, 83
Shostrum, Everett L., 153
Silverstein, Louise B., 21, 26, 30
Silverstein, Olga, 15
Skee–Lo, 120
social constructionist view, 22, 25–28, 182, 184, 185
Sokolove, Michael, 76–77

Sommers, Christine Hoff, 24
Soprano, Tony, 13
spirituality, 2, 5, 18, 23, 28, 40–45
sports, 3, 60, 85–86, 97
sports program, 90–92
Springsteen, Bruce, 195
Stallone, Sylvester, 13
standards movement, 172–73
Steigmeier, Carolyn, 19
Sternberg, Robert J., 167
steroid use, 79
Stiller, Ben, 13
Stoltenberg, John, 25
stress, 52, 65, 89, 97, 102, 109, 134
  stress reduction, 52, 89, 171, 202
  posttraumatic, 65–66
Stringer, Korey, 49, 50, 77, 78, 79, 107
Strohl, James E., 188
substance abuse, 15, 17–18, 200
Sumedho, Ajahn, 34
Sweeny, Thomas J., 198

Taliban, 124
Teachout, Terry, 13
Tepp, Alan, 17
Thomas, Kenneth R, 175
Thompson, Michael, 2, 10, 16, 29–30, 99, 124
Thurman, Robert, 4, 187
tipping point, 92
transpersonal psychology, 180, 187
trauma, 17, 19, 133, 140, 141, 191, 199
Trungpa, Chogyam, 4, 183
Tuaolo, Esea, 82
twelve step program, 181
Vimalakarti, 195
violence, 15, 84, 97, 103, 175
  in schools, 9–10, 17, 38, 65, 191, 200
vipassana. see meditation
visualization, 4, 104, 107, 137, 162

Waldear, Debbi, 86
Warner, Curt, 136
warrior, 23, 127–28, 182–83
Washington, Gene, 81
Weaver-Hightower, Marcus, 13, 15
Webster, Mike, 80
weight loss, 98–99
Weinrach, Stephen G., 41–42, 175
Welch, Lew, 193, 194
Welch, Sharon, 27
Welwood, John, 5
Wessler, Ruth, 48, 169
Wexler, Phillip, 44–45
White, Michael, 183, 184
White, Rhea A., 51, 86
Wilber, Ken, 4, 30, 45, 169, 175, 184, 197
Willis, Ellen, 14
Winston, Diane, 195–96
wisdom, 167–68, 180, 181, 196
Witmer, Melvin, 198
Wolff, Rick, 70–71

work, 191–92, 200
World Trade Center, 12, 124
women, 11, 12, 82, 113–21, 124
yoga, 33, 34, 93, 198

zero tolerance, 38
zen, 85, 191, 194
zone the, 1–2, 3, 6, 52, 85–88, 93,
    97, 110, 117, 123, 136, 138, 140,
    145, 159, 163, 164, 167, 204

COUNTERPOINTS

Studies in the Postmodern Theory of Education

General Editors
Joe L. Kincheloe & Shirley R. Steinberg

Counterpoints publishes the most compelling and imaginative books being written in education today. Grounded on the theoretical advances in criticism, feminism, and postmodernism in the last two decades of the twentieth century, Counterpoints engages the meaning of these innovations in various forms of educational expression. Committed to the proposition that theoretical literature should be accessible to a variety of audiences, the series insists that its authors avoid esoteric and jargonistic languages that transform educational scholarship into an elite discourse for the initiated. Scholarly work matters only to the degree it affects consciousness and practice at multiple sites. Counterpoints' editorial policy is based on these principles and the ability of scholars to break new ground, to open new conversations, to go where educators have never gone before.

For additional information about this series or for the submission of manuscripts, please contact:

Joe L. Kincheloe & Shirley R. Steinberg
c/o Peter Lang Publishing, Inc.
275 Seventh Avenue, 28th floor
New York, New York 10001

To order other books in this series, please contact our Customer Service Department:

(800) 770-LANG (within the U.S.)
(212) 647-7706 (outside the U.S.)
(212) 647-7707 FAX

Or browse online by series:
www.peterlangusa.com